T0374547

THE

PUBLICATIONS

OF THE

SURTEES SOCIETY

VOL. CLXXV

Made and Printed in Great Britain
by Northumberland Press Limited
Gateshead on Tyne

THE

PUBLICATIONS

OF THE

SURTEES SOCIETY

ESTABLISHED IN THE YEAR
M.DCCC.XXXIV

VOL. CLXXV

FOR THE YEAR M.CM.LX

At a COUNCIL MEETING of the SURTEES SOCIETY held in Durham Castle on December 3rd, 1963, the President in the Chair, it was ORDERED—

"That a third volume of Miscellanea be published by the Society, to comprise:

i. The completion of Mr C. R. Hudleston's edition of the registrations of Durham recusant estates 1717-1778.

ii. Dr Ann Forster's extracts from the Recusants' Roll for 1636-7."

H. S. Offler,
Secretary.

MISCELLANEA

VOL. III

comprising

I.

DURHAM RECUSANTS' ESTATES 1717-1778, PART II

II.

DURHAM ENTRIES ON THE RECUSANTS' ROLL 1636-7

PUBLISHED FOR THE SOCIETY BY
ANDREWS & CO., SADLER STREET, DURHAM
and
BERNARD QUARITCH, 11 GRAFTON STREET
NEW BOND STREET, LONDON W.1
1965

CONTENTS

BOOKS REFERRED TO IN THE FOOTNOTES

The following abbreviations are used:

EP	*The English Catholic Nonjurors of 1715*, by the Very Rev. Edgar E. Estcourt and John Orlebar Payne (1855).
GEC	*The Complete Peerage*, by G. E. C[ockayne], 2nd edition (1910-1959).
NCHN	*The New County History of Northumberland.*
Rec. EC	*Records of the English Catholics of 1715*, by John Orlebar Payne (1889).
SP Dom.	State Papers Domestic, in the Public Record Office, London.
Surtees	*History and Antiquities of the County Palatine of Durham*, by Robert Surtees (1816-1840).
SS	Surtees Society.
VCH	*Victoria County History.*

I

DURHAM RECUSANTS' ESTATES

1717 - 1778

PART II

edited by

C. ROY HUDLESTON

INTRODUCTION

Volume 173 contained the registrations in alphabetical order of Durham recusants' estates for 1717-1778 as far as the registration of Bryan Salvin. The remaining certificates are now printed, together with an appendix containing six registrations from the first book of enrolments covering the period 1 May 1717 to 1 October 1722. This book only came to light when the muniments in the old Shire Hall at Durham were moved to the County Record Office in the new County Hall, at which time the printing of Volume 173 was far advanced and it was too late to add new material. The registrations are now printed, and use has been made of some of the enrolled deeds in the book which contain genealogical information.

I am grateful to Dr. W. A. L. Seaman, the County Archivist, and his staff for never failing kindness and help and my thanks are also due to the Clerk of the Peace for permission to print these documents.

C.R.H.

134-5. EDWARD SALVIN 1751

The registry of me Edward Salvin of Tudhoe in the County of Durham gentleman of and concerning my messuages lands tenements and hereditaments in the township of Tudhoe within the parish of Bransepeth . . . to wit

One capital messuage or tenement in Tudhoe . . . with the stables garden and appurtenances thereunto belonging late in the possession of Ralph Dunn and now in the possession of John Dunn the younger as tenant at will for which he is to pay no rent but is to live in the said messuage or tenement for taking care of the gardens and keeping them in order

One other messuage or tenement and farm in Tudhoe . . . with the appurtenances now in the possession or occupation of Thomas Wilson as tenant thereof by lease bearing date 4 February 1746 to hold the pasture ground from Lady Day and all the rest of the premisses thereby demised from 1 May next after the date thereof for the term of nine years at . . . the yearly rent of £90. One close called Spark's croft in Tudhoe . . . now likewise in the possession . . . of the said Thomas Wilson as tenant or farmer thereof from year to year at . . . the yearly rent of £2 5s.

Two rooms or chambers used as a granary in the house at Tudhoe aforesaid where John Maw now lives now likewise in the possession . . . of the said Thomas Wilson as tenant or farmer thereof from year to year at . . . the yearly rent of 7s. One other messuage or tenement and farm in Tudhoe . . . with the appurtenances thereunto belonging late in the possession of John Priss and now in the possession of Thomas Priss son of the said John Priss as tenant or farmer . . . by lease made to the said John Priss . . . bearing date 1 December 1747 to hold the pasture ground from Lady day and all the said rest of the premisses thereby demised from 1 May next after the date thereof for the term of nine years at . . . the yearly rent of £45

One other messuage or tenement and farm in Tudhoe . . . with the appurtenances now in the possession or occupation of George Greenwell as tenant or farmer thereof by lease bearing date 4 February 1746 to hold the pasture ground from Lady day and all the rest of the premisses thereby demised from 1 May next after the date thereof for the term of nine years at . . . the yearly rent of £70

One other messuage or tenement and farm in Tudhoe . . . with the appurtenances now in the possession or occupation of Elizabeth Harrison widow as tenant or farmer thereof by lease bearing date 1 December 1747 to hold the pasture ground from Lady day and all the rest of the premisses thereby demised from 1 May next after the date thereof for the term of six years at . . . the yearly rent of £45

Two other messuages or tenements and farms in Tudhoe . . . with the appurtenances now in the possession or occupation of John Pickering as tenant or farmer . . . by lease bearing date 1 December 1749 to hold the pasture ground from Lady day and all the rest of the premisses . . . from 1 May next after the date thereof for the term of six years at . . . the yearly rent of £94 one of which said last mentioned farms was late in the possession of Thomas Foreman as tenant or farmer thereof.

One other messuage or tenement and farm in Tudhoe . . . with the appurtenances now in the possession or occupation of Edward Crosby as tenant or farmer thereof by lease 1 December 1747 to hold the pasture ground from Lady day and all the rest of the premisses thereby demised from 1 May next after the date thereof for the term of nine years at . . . the yearly rent of £48. One other messuage or tenement and farm in Tudhoe . . . with the appurtenances now in the possession or occupation of Henry Hutchinson as tenant or farmer thereof by lease . . . 1 December 1748 to hold the pasture ground from Lady day and all the rest of the premisses thereby demised from 1 May next after the date thereof for the term of nine years at . . . the yearly rent of £20 10s. One other messuage or tenement and stable in Tudhoe . . . with the appurtenances now in the possession or occupation of Michael Hills as tenant or farmer thereof from year to year at the yearly rent of £1 9s. 6d.

One other messuage or tenement and farm in Tudhoe . . . with the appurtenances now in the possession or occupation of John Dunn the elder as tenant or farmer thereof from year to year at the yearly rent of £10. One other messuage or tenement in Tudhoe . . . with the garth and appurtenances thereunto belonging now in the possession or occupation of Robert Burn as tenant or farmer thereof from year to year at the yearly rent of £1 11s.

One other little close in Tudhoe . . . late in the possession of the said Robert Burn and now in my own possession of the yearly value of 15s. or thereabouts.

Four closes or parcells of ground in Tudhoe . . . with the appurtenance late in the possession or occupation of Ralph Dunn and now in the possession or occupation of John Dunn the younger as tenant or farmer thereof from year to year at the yearly rent of £18. One other messuage or tenement in Tudhoe . . . with the lands and appurtenances thereunto belonging late in the possession or occupation of Thomas Crosby and now in the possession or occupation of William Pickering as tenant or farmer thereof from year to year at the yearly rent of £4 10s. One other close or parcell of ground in Tudhoe . . . with the appurtenances late in the possession or occupation of John Dunn the younger and now in my own possession of the yearly value of £5 10s. or thereabouts. One other close or parcell of ground in Tudhoe . . . with the byer and appurtenances thereunto belonging now in the possession or occupation of Thomas Pickering as tenant or farmer thereof at . . . the yearly rent of £5. One cottage house in Tudhoe . . . with the appurtenances now in the possession or occupation of John Maw as tenant or farmer thereof from year to year at . . . the yearly rent of 18s. One other cottage house in Tudhoe . . . with the appurtenances late in the possession of Jane Catton which is now untenanted and is so ruinous and decayed that it is falling down. One other cottage house in Tudhoe with the appurtenances late in the possession of William Makepeace which is likewise untenanted and so ruinous and decayed that it is falling down. One other cottage house and garth in Tudhoe . . . now in the possession of Catherine Wheatley as tenant . . . from year to year at . . . the yearly rent of 14s. One other cottage house called the Schoolhouse in Tudhoe late in the possession . . . of Thomas Craggs and now in the possession of John Haswell as tenant . . . from year to year at . . . the yearly rent of 8s. One other cottage house and garth in Tudhoe . . . in the possession . . . of Frances Hunt as tenant . . . from year to year at the yearly rent of £1. One other cottage house and garth in Tudhoe . . . in the possession . . . of Thomas Thornberry as tenant . . . from year to year at the yearly rent of 12s. One other cottage house in Tudhoe . . . late in the possession . . of Anne Spark which is now untenanted and so ruinous and decayed that it is falling down. One other cottage house in Tudhoe . . . late in the possession . . . of Thomas Jobling and now in the possession of John Ridley as tenant . . . from year to year at the yearly rent of 12s. One other cottage house and garth in Tudhoe . . . now in the possession . . . of [*illegible*] Taylor as tenant . . . at the yearly rent of 16s.

Out of which said severall yearly rents there are severall outgoings or deductions made and paid yearly for the lime laid upon the tillage ground belonging to the said premisses which amounts yearly and every year to the sum of £12 5s. or thereabouts one year with another over and besides the land tax windows sess bridge and rogue sess and all necessary repairs for the said premisses which are likewise paid or allowed by me the said Edward Salvin forth and out of the said severall yearly rents. And there is also a yearly rent called the Crown rent or fee farm rent of £24 8s. 9½d. and one pound of pepper valued at 1s. 8d. paid or payable yearly and every year forth and out of the whole township of Tudhoe of which I . . . pay yearly and every year £12 8s. 3½d. for my share and proportion for and in respect of the said premisses. And there is likewise a prescript rent of £1 10s. payable yearly and every year forth and out of the whole township of Tudhoe to the Rector of Brancepeth . . . for and in lieu of the tyth hay of the said township of which I . . . pay yearly and every year 15s. 11½d. for my share and proportion for and in respect of the said premisses and there is also another yearly out rent of 11s. 5½d. payable yearly and every year to the Dean and Chapter of Durham forth and out of that part of the premisses called the Welling Farm. In all which said messuages lands tenements and hereditaments I . . . have or claim to be intitled to an estate for my own life without impeachment of waste with remainder to my first and other sons in tail male by and under the last will and testament of my late brother Bryan Salvin deceased subject to the payment of £4,000 thereby charged upon the said premisses and to the payment of £2000 more and £550 prior charges and incumbrances respectively affecting either the whole or some part or parts of the said messuages lands tenements or hereditaments and for which the same or some other part thereof was or were formerly mortgaged or charged.

All which matters and things before mentioned and set forth I . . . do by this writing under my hand desire the Clerk of the peace of and for the County of Durham or his lawful Deputy to register and enter in the parchment book or books roll or rolls which are or shall be by him made or kept for that purpose in the manner and in the words before mentioned. In witness whereof I . . . have hereunto sett my name 1 October 1751.

Edward Salvin

The name of the said Edward Salvin was subscribed to this registry by Hendry Hopper gentleman his attorney thereunto authorized by letter of attorney under his hand and seal the execution whereof was proved by two witnesses and the said subscription and proof were made in open court at the general quarter sessions of the peace holden at the City of Durham in and for the County Palatine of Durham 9 October 1751 before us Hen. Lambton J. Davison

One of the sons of no. 133 and younger brother of no. 139. Died unmarried 21 December 1757, buried at St. Pancras, London (Surtees iv, 120).

136. JERRARD SALVIN 1717

(enrolled 23 April 1717)

I Jerrard Salvin of Croxdale in the parish of St. Oswald in the County Palatine of Durham Esqr. . . .

Imprimis Croxdale all the manor or lordship or reputed manor or lordship of Croxdale . . . with the capital messuage or mansion house there and several lands tenements and hereditaments therewith used being now unlet and in my own hands and possession being together of the yearly value of £160.

Item a water corn mill there and two closes therewith held and enjoyed with the appurtenances in the possession of Mary Arrowsmith widow as tenant from year to year under the yearly rent of £24

Item a paper mill with the appurtenances in the possession of Edward Clarke as tenant . . . to whom I have let the same for three years to begin . . . from 1 May next ensuing under the yearly rent of £9

Item a farmhold or tenement called the Broad Close farm with all lands and grounds thereunto belonging . . . in Croxdale . . . in the possession of John Pickering yeoman as tenant . . . from year to year under the yearly rent of £52 10s.

I pay for the freehold part of the farm to the Bishop of Durham yearly an out rent of 8s. 3d. and for that part of the said farm which is leasehold as hereinafter is mentioned.

I pay for all the tithes of corn and hay for all the freehold lands of Croxdale a yearly prescript rent of £1 0s. 10d. to the curate of Croxdale Chappelry and for the petty tithes of the whole lordship as I can agree for the same with the curate. The last year I paid for the said tithes £3 15s.

The said tenants have their farms tithe free and I pay or allow them for all repairs and all taxes.

Sunderland All that messuage or tenement and farm . . . in the township of Sunderland nigh the Bridge in the said parish of St. Oswald in the possession of Mary Brown widow as tenant thereof from year to year under the yearly rent of £45

Item A messuage tenement and farm at Sunderland aforesaid in the possession of Robert Darnton yeoman as tenant thereof from year to year under the yearly rent of £45

Item a messuage or tenement therewith a smith's shop thereunto belonging in the possession of Humphrey Darnton, smith, as tenant . . . from year to year under the yearly rent of £4

There is payable out of my said estate at Sunderland bridge a yearly prescript rent of 14s. for the tithes of hay and an out rent to the Crown of £7 to Edward Noell Esq., his heirs and assigns and I allow to the tenants of Sunderland bridge out of their said rents all repairs and they pay the said prescript rent of 14s., and also the said yearly rents of £7.

Shotton A messuage or tenement at Shotton in the parish of Sedgefield in the said county of Durham in the possession of John Lynn as tenant or farmer . . . for the remainder of a term of seven years (which commenced 1 May 1715) under the yearly rent of £93 by vertue of a memorandum in writing under the hand of Thomas Ord my steward

Item a messuage or tenement at Shotton . . . in the possession of Humphrey Arrowsmith yeoman as tenant . . . for the remainder of a term of seven years which commenced at Mayday 1715 under the yearly rent of £87 by vertue of a memorandum in writing under the hand of the said Thomas Ord my steward

I allow the said tenants at Shotton out of their rents half of all the lime at the Kiln which they lay upon their said farms and all taxes and assesments . . . except poor sess. There is a yearly prescript rent of £1 13s. 4d. paid for the said tenements at Shotton which the tenants pay

Bruntoft: Wolveston. A messuage or tenement at Wolveston in the parish of Billingham and at Bruntoft in the parish of Elwick both in the said county of Durham in the possession of Robert White yeoman as tenant thereof for the remainder of a term of three years which commenced at May Day 1715 under the yearly rent of £94 by vertue of a memorandum in writing under the hand of my said steward but part of this farm, to wit the lands called Padclose pasture little Dove Coatfeild and the out moore are by the settlement made upon the marriage of my son Bryan Salvin with Anne his now wife settled upon him and his issue by his said wife in part of his present maintenance so that my proportion of the said farm and rent is only £50

The said tenant hath allowed him out of his rent all repairs all lime and all taxes and assessments . . . poor sess excepted

Tofts Wolveston A messuage or tenement . . . at the Tofts in the parish of Elwick and at Wolveston . . . in the possession or occupation of William Duell yeoman tenant . . . for the remainder of a term of three years by me made to him . . . which commenced at May day 1715 under the yearly rent of £50. The said tenant hath allowed to him out of the said rent all lime at the Kill which he shall lay upon his said farm and all taxes and assessments as well parliamentary as parochial, poor sesse excepted

Butterwick A messuage farmhold or tenement commonly called Butlers farm . . . at Butterwick in the parish of Sedgefield . . . in the possession of Lancelott Clark and Thomas Lamb tenants thereof from year to year under the yearly rent of £50. I allow to the said tenants all lime which they lay upon the farm and all taxes and assessments except poor sesse. I pay to Philip Papilion Esq for this farm a yearly rent of £1 13s. 4d.

And I have such estate and interest in and to the said several premises as followeth (that is to say) as to part of the said premises above mentioned to be unlet and in my possession of the yearly value of £8 10s. and as to part of the said Broad Close farm in the possession of John Pickering of the like yearly value of £8 10s.

I am intitled thereunto for the residue of a term of 21 years thereof granted to me by the Dean and Chapter of Durham by indenture [*date left blank*] at . . . the yearly rent of £2 13s. 4d. which said lease is usually renewed every seven years at an arbitrary fine paid to the said Dean and Chapter beside the lease and seal fees. And as to the messuage farm and lands at Butterwick called Butlers farm I am intitled thereunto to me and my heirs and as to all the rest of the said premises . . . at . . . Sunderland near the Bridge Croxdale Butterwick Bruntoft Toft Wolveston and Shotton or elsewhere in the parishes of St. Oswald's, Sedgefield, Elwick and Billingham I am intitled thereunto for the term of my natural life with only the remainder or reversion to me and my heirs after the death of my said son Bryan Salvin and failure of issue male of his body subject to an estate limited to Mary my wife for her life, if she shall survive me of and in the said premises of Shotton and the said premises called Toft and the premises at Wolveston therewith letten and enjoyed and subject to a term of 400 years commenced from my death of all the premises whereof I am herein mentioned to be tenant for life other than the said premises limited to my said wife for her life to Sir Nicholas Tempest Thomas Maire and Ralph Shipperdson for the raising of £1500 for the portion of Katherine Salvin my daughter with interest and subject to a further term limited thereof and of the reversion of the said premises limited to my said wife for her life and of other lands of the yearly value of £400 to a further term limited thereof and of the reversion of the said premises limited to my said wife for her life and of other lands of the yearly value of £400 or thereabouts which upon the marriage of my said son Bryan Salvin were settled upon him for his maintenance to Sir Carnaby Haggerston John Tempest and Thomas Ord for 500 years in remainder after the death of my said son for the raising of such annuities and portions for the daughters and younger sons of the said Bryan Salvin by his now wife as in the said settlement made upon his marriage is mentioned and subject to a further term of 1000 years limited of all the said premises in remainder after failure of issue male of my said son Bryan Salvin by his now wife to Sir Marmaduke Constable Robert Shaftoe and William Bacon for the raising portions for the daughter or daughters of my said son and his now wife in case of failure of issue male of their bodies —to wit £3,000 if one such daughter and £4,000 if two or more with an augmentation of £2000 more in case of failure of issue male of the said Bryan Salvin by his now wife or any other wife and for the raising maintenance for such daughters until the said portions shall be raised and paid with the usual powers for me and my said son to grant leases of the said premises not exceeding 21 years at the rack rent and subject to the sum of £1000 charged and chargeable upon the said premise in Croxdale Sunderland Shotton Butterwick Bruntoft Wolveston in part of the portion of Anne daughter of the said Jarrard Salvin and late wife of Walter Strickland Esq and by the said settlement made upon the marriage of my said son which by lease and release I . . . have conveyed or therein made mention to convey to the said Robert Shaftoe and William Bacon their heirs and assigns all my lands and tenements in Croxdale . . . to the uses therein mentioned and in case the said leasehold lands do pass thereby then my interest in the said leasehold premises late of the said Dean and Chapter is vested in the said Robert Shaftoe and William Bacon in trust for me . . . for my life

Owton Item a messuage farmhold or tenement with all houses buildings lands closes and parcels of ground thereunto belonging or therewith held and enjoyed . . . at Owton in the parish of Stranton in the said County of Durham in the possession of Ralph Steel gen, Ralph Ord, yeoman as tenants . . . for the remainder of a term of four years which commenced 1 May 1715 granted thereof by me to them under the yearly rent of £126

The tenants have allowed them out of the said rents all repairs and all taxes parliamentary and parochial

Item a messuage or tenement and farm with all houses and buildings lands closes and parcels of ground thereunto belonging in the possession of Luke Elstobb yeoman as tenant . . . situate . . . at Owton . . . under the yearly rent of £80 by vertue of a memorandum in writing under the hand of Thomas Ord my steward whereby the said premises were let to the said Luke Elstobb for four years which commenced from 1 May 1715

The tenant hath allowed him out of the said rents all taxes and assessments parliamentary and parochial

Item Several closes and parcels of ground . . . at Owton . . . in the possession of John Knaggs as tenant . . . for the remainder of a term of six years which commenced 1 May 1716 under the yearly rent of £36 by vertue of a memorandum in writing signed by the said Thomas Ord. . . . The tenant has allowed him out of his rents all taxes and assessments whatsoever as well parliamentary as parochial

There is also issuing and payable out of the said manor and

premises at Owton to the owner of the Manor of Tinmouth in lieu of and for all tithes and yearly prescript rents of £2 13s. 4d. Which said manor of Owton and the said premises in Owton and Seaton Carew I am intitled to me my heirs and assigns subject to and charged and chargeable with the payment of £40 yearly to Troth Saltmarsh spinster for her life and also subject to the sum of £500 charged upon all the said premises at Owton (except Raintons Close Hubbocks Pasture Wrenns Close and Braffertons Close) for other part of the portion of the said Ann Strickland my daughter with interest and also subject to a term of 2,000 years granted of all the said manor and premises at Owton (except the last mentioned to be excepted closes) by me to Thomas Ord and Bryan Gray Esq by indenture bearing date about a year ago but the certain date not having the same in my custody I cannot set forth for the security and paying thereout as well the said £1000 as the said £500 being the portion of the said Ann Strickland with interest and for the indempnifying and discharging the estates comprized in the said settlement made upon the marriage of my said son Bryan Salvin of and from the same

In witness whereof I have hereunto set my hand 18 April 1717

Jar: Salvin

The name of the said Jerrard Salvin was subscribed to this registry by David Dixon gen his attorney thereunto authorized by warrant of attorney under his hand and seal, the execution whereof was proved by two witnesses at the general quarter sessions of the peace held for the County of Durham 1 May 1717 and the said subscription was made at the said general quarter sessions of the peace held by adjournment 27 June 1717 in the presence of Jno Rudd Antho: Hall.

Son and heir of Bryan Salvin and his wife Katherine, daughter of Sir Thomas Tempest, Bart. of Stella. Aged 12 on 18 August 1666 (Vis. pedigree), married (lic. 20 June 1676) Mary, daughter of Ralph Clavering of Callaly. He was then 22 and she 19, marriage certificate given by Matthew Burnly, Rector of St. Trinity, Micklegate, York. Pass to travel with Mary his wife and William Salvin beyond the seas granted 23 April 1679 (Cal. S.P. Dom. 1679/80 p. 341), pass to travel from Croxdale to Callaly granted 31 May 1679 (Salvin papers). His house searched for arms 1689 (Sharp MS. 110).

Died 5 February 1722/3 aged 69, buried at St. Oswald's, Durham, 7

February. Will dated 20 January 1721, in which he leaves to his loving and dearly beloved wife Mary Salvin, all his manor or lordship of Owton and all his messuages etc. in Buterwick for her life, and then to his well beloved and only son Bryan Salvin, to whom he left all other his manors, messuages and lands in the county of Durham, and also all pictures, furniture and ornaments "within my great dining room at Croxdale and in the room and chambers over and above the same and my large silver tankard and two silver candlesticks with my family's coat of arms engraven thereupon". He leaves to his well beloved daughter Katherine Salvin £1,500, and appoints his wife and son executors. The witnesses were Tho. Ord, Laurence Liddell and Dav. Dixon. The will was enrolled at Durham Quarter Sessions on 24 May 1723.

137. MARY SALVIN 1723

To the Clarke of the peace for the county Palatine of Durham and Sadberge or his Lawfull Deputy

I Mary Salvin of Croxdale in the parish of Saint Oswald in the said County widdow and relict of Jarrard Salvin Esqr late of Croxdale aforesaid deceased

Imprimis Shotton

a messuage and farm in Shotton in the parish of Sedgfield in the said County of Durham in the possession of John Lynn as tenant or farmer thereof being let by me to him for the terme of three years comencing as to part of the premisses from Lady day last and as to the rest of the premisses from 1 May last at and under the yearly rent of £99

Item a messuage and farme at Shotton . . . in the possession of Humphrey Arrowsmith yeoman as tennant or farmer thereof being lett by me to him for the terme of three years comencing as to part of the premisses from Lady day last and as to the rest of the premisses from 1 May last at and under the yearly rent of £93

there is a yearly prescript of £1 13s. 4d. paid for the said Lands at Shotton which the said tennants pay

Tofts and Wolveston

Item a messuage and farme scituate lying and being part thereof at Tofts in the parish of Elwicke and the residue thereof at Wolveston in the parish of Billingham both in the said County of Durham in the possession of William Duell yeoman as tennant or farmer thereof being let by me to him for the terme of three years comencing as to the pasture ground from Lady Day last and as to the rest of the premisses from 1 May last under the yearly rent of £48 15s. To all which . . . lands and premisses I am intitled for the terme of my naturall life

Item Butterwick

A messuage and farmhold commonly called Butlers farme scituate . . . at Butterwick in the parish of Sedgfield . . . now in the possession of Thomas Lamb yeoman as tennant or farmer thereof being let by me to him for the terme of three years which comenced as to the pasture ground from Lady Day last and as to the rest of the premisses from 1 May last past under the yearly rent of £50

I allow to the said tennant all assessments and taxes whatsoever except poor sess and I pay to Phillip Papilion Esqr for the said farme a yearly out rent of £1 13s. 4d.

Owton

Item a messuage and farmhold scituate . . . att Owton in the parish of Stranton . . . in the possession of Ralph Steel gentleman and Ralph Ord yeoman as tennants or farmers thereof for the terme of three years comencing as to the pasture ground from Lady Day last and as to the rest of the premisses from 1 May last past under the yearly rent of £121

Item Owton

a messuage and farmhold scituate . . . at Owton . . . now in the possession of Luke Elstobb yeoman as tennant or farmer thereof for the terme of three years comencing as to part of the premisses from Lady Day last and as to the rest of the premisses from 1 May last past under the yearly rent of £80

Item several closes and parcells of ground scituate . . . at Owton in the possession of John Stoddart and Thomas Yeild yeomen as tennants or farmers thereof for the terme of three years comencing as to part of the premisses from Lady Day last and as to the rest of the premisses from 1 May last past under the yearly rent of £34 out of which said lands and tenements of Owton there is issuing and payable to the owner of the Honor of Tinmouth in liew of and for all tythes a yearly prescript rent of £2 13s. 4d.

To which said messuages lands and tenements lying at Butterwick and Owton . . . I am intitled for the terme of my naturall life by vertue of the last will and testament of my said late deceased Husband all which said mannor of Owton and lands at Butterwicke are subject to and charged and chargeable with the sume of £500 (excepting Raintons Close Hubbock Pasture Wrenns Close and Braffertons Close) for part of the portion of my Daughter Anne Strickland widdow with interrest and also subject to a terme of 2,000 years or some such terme granted of all the said mannor and premisses at Owton (except the last mentioned to be excepted Closes) by me said late husband to Thomas Ord and Bryan Gray Esqr by deed or indenture but the certain date thereof (not having the same in my custody nor knowing where the same is I cannot set forth) for the securing raseing and paying thereout as well the sume of £1,000 as of the said £500 being the portion of my said daughter Strickland with interrest and for the indempnifying and discharging the estate comprised in the settlement made upon the marriage of my son Bryan Salvin of and from the same but the purport of the said deed I cannot sett forth otherwise than as aforesaid.

Mary Salvin

The name of the said Mary Salvin was subscribed . . . by David Dixon Gent her attorney . . . in open court at the General Quarter Sessions of the peace held at the City of Durham for the county of Durham 17 July 1723 in the presence of us Jno Rudd Nich. Tempest Tho. Stonhewer Cler. pacis

Widow of the last. Buried at St. Oswald's, Durham, 16 February 1727/8, aged 75.

138. RALPH SALVIN 1717

(enrolled 23 April 1717)

I Ralph Salvin of Tuddoe in the parish of Brancepeth in the county of Durham Esqr. . . .

Imprimis all that capital messuage mansion house or tenement . . . in the town of Tuddoe . . . wherein I now dwell with all orchards gardens lands and closes therewith held and enjoyed with their appurtenances of the yearly value (as near as I can compute) of £62 10s.

Item all that messuage tenement and farm with the appurtenances

. . . in Tuddoe . . . in possession of Thomas Wilson tenant thereof from year to year under the yearly rent of £52 10s.

Do. in the possession of John Readleach as tenant . . . £35 10s.

Do. in the possession of George Dunn . . . £19 17s.

Do. in the possession of George Biggins . . . £8.

Item a messuage tenement and croft in Tuddoe . . . with the appurtenances in the possession of Ralph Dunn tenant . . . from year to year under the yearly rent of £7 10s.

Do. in the possession of William Griffin . . . £4.

Item a messuage tenement and farm in Tuddoe . . . with the appurtenances in the possession of Thomas Harrison tenant thereof under the yearly rent of £45 for the term of three years by vertue of a lease in writing from me to him . . . which term commenced 1 May 1715 in which said lease there is comprized some lands late belonging to William Ettricke Esq for his life of the yearly value of £8 being part of and to make the said yearly rent of £45.

Item a messuage tenement and farm with the appurtenances in Tuddoe . . . in the possession of George Pickering tenant thereof from year to year under the yearly rent of £48 10s. which said last mentioned farm and lands were also late the estate of the said William Ettricke

Item a cottage in Tuddoe . . . with the appurtenances in the possession of John Dunn tenant . . . under the yearly rent of £1 10s.

Item a cottage . . . in Tuddoe . . . in possession of Ralph Hill tenant . . . under the yearly rent of 20s.

Item a cottage in Tuddoe . . . in possession of Anne Langstaffe widow under the yearly rent of 20s.

Item a cottage or dwelling house in Tuddoe . . . in possession of Peter Craggs under the yearly rent of 20s. late part of the estate of the said William Ettricke

[The following cottages in Tuddoe let to Thomas Thornbury 12s. per annum. part of the estate of William Ettricke, let to Eliz. Kirkley spinster 12s. per annum, let to Ralph Cosser at 10s. per annum, let to Isabell Pearson widow at 8s. a year, all these being tenants from year to year.]

I pay or allow to all the tenants aforesaid out of their rents for all repairs, taxes and assessments, parliamentary and parochial, excepting Thomas Harrison, who pays church sess and poor sess for his farm.

The whole township of Tuddoe pays a prescript rent for tithes of hay 30s. my share thereof (as tis yearly collected and I believe tis truly proportioned) amounts unto 11s. 10d. two farthings.

The township of Tuddoe also pay for the Nouke hills and Welling farm in Tuddoe to the . . . Dean and Chapter an out rent of 20s. per annum my proportionable rent whereof is 8s. 2d. per annum.

The said township also pays yearly for a crown rent to Philip Papilion Esq £24 8s. 9d. two farthings, my proportionable part thereof amounts to £8 17s. 6d.

I am intitled to the said messuage cottages lands and grounds herein mentioned to have been late part of the estate of the said William Ettricke for the life of the said William Ettricke and I am intitled to the residue of the said premises for my life with remainder to me and the heirs male of my body and failing such issue to me and my heirs subject to a term of 500 years commencing from and after my death thereof limited by the settlement upon my marriage with my late wife to the Honble Thomas Radclyffe Esq and Nicholas Kennett Esq upon trust by mortgage or demise of the same premises or any part thereof to raise such sum or sums as I shall direct not exceeding £1000 in the whole to be paid as I shall appoint and also £1000 for the portion of Dorothy my daughter by my said late wife

Ral: Salvin

The name of the said Ralph Salvin was subscribed to this registry by David Dixon gent his attorney thereunto authorized by warrant of attorney under his hand and seal the execution whereof was proved by two witnesses at the general quarter sessions of the peace held for the County of Durham 1 May 1717 and the said subscription was made at the said general quarter sessions of the peace held by adjournment 27 June 1717 in the presence of Jno Rudd Antho: Hall

138. RALPH SALVIN 1718

I Ralph Salvin of Tuddoe . . . Esqr . . . a messuage farme or tenement with severall closes and parcells of ground arable meadow and pasture therewith held . . . now in the possession . . . of John

Richardson of Tuddoe . . . yeoman . . . at . . . the yearly rent of £40 payable . . . att . . . Martinmas and May-day be equall portions by vertue of a lease in writing . . . 20 December 1712 made between William Ettricke of Sunderland by the Sea . . . Esqr of the one part and the said John Richardson of the other part under the hands and seals of both the said parties to hold the said premisses to the said John Richardson in manner following . . . the arable and pasture grounds from 25 March then next ensuing and the meadow grounds and other the premisses from 3 May then next after the terme of six years to commence from the severall days of entry, the first payment to begin and to be made at Martinmas then next after I pay all taxes and assessments whatsoever (window sess only excepted which the tennant payes) as by the said lease more fully may appear one other messuage farm or tenement with severall closes and parcells of ground arable meadow and pasture therewith held and enjoyed now in the possession . . . of Edward Crosby of Tuddoe . . . yeoman as tennant or farmer thereof att . . . the annual . . . rent of £40 . . . payable at two terms in the year vizt Martinmas and May day by equall portions by vertue of a lease in writing bearing date 1 January 10 Anne [1711-12] made by the said William Ettricke . . . and the said Edward Crosby . . . to hold the said premisses to the said Edward Crosby in manner following vizt the pasture ground from 25 March then next ensuing and the meadow grounds and other the premisses from 3 May then next after for the term of nine years to commence from the said severall dayes of entry the first payment to begin at Martinmas then next ensuing I pay all taxes and assessments . . . (window sess only excepted which the tennant payes) as by the said lease more fully may appear

One other messuage farmhold or tenement with severall closes and parcells of ground arable meadow and pasture therewith held and enjoyed now in the possession of Richard Arrowsmith of Tuddoe . . . yeoman as tennant or farmer . . . att . . . the annuall . . . rent of £42 10s. . . . payable at two terms . . . vizt Martinmas and May-day by equall portions by vertue of a lease in writing bearing date 22 December 1712 made between the said William Ettricke . . . and the said John Richardson then of Kelloe . . . yeoman . . . to hold the said premises to the said Richard Arrowsmith in manner following vizt the arable ground from 25 March then next ensuing and the meadow grounds and other the premises from 3 May then next after for the terme of one year to commence from the said severall dayes of entry the first payment to begin at Martinmas then next ensuing

I pay all taxes and assessments . . . window sess only excepted which the tennant payes as by the said lease more fully may appear

One other messuage or cottage farme or tenement with some small parcells of ground therewith held and enjoyed now in the possession . . . of Thomas Johnson of Tuddoe . . . yeoman as tennant . . . at . . . the annuall . . . rent of £4 8s. . . . payable . . . at May day and Martinmas by equall portions by vertue of a lease parol which began . . . on or about 11 November last past to hold to him the said Thomas Johnson for the terme of one whole year from thence next ensuing I pay all sesses and taxes (window sess only excepted which the tennant payes)

All . . . which severall messuages farm lands tenements and hereditaments are scituate . . . within the townshipp townefields precincts and territories of Tuddoe . . . and were by good and sufficient conveyances and assurances in the law thereof duly made [*rubbed*] by William Ettricke of Sunderland by the sea . . . gent son and heir apparent of the said William Ettricke of the same place esqr and the said William Ettricke the father granted and conveyed to Marke Shafto of Whitworth his heires and assignes to hold to him . . . his heires and assignes to and for such uses trusts and agreements as are therein expressed and declared (that is to say) to the use and behoofe of the said William Ettricke the father his executors administrators and assignes for during and unto the full end and term of 500 years from the day of the date of the said conveyances fully to be compleat and ended without impeachment of waste with a provisoe for making void the said terme of 500 years upon the payment of £2000 . . . by the said Marke Shafto his heirs executors administrators or assignes to the said William Ettricke his executors administrators and assignes with interest for the same after the rate of £4 per centum per annum upon 1 May 1719 without any abatement or deduction of or for any taxes assessments or any other matter or thing whatsoever And from and after the end and expiration or other sooner determination of the said terme of 500 years then to the use and behoofe of the said Marke Shafto his heirs and assignes for ever which said conveyances and assurances and the interest thereof vested in the said Marke Shaftoe are by a deed or declaration of trust . . . duly executed by the said

Marke Shaftoe bearing date some short time after the date of the conveyances and assurances before mentioned declared to be in trust in the first place for securing to the said Marke Shaftoe his executors administrators and assignes . . . £200 . . . now oweing unto him . . . from me the said Ralph Salvin upon my bond or obligation by me made given and entred unto the said Marke Shaftoe with the interest thereof payable as in the condition of the said bond is mentioned and also for the securing of all such other summe and summes of money as I . . . then was or should thereafter be indebted unto the said Marke Shaftoe with interest for the same and then in trust for me . . . my heirs and assignes for ever

And I . . . have and am entituled to such right estate and interest in and to the premisses as is before mentioned and set forth by and under the said deeds conveyances and declaration of trust and I am now indebted to the said Marke Shaftoe the said summe of £200 with the interest thereof and no more and the said £200 with the interest thereof is still resting due and unpaid to the said William Ettricke the elder and the said estates uses and trusts raised by the said conveyances and declaration of trust are still in force and unaltered Witnesse my hand 3 September 1718

Ralph Salvin

The name of the said Ralph Salvin was subscribed to this registry by David Dixon gent his attorney thereunto authorized by warrant of attorney under his hand and seal the execution whereof was proved by two witnesses and the subscription and proof was made in open court at the generall quarter sessions of the peace held at the City of Durham for the County of Durham by adjournment 21 October 1718 before us Jno Rudd John Bowes

138. RALPH SALVIN 1723/4

I Ralph Salvin of Tudhow in the County of Durham Esquire. . . .

A cottage in Tudhow in the occupation of Jane Allan at the yearly rent of 15s.

A house and Garth in Tudhow . . . in the occupation of Robert Spark at the yearly rent of £1 5s. and another Cottage in Tudhow in the occupation of William Corser att the yearly rent of 10s.

All which premisses are lying and being in the said County of Durham and are held by the said severall persons from year to year at the yearly rents before mentioned. All which said houses lands and tenements were conveyed to and are vested in John Rudd of the City of Durham Esqr and his heirs for securing the payment of £20 with interest to the said John Rudd and subject thereunto in trust for me and my heirs and I am intitled in equity to the premisses to me and my heirs subject to the payment of the said £20 with interest to the said John Rudd.

Ralph Salvin.

Subscribed . . . in open Court at the General Quarter Sessions of the peace held at the City of Durham by Adjournment 7 February 1723 before Jno Rudd Fr Cornforth mayor

Only son of William Salvin of Brandon and Elvet, by Dorothy his first wife. Inherited estate in Tudhoe from his uncle Ralph Salvin in 1705 and bought more property there in 1717/18 (Salvin papers). Married at Kelloe 10 June 1708 (post-nuptial settlement 3 February 1708/9) the Hon. Barbara Browne, daughter of Henry 5th Viscount Montagu, and had one daughter, Dorothy. Barbara was buried 13 December 1709. Ralph Salvin was buried at St. Oswald's, Durham, 27 August 1729. Will dated 12 August 1729, delivered to Bryan Salvin of Croxdale, who enters into a bond 26 August following. In it the testator leaves to Gerrard Salvin, eldest son of his cousin Bryan Salvin, all his messuages and lands in Tudhoe and elsewhere, "and in case the said Gerrard Salvin shall marry and have two sons my will and desire is that his second son shall be called Ralph and in such case I give the said messuages and lands after the death of the said Gerrard Salvin to such second son as he shall have and called by the name of Ralph Salvin and for default I give the said messuages and lands to the said Gerrard Salvin and his heirs and for default to Bryan Salvin, younger son of my said cousin Bryan Salvin." He leaves to his cousin Katharine Salvin, sister of the said Bryan, his gold watch and all his trinkets and a gold ring of the value of 20s.

To his cousins Ann Strickland, James Salvin and his wife, Anthony Salvin, Elizabeth Salvin and her sister Katharine Salvin he leaves mourning rings of the value of 20s. To his cousin Dr. William Howard "all the horses, mares and geldings which I shall have at the time of my death and likewise my chaise". The residue is bequeathed to his said cousin Bryan Salvin, the elder of Croxdale, whom he names executor.

139. WILLIAM SALVIN 1745

The registry of me William Salvin of Croxdale . . . Esquire of and concerning my messuages and lands . . . in the township of Tudhoe within the parish of Brancepeth . . .

one capital messuage or tenement in Tudhoe . . . with the stables gardens and appurtenances . . . now in the possession of Ralph Dunn as tenant at will for which he is to pay me no rent but is to live in the said messuage . . . for taking care of the gardens and keeping them in order

One other messuage or tenement and farm and the lands therewith used in Tudhoe aforesaid with the appurtenances now in the possession or occupation of Thomas Wilson as tenant thereof from year to year at the yearly rent of £90

One other messuage or tenement and farm and the lands therewith used in Tudhoe aforesaid with the appurtenances now in the possession . . . of John Priss as tenant thereof under a lease made to Robert Forster by my father Bryan Salvin senior of Croxdale Esquire . . . 1 February 1739 to hold the pasture ground from Lady day next and the rest of the premisses from May day then next ensuing for the term of nine years at the yearly rent of £47

One other messuage or tenement and farm and the lands therewith used at Tudhoe . . . with the appurtenances now in the possession . . . of George Greenwell as tenant thereof under an agreement in writing made between him and my father Bryan Salvin 3 December 1743 to hold from Lady day the pasture ground and the rest of the premisses from May day 1744 for the term of three years from thence next ensuing at . . . the yearly rent of £70.

One other messuage or tenement and farm and the lands therewith used in Tudhoe . . . with the appurtenances now in the possession . . . of Elizabeth Harrison widow as tenant from year to year at the yearly rent of £45.

One other messuage or tenement and farm and the lands therewith used in Tudhoe . . . with the appurtenances now in the possession . . . of John Pickering as tenant . . . from year to year at the yearly rent of £36.

[*Other messuages in Tudhoe in possession of the following at the rents specified:* Edward Crosby £48 Thomas Foreman £58 Henry

Hutchinson £20 10s. Michael Hills £3 14s. 6d. John Dunn £10 Robert Burn £2 6s.]

Four closes . . . of ground in Tudhoe . . . with the appurtenances now in the possession . . . of Ralph Dunn as tenant from year to year at the yearly rent of £18

One other messuage or tenement and the lands therewith used in Tudhoe . . . with the appurtenances now in the possession . . . of Thomas Crosby as tenant . . . from year to year at the yearely rent of £4 10s.

One other close . . . in Tudhoe . . . with the appurtenances now in the possession . . . of John Dunn the younger as tenant thereof from year to year at the yearly rent of £5 10s.

One other close . . . in Tudhoe . . . with the byer and appurtenances now in the possession . . . of Thomas Pickering as tenant . . . from year to year at the yearly rent of £5

One other cottage house in Tudhoe . . . with the appurtenances now in the possession . . . of John Maw as tenant . . . from year to year at the yearly rent of 18s.

One granary in Tudhoe . . . with the appurtenances now in the possession . . . of Thomas Wilson as tenant thereof from year to year at the yearly rent of 7s.

(Cottage houses in Tudhoe tenanted by Jane Catton 8s. a year rent. William Makepeace 12s. A cottage house and garth in Tudhoe tenanted by Catherine Wheatley at 13s. a year.)

One other cottage house called the School House in Tudhoe . . . with the appurtenances now in the possession of Thomas Craggs as tenant . . . at the yearly rent of 12s.

(Cottage houses and garths in Tudhoe tenanted by Edward Hunt at £1 rent. by Thomas Thornberry at 12s. A cottage house in Tudhoe tenanted by Anne Spark at 6s. A cottage house and stable, tenant Thomas Joblin at 15s. A cottage house and garth, tenant Benjamin Taylor, at 16s.)

Out of which . . . severall yearly rents there are severall outgoings or deductions and allowances made yearly and every year for the lime laid upon the tillage ground belonging to the said premisses which amounts yearly to the sum of £20 and upwards one year with another over and besides the Land Tax and the Window Sess and Bridge Sess for the said premisses which are yearly paid or allowed by me the said William Salvin and there is also a yearly out rent called the Crown rent of £9 18s. 4d. and a quarter of a pound of pepper valued at 5d. payable yearly and every year forth and out of the said premisses and likewise a prescript rent of 11s. 11d. payable yearly . . . to the Rector of Brancepeth . . . for and in lieu of the tyth hay of the said premisses

And there is also another yearly out rent of 11s. 5½d. payable yearly . . . to the Dean and Chapter of Durham forth and out of that part of the said premisses called the Welling Farm

In all which said messuages lands tenements and hereditaments I the said William Salvin have or claim to be intitled to an estate during the joint lives of me and my father Bryan Salvin by and under the will of my late brother Bryan Salvin deceased subject nevertheless to £4,000 thereby charged and also to £550 and £2,000 prior charges respectively affecting either the whole or some parts of the said messuages lands tenements and hereditaments.

26 September 1745 William Salvin.

The name of the said William Salvin was subscribed to this registry by John Reed gentleman his attorney . . . in open Court at the Generall Quarter Sessions of the peace holden at the City of Durham in and for the County Palatine of Durham by adjournment 1 November 1745 before us Ralph Carr Antho. Wilkinson Justices of the peaces.

139. WILLIAM SALVIN 1752

To the Clerk of the Peace for the County of Durham and Sadberge or his lawful deputy.

I William Salvin of [*illegible*] in the parish of St. Oswald in the said county esquire son and heir of Bryan Salvin Esquire late of Croxdale aforesaid deceased . . .

A true particular of the severall messuages lands tenements and hereditaments scituate . . . in the County of Durham whereof I . . . am come into the possession of since the death of Bryan Salvin my late father deceased. . . . Imprimis the manor or lordship or reputed lordship of Croxdale in the parish of Saint Oswald aforesaid with the capital messuage or mansion house there and severall lands tenements and hereditaments therewith used being now unlet and in my own hands and possession together of the yearly value of £123 or thereabouts. Item a farm of land consisting of four closes part of the said manor . . . let to Mathew Corner from year to year at the yearly rent of £40 out of which he has an allowance of all taxes sesses and repairs. Item a water corn mill there and a close adjoining upon the chappel at Croxdale lett to Joseph Ayers the younger from year to year at the yearly rent of £32 10s. out of which he has an allowance of all taxes sesses and repairs. Item a paper mill and a close therwith now lett to Joseph Ayers the elder from year to year at the yearly rent of £25 out of which he has an allowance of all taxes sesses and repairs. Item a farmhold or tenement called the Broad Close farm with all lands and grounds thereunto belonging scituate . . . in Croxdale in the possession of William Worthy yeoman as tenant thereof till May day next under the yearly rent of £90 There is a yearly out rent of 8s. 3d. payable out of the freehold part of this farm to the Bishop of Durham and for that part of the said farm which is leasehold as hereinafter is mentioned. There is a payment or yearly prescript rent of £1 0s. 10d. payable to the Curate of Croxdale for and in lieu of all the tythes of corn and hay in all the freehold lands at Croxdale . . . and a payment for the petty tythes of the whole lordship as the tenants can agree for the same with the said curate. The said William Worthy present tenant pays a third part of the said prescript rent a third part of the petty tythes and a third part of the church and poor sess and has no allowance out of this said rent for the same or any other sesses and taxes save for half of the lime used upon the said farm and repairs.

Sunderland Bridge Imprimis all that messuage or tenement and farm scituate . . . within the township of Sunderland near the Bridge in the parish of Saint Oswald . . . in the possession of William Wilkinson as tenant thereof at the yearly rent of £73 10s. from year to year out of which said rent the tenant has an allowance for all repairs and for half of the lime used upon the said farm.

Item a messuage or tenement and farm at Sunderland aforesaid . . . in the possession of William Fairman as tenant thereof from year to year at the yearly rent of £60 out of which said rent the tenant has an allowance for all repairs and for half of the lime used upon the said farm. Item a messuage or tenement there with a smiths shop therewith letten and thereunto belonging in the possession of Thomas Fawell tenant thereof from year to year at the yearly rent of £10 out of which the tenant has an allowance for all repairs.

There is payable out of my said estate at Sunderland bridge a yearly rent of 14s. for the tyth of hay and a yearly out rent or fee farm rent of £7. The said William Wilkinson and William Fareman pay the prescript rent of 14s. and said William Fareman pays the out rent of £7 out of their respective farms at Sunderland bridge over and besides their rent.

Butterwick Imprimis a messuage farm and lands . . . at Butterwick in the possession of William Todd as tenant thereof under a lease for six years commencing at May day next at the yearly rent of £190 out of which he has an allowance made for repairs and for one half of the lime used upon the premisses. . . . Item a messuage or tenement and farm at Butterwick aforesaid in the possession of John Wilkinson as tenant thereof under a lease for three years commencing at May day next at the yearly rent of £105 out of which he has an allowance made for repairs and for one half of the lime used upon the premisses out of which said two farms at Butterwick there is a yearly rent of £5 13s. 4d. payable to the Lord Bishop of Durham and his successors, I pay the said out rent.

Item a messuage and farmhold commonly called Butlers Farm scituate . . . at Butterwick . . . now in the possession of Emanuel Peverley tenant thereof under a lease for three years commencing at May day next at the yearly rent of £54 out of which I pay to Philip Papillion Esquire for a fee farm rent £1 13s. 4d. and make an allowance to the tenant for repairs and half of the lime used upon the premisses.

Owton. Imprimis a messuage and farmhold scituate . . . at Owton in the parish of Stranton in the said county . . . in the possession of Thomas Collin tenant thereof under a lease thereof for seven years comencing at May day next att the yearly rent of £131 out of which he has an allowance of £6 yearly for lime and also an allowance for repairs. Item a messuage and farmhold . . . at Owton . . . in the possession of Richard Elstob at tenant thereof under a lease for two years commencing at May day next at the yearly rent of £85 out of which he has an allowance for repairs and for one half of the lime used upon the said premisses. Item severall closes and parcells of ground . . . at Owton . . . in the possession of Thomas Yielid as tenant . . . at the yearly rent of £43 out of which he has an allowance for repairs and half of the lime used upon the said premisses under lease for two years comencing at May day next.

Shotton. Imprimis a messuage and farm in Shotton in the parish of Sedgfield . . . in the possession of John Lynn as tenant . . . under a lease for two years commencing at May day next at the yearly rent of £125 out of which he has an allowance for all repairs and half of the lime used upon the said premisses. Item a messuage and farm at Shotton . . . in the possession of John Cole as tenant . . . under a lease for two years comencing at May day next at the yearly rent of £120 out of which he has an allowance for repairs and half of the lime used upon the premisses and the tenants pay a yearly prescript rent of £1 13s. 4d. paid for the said lands at Shotton.

Bruntoft and Wolveston. Imprimis a messuage and farmhold at Wolveston in the parish of Billingham and at Bruntoft in the parish of Elwick . . . in the possession of John White tenant thereof under a lease for six years commencing at May day next at the yearly rent of £100 out of which he has an allowance for repairs and half of the lime used upon the premisses.

Tofts. Imprimis a messuage and farm, part thereof . . . at Tofts in the parish of Elwick and the residue . . . at Wolveston in the said parish of Billingham in the possession of James Thompson tenant thereof under a lease for four years commencing at May day next at the yearly rent of £50 out of which he has an allowance made for all repairs and half of the lime used upon the said premisses.

Old Elvett. A freehold messuage tenement or dwelling house with a garden behind the same in Old Elvett now in the possession of George Clavering Esquire who by agreement with me has been in the possession thereof since Martinmas last and is to continue tenant thereof untill May day next for which and for the use of the furniture in the said house belonging to me the said George Clavering is to pay at May day next the sum of £20 and I am to pay all taxes and repairs and the said premisses are subject to a mortgage of £700 and interest to the Honourable Christopher Dawney Esquire and the same is subject to a yearly out rent of 4s. 4d. to the Dean and Chapter of Durham and also to another yearly out rent of 9s. due to the Lord Feversham.

Item all that farm and lands called the Close in the said parish of Elwick in the possession of William Arrowsmith tenant thereof under a contract for 13 years commencing at May day next at the yearly rent of £117 out of which he has an allowance for repairs and for half of the lime used upon the said premisses.

Item one other messuage and farm in the said parish of Elwick called the Red Gapp alias the Close . . . in the possession of George Wilkinson tenant . . . under a lease for two years commencing at May day next under the yearly rent of £100, out of which he has an allowance for repairs and half of the lime used upon the said premisses. There is also payable out of the said two last mentioned farms a yearly out rent of £13 6s. 8d. to Edward Noell Esquire his heirs or assigns which I pay and a modus or prescript rent of 20s. a year to the parson of Elwick for tyths of hay and corn which is paid by the tenants.

And I have such estate and interest in and to the said severall premisses as followeth . . . as to part of the said premisses above mentioned to be unlett and in my possession of the yearly value of £8 10s. and as to part of the said Broad Close farm in the possession of William Worthy of the like yearly value of £8 10s. I am intitled thereto for the residue of a term of 21 years thereof granted to my said late father by the Dean and Chapter of Durham by indenture . . . 9 April 1747 at . . . the yearly rent of £2 13s. 4d. which said lease is usually renewed every seven years at an arbitrary fine paid to the said Dean and Chapter besides the lease and seal fees and as to all the rest and residue of the premisses I am intitled thereunto in fee simple. And the said premisses are charged as hereinafter is mentioned (to witt) the lands of Croxdale with the payment of £1500 to my aunt Catherine Salvin for her portion and the further sum of £3000 to my sister Mary Salvin now Mary Markham for her portion and the said lands at Owton and Peverleys Farm at Butterwick stand charged with the payment of £1500 to the representatives of Sir Francis Child knight late deceased upon a mortgage made to him . . . and my said late father charged the said lands at Owton and Peverleys Farm . . . with . . . £2500 payable to my brother Edward Salvin and also charged the said lands with . . . £500 to my sister Mary now the wife of George Markham and there is likewise a yearly prescript rent of £2 13s. 4d. issuing and payable forth and out of the said lands and tenements at Owton and other lands there to the owner of the Honour of Tinmouth in lieu of and for all tyths.

In witness whereof I have hereunto subscribed my name with my own hand 1 January 1752.

William Salvin

The name of the said William Salvin was subscribed to this Registry by Pexall Forster gentleman his attorney thereunto authorized by letters of attorney under his hand and seal the execution whereof was proved by two witnesses and the said subscription and proof were made in open court at the General Quarter Sessions of the peace holden at the City of Durham in and for the County Palatine of Durham 15 January 1752 before us Hen. Lambton Robt. Wharton

Son and heir of no. 133. Born 28 November 1723, died 20 January 1800. Married first Mary, eldest daughter of Sir Edward Gascoigne, fifth baronet. She died 7 May 1756, after giving birth to a still-born child, and he married secondly, in 1758, Catherine, only child and heiress of Thomas Thornton of Nether Witton.

140. CATHERINE SELBY 1717

(enrolled 22 April 1717)

I Catherine Selby of the Town and County of Newcastle upon Tine widdow. . . .

I . . . am in possession and the receipt of an annual sum or yearly rent charge of £12 per annum secured to me by indenture of demise 1 May 1686 made . . . between Ralph Widdrington of Cheesburne Grainge in the county of Northumberland Esq of the one part Anne Hodshon of the town and county of Newcastle upon Tyne widdow since deceased and me the said Catherine Selby by the name of Catherine Hodshon of the said town and county of Newcastle upon Tyne spinster of the other part for the consideration therein mentioned did give grant and confirm to the said Anne Hodshon and me our executors administrators and assigns one annuity or yearly rent charge of £12 . . . to be issuing and coming forth and out of all those the said Ralph Widdrington his third part of all the tiths of corn and grain lamb wool and hay and other tithes whatsoever as well as p^r^diall personall as next yearly happening chancing renewing coming or growing due within the parish of Lanchester in the county of Durham to be paid at four feast days or terms in the year, that is to say the feast of St. Peter ad vincula commonly called Lammas day, the feast of St. Martin the

Bishop in Winter commonly called Martinmas day, the feast of the purification of the Blessed Virgin Mary commonly called Candlemas day and the feast of St. Philip and James commonly called May day by even and equal portions, to hold for the term of four score and nineteen years (if the said Anne Hodshon and I the said Catherine should so long live) with power of distress for nonpayment of the said annuity . . . by vertue of which said indenture and the death of the said Anne Hodshon I am intitled to and am in possession of the said rent charge of £12

Catherine Selby

The name of the said Catherine Selby was subscribed to this registry by Edwd Riddell gent her attorney . . . in open court at this quarter sessions of the peace held for the county of Durham 1 May 1717 in the presence of Jno Rudd Fr. Carre

Daughter of Anne Hodshon, widow of Newcastle, whose will dated 16 May 1686 she proved at Durham on 16 February 1690/1 (Anne was buried at St. Nicholas, Newcastle, on 7 November 1690). Before 18 March 1698 she married Thomas Selby of Newcastle (*SS.* cxxxi, 52), whose will, dated 1 October 1715, she proved at Durham on 31 March 1716. In it he leaves to his dear and well beloved wife Catharine Selby £100 in the hands of Mr. John Turner, "executor of my cousin Henry Jefforis, who left me the said £100 and at the death of my said wife . . . £50 to my loving sister Margarett Tosier and £50 to my loving kinsman Lancelot Tomson". The witnesses were John Clavering, George Sanderson, Ephr. Selby and Austin Gwyn. Catherine Selby, widow, was buried at St. Nicholas, Newcastle on 16 November 1727. Her will, as of the parish of St. John's, Newcastle, is dated 15 October 1719, and mentions her loving brother Albert Hodshon, to whom she leaves a guinea in gold, her loving nephew Thomas Hodshon, and her dear sister Margaret Tosier, whom she appoints sole executrix. The will was proved at Durham by Margaret Tosier, widow, of Newcastle on 27 February 1727/8.

141. THOMAS SHIRLEY 1723/4

I Thomas Shirley of New Elvett near the City of Durham . . . joyner. . . .

One Burgage or tenement sett lying and being in New Elvett within the suburbs of the City of Durham held by lease for 40 years under the Dean and Chapter att the yearly rent of 2s. and now in my own possession of the yearly rent of £6

Thomas Shirley junr

Subscribed by the said Thomas Shirley jun in open court held by Adjournment at the City of Durham 31 January 1723 before Jno Rudd Fr. Cornforth

Thomas Shirley of the City of Durham, joiner, obtained a lease from the Dean and Chapter of Durham on 12 November 1719 of a burgage in Elvett, between a tenement in the tenure of Margaret Thornton on the south, and one of Hugh Dixon on the north, and adjoining on a close belonging to Henry Reah on the east and the King's high street on the west, late in the tenure of Henry Sheeles at the annual rent of 2s. (Reg. Montague 1714-20, ff. 259-260). The lease was renewed in 1733, 1747 and 1765.

Elizabeth, daughter of Thomas and Elizabeth Shirley, died 3 May 1722; Elizabeth second wife of Thomas Shirley, junior, died 19 April 1733 aged 31, m.i. St. Oswald's Churchyard, Durham.

Mr. Thomas Shirley senior was buried in St. Oswald's Churchyard, Durham on 30 March 1737.

142. RICHARD SKELTON 1717

(enrolled 17 April 1717)

I Richard Skelton of Wycliff in the county of York Esqre. . . .

Imprimis a messuage or tenement with two barns two stables and outhouses and several closes or parcells of arable meadow and pasture ground . . . within the parish of Great Aycliffe in the . . . county of Durham known by the name of Gambwells farm in the occupation of William Gambwell let by me to the said William Gambwell by lease in writing at the yearly rack rent of £100 with allowances of taxes and repairs and pursuant to the said lease

Item another farm called Goodburns farm in the occupation of Richard Goodburn containing a tenement with a barn a stable and several closes of arable meadow and pasture ground thereto belonging . . . within the parish . . . aforesaid let by me to the said

Richard Goodburn by lease in writing at the yearly rack rent of £20. In which said premises I . . . have and hold an estate to me and my heirs by vertue of a lease granted from the Lord Bishop of Durham for the terme of three lives which said premises are subject and lyable to such yearly rents charges and other incumbrances as are issueing out and charged upon the same

Richard Skelton

The name of the sd Richard Skelton was subscribed . . . by John Lodge gent his attorney . . . in open court at the Generall Quarter Sessions of the peace held for the county of Durham 1 May 1717 in the presence of Jno Rudd William Ettricke

According to Samuel Jefferson, *History and Antiquities of Leath Ward, Cumberland,* 224-225, Richard Skelton was eldest son of John Skelton of Armathwaite Castle, Cumberland, by his wife Elizabeth, daughter of Jarrard Salvin of Croxdale. He was baptized on 18 September 1651, was 13 when Dugdale made his Visitation of Cumberland on 28 March 1665, and married Mary, daughter of George Meynell of Dalton Ryal, Yorks, by whom he had a son and heir John, nine other sons and six daughters. In 1703-4 with his wife and son John he made a settlement of the Armathwaite estate (Heysham-Mounsey MSS, Record Office, Carlisle). He sold the property to William Sanderson in 1712.

His son Nicholas Skelton, born in Cumberland 17 December 1691, became a priest. He died at Lancaster on 13 November 1766 (*Catholic Rec. Soc.* xxviii). Nicholas was arrested in December 1745 on suspicion of assisting the Jacobites at Manchester. He was a prisoner in Lancaster Castle in September 1746, when he petitioned for release (S.P. Dom. 36/87 no. 11). His will, as of Lancaster, gentleman, dated 4 October 1766, was proved in the Archdeaconry of Richmond by the Hon. Edward Clifford of Park Hall in Quarmore, on 17 February 1767, power being reserved to Thomas Winder Faithwaite of Pottyeats in Littledale gentleman and William Pennington gentleman the other executors. Edward Clifford and Thomas Winder Faithwaite were the only legatees named in the will.

The property in Great Aycliffe which Richard Skelton registered was presumably the fourth part of Ricknall Grange, which is mentioned in *SS*. clxxiii, 142, 144, 189. Its history may be traced in two enrolled deeds of 27 and 28 April 1721. To the latter deed of release the parties were (1) Richard Skelton of Wycliffe, Yorks., gent. (son and heir of John Skelton late of Armathwaite, Cumberland esq.), Richard Skelton the younger of Berwickside, Cumberland, gent., one of the sons of the said Richard Skelton, and John Skelton of Berwickside aforesaid in the parish of Heskett, Cumberland, gent.; (2) Elizabeth and Katherine Salvin, both of New Elvet, Durham, spinsters and executrixes of Anthony Salvin the younger their late brother deceased who was executor of Anthony Salvin the elder late of Old Elvet gent. their late father deceased and James Salvin of Sunderland nigh the Bridge, Co. Durham gent., eldest son and heir of the said Anthony Salvin the elder; (3) Christopher Maire of Hart Bushes gent., John Maire formerly of the City of Durham and now of Hart Bushes gent., brother of the said Christopher, Mary Maire of Gilligate spinster executrix of Ralph Maire gent., her late father deceased, who was executor of John Maire late of Gilligate, gent., deceased, John Jennison of Walworth, gent., executor of John Lamb esq deceased, Thomas Rawdon of Sizergh, Westmorland, gent.; (4) William Hutchinson of Barnard Castle, gent. It is therein recited that Nathanael, Bishop of Durham, leased his capital messuage called Ricknall Grainge with a water corn mill upon the water of Skerne called Ricknall mill to the Hon. James Darcy of Witton Castle. The lease was dated 13 May 1687 and was for the lives of Mark Shaftoe esq., Gerard Skelton second son of the said John Skelton and Lancelott Garth, only son of Lancelot Garth of Armathwaite yeoman, at the yearly rent of £30 for the Grainge and £3 10s. for the mill. A week later Darcy assigned a quarter of the property to John Skelton. In April 1705 Richard Skelton and his eldest son John mortgaged it for £907 17s. 6d. to Joseph Relfe of Cockermouth gent., and in March 1706 Skelton and his son John with Joseph Porter of Cockermouth gent., the said Joseph Relfe, and Thomas Rawdon, conveyed it to Anthony Salvin the elder for £1330. Salvin was merely trustee for Christopher and John Maire, who paid £630, and for John Lamb, who paid £550, and for Thomas Rawdon, who paid £150. By mistake John Maire was described as of Gilligate, but it was a namesake who lived there and the John Maire who provided part of the money lived in or near the City of Durham, and was a party to the deed, whereas John of Gilligate was dead. Lamb was also dead, and Jennison was his executor. The property was acquired for £2,550 by William Hutchinson, the Maires receiving £647 6s. 6d., Jennison £565 2s. 6d., Rawdon £154 2s. 6d., and Richard Skelton and his son Richard £1183 8s. 6d. William Gamble was the tenant. In Thomas Rawdon's register (*SS*. clxxiii, 189) this name is printed William Greenwell. The name is badly written, but appears to be Gamwell. The question mark after Stearsby in *SS*. clxxiii, 189 should be deleted. For biographical details of Thomas Rawdon see *Catholic Record Society*, xxxii, 45 ff. and *The Ushaw Magazine*, lxxiii, 99f. Mr. Henry Hornyold-Strickland F.S.A., of Sizergh Castle, Westmorland, tells me that he can find no record of Rawdon's having served there as chaplain. He was buried at Kendal 1 November 1741.

143. WILLIAM SLEIGH 1723/4

I William Sleigh of Stockton upon Tease in the county of Durham . . . merchant. . . .

I am seized in reversion after the death of Elizabeth Hall my mother of in and to the severall messuages cottages farms and grounds hereinafter mentioned. . . .

to one farm now in the possession of Robert Wastell now lett at £22 per annum to one other farme now in the possession of William Fenwick now lett at £25 5s. per annum

Some old cottages in the possession of John Featham att the yearly rent of 40s. To a seat house lying and being within the parish of Haughton in the said County of Durham

William Sleigh

The name of William Sleigh was subscribed . . . by John Man gent his attorney thereunto authorized by letter of Attorney under his hand and seal . . . and the said subscription and proofe was made in open Court att the Generall Quarter Session of the peace held att the City of Durham in and for the County of Durham by adjournment 9 March 1723 before Jno Rudd J. Fawcet

144. GEORGE SMITH

(enrolled 23 April 1717)

(An adequate abstract is printe' in SS. cxxxi, 129. The register was subscribed in the presence of ,ohn Rudd and Anthony Hall.)

145. JOHN SMITH

(enrolled 7 October 1717)

I John Smith of Cornesey raw in the parish of Lanchester and County of Durham yeoman

Imprimis one tenement or farmhold with the appurtenances . . . in Biggin in the parish aforesaid let as hereafter mentioned (to wit) part thereof let at £9 15s. per annum to Christopher Burrow and Isable Kirkley for one year ending at May day next other part thereof to George Taylor for the like term under the rent of £2 10s. per annum which said premises are held by coppy or court roll of the Bishop of Durham and I have an estate or am interested [?] therein to me and my sequells according to the custom of the manor of Lanchester wherein they lie and pay thereout yearly rent of 6s. 4d. to the said Bishop

One messuage and farmhold with the appurtenances . . . at Cornsey low raw in the parish aforesaid now in my possession

A farmstead in Cornsey in the parish aforesaid and two closes or parcels of ground undivided in Cornsey town fields part let and part in my own hands, that part so let is let to Richard Carrett for a term ending at May Day come twelve months under the rent of £8 10s. per annum since which time the house buildings being burnt down the rent is thereby lessened 40s. per annum

Also several dales or little parcels of ground lying and dispersed undivided in the said town fields computed to be about five acres all which said last mentioned places are freehold wherein I have an estate in fee and there (*sic*) said parcel there in my own possession is valued at £4 14s. per annum for which premises at Cornsey rawe and Cornsey I pay an out rent of 2s. 6d. per annum to the Bishop of Durham and a crown rent of 8s. 3d. per annum and other taxes sesses and repairs and for lime and also a clear annuity . . . of £10 to Thomas Smith of Cornsey rawe . . . for . . . his natural life who is yet living

John Smith

Subscribed . . . in open Court at the general Quarter Sessions of the peace held at the City of Durham 9 October 1717 in the presence of Jno Rudd James Fynney

146. THOMAS SMITH 1717

(enrolled 25 April 1717)

I Thomas Smith of Broomledges in the county of Durham yeoman. . . .

One messuage or tenement and outhouses and a farm of land . . . at Iveston in the parish of Lanchester . . . and now let by me by paroll to John Lisle, who is in the possession thereof at the yearly rent of £24; the messuage or tenement and outhouses and a part of the said farm of land I hold by lease from the Dean and Chapter of Durham for the term of 21 years, and is worth £7 per annum, although the rent thereof is not distinguished from the rent of the other part of the said farm of land and I pay a yearly out rent to the Dean and Chapter of 10s. for the same. other part of the said farm of land is copyhold and in and to which I claim an estate of inheritance and the same is worth £8 10s. per annum, although the rent thereof is not distinguished from the rent of the other part of the said farm and I pay a yearly rent only of the same of 3s. 2d. to Mr James Clavering; and the residue of the said farm of land is a freehold and in and to which I claim an estate of inheritance in fee simple; and the same is worth £8 10s. per annum although the rent thereof is not distinguished from the rent of the other part of the said farm, which said freehold part of the farm I did heretofore mortgage to Mr Francis Richardson of Ferryhill for £100 and the same is still owing and unpaid by me and I allow the said tenant £3 a year out of his said whole rent for lime and I pay or allow several other taxes or sesses yearly

Tho: Smith

The name of the said Thomas Smith was subscribed to this registry by Anthony Wilkinson gent his attorney . . . in open court at the general quarter sessions of the peace for the county of Durham held by adjournment 2 September 1717 in the presence of John Bowes Anth: Hall

147. SIR EDWARD SMYTHE 1741

I Sir Edward Smythe of Acton Burnell in the County of Salop Baronett.

one farm of land with the appurtenances . . . at Nunstainton in the parish of Aycliff . . . let by me by lease parole to Ralph Smithe who is in the possession thereof at the yearly rent of £128

one other parcell of land with the appurtenances . . . at Nunstainton aforesaid . . . let by me by lease parole to John Arrowsmith who is in the possession thereof at the yearly rent of £132

one water corn mill and land with the appurtenances . . . at Nunstainton let by me to John Thompson who is in the possession thereof at the yearly rent of £15 and of which said farms lands and mill there is issuing a yearly out rent of 30s. payable to the heirs or assigns of the late Honourable John Lord Somers and I allow the repairs of the said mill and houses upon the premisses at Nunstainton out of the said rents thereof

One farm of land with the appurtenances . . . at Woodham in the . . . parish of Aycliff let by me by lease parole to Robert Walker who is in the possession thereof at the yearly rent of £84 5s. out of which rent he hath a yearly allowance for lime of £5

One other farm of land with the appurtenances . . . at Woodham . . . let by me by lease parole to John Hutton who is in the possession thereof at the yearly rent of £25

One other farm of land with the appurtenances . . . at Woodham . . . lett by me by lease parole to Michael Leedley who is in the possession thereof at the yearly rent of £42 10s. out of which rent he hath a yearly allowance from me of £4 for lime and one other farm of land there let by lease parole to Robert Mitchell at the yearly rent of £30 and of all which said lands and tenements at Woodham . . . there is issuing a yearly out rent of 8s. payable to the Dean and Chapter of Durham

One farm of land with the appurtenances . . . at Herrington in the parish of Houghton in the Spring and County of Durham let by me by lease parole to Ralph Reed who is in the possession thereof at the yearly rent of £60

One other farm of land with the appurtenances . . . at Middle Herrington in the parish of Houghton in the Spring . . . let by me by lease parole to Thomas Tayler who is in the possession thereof at the yearly rent of £57 out of which . . . lands and tenements at Herrington and Middle Herrington there is issuing a yearly out rent of £3 3s. 11d. payable to the Lord Bishop of Durham

One farm of land with the appurtenances . . . at Low Marley in the parish of Houghton in the Spring . . . let by me by lease parole to Elizabeth Haddock who is in the possession thereof at the yearly rent of £10

The mansion house of Esh and yard in my own possession at the yearly value of £3

One farm of land with the appurtenances . . . at Esh in the parish of Lanchester and Chapplery of Esh and County of Durham let by me by lease parole to Jane Jackson who is in the possession thereof at the yearly rent of £21 10s.

One other farm of land with the appurtenances . . . at Esh . . . let by me by lease parole to Francis Bradshaw who is in the possession thereof at the yearly rent of £24 10s.

One other farm of land with the appurtenances . . . at Esh . . . let by me by lease parole to William Kay who is in the possession thereof at the yearly rent of £5 5s.

One other farm of land with the appurtenances . . . at Esh . . . let by me by lease parole to Thomas Pinckney who is in the possession thereof at the yearly rent of £23

One other farm of land with the appurtenances . . . at Esh . . . let by me by lease parole to Michael Batmanson who is in the possession thereof at the yearly rent of £4

One other farm of land with the appurtenances . . . at Esh . . . let by me by lease parole to John Hixon who is in the possession thereof at the yearly rent of £80 out of which rent the said John Hixon hath a yearly allowance from me of £5 for lime and 2s. 6d. for keeping the Lowd Wall in repair

One other farm of land at Esh . . . let by me by lease parole to Thomas White who is in the possession thereof at the yearly rent of £7 out of all which lands and tenements at Esh aforesaid there is issuing a yearly out rent of £1 18s. 8d. payable to the Lord Bishop of Durham

One farm of land with the appurtenances . . . at Ushaw in the . . . parish of Lanchester and Chapplery of Esh . . . let by me by lease parole to Miles Pinckney who is in the possession thereof at the yearly rent of £39 10s. out of which rent 2s. 6d. is payable to the Bishop of Durham

One other farm of land with the appurtenances . . . at Ushaw . . . lett by me by lease parole to Michael Batmanson who is in the possession thereof at the yearly rent of £31 10s.

One other farm of land with the appurtenances . . . at Ushaw . . . let by me by lease parole to Thomas Hills who is in the possession thereof at the yearly rent of £10 19s.

The prebendary of Esh consisting of the tythe of corn and grain of severall lands and grounds in the said parish of Lanchester and Chapplery of Esh let by me by lease parole to Francis Bradshaw who is in the possession thereof at the yearly rent of £50 out of which tyth of corn and grain there is issuing a yearly out rent of £8 13s. 4d. payable to Anthony Duncombe Esquire

One farm of land with the appurtenances . . . at Heigh in the . . . Chapplery of Esh . . . lett by me by lease parole to John Grainger who is in the possession thereof at the yearly rent of £30 out of which rent he hath an allowance of 40s. per annum for lime

One farm of land with the appurtenances . . . at Rowley in the . . . Chapplery of Esh . . . lett by me by lease parole to George Greenwell who is in the possession thereof at the yearly rent of £34 out of which rent he hath an allowance of from me of 40s. per annum for lime and I pay parish and County Sesses for that farm

One farm of land with the appurtenances . . . at Cockside House in the parish of Brancepeth and County of Durham lett by me by lease parole to Michael Peet who is in the possession thereof at the yearly rent of £18 10s. out of which farm there is issuing a yearly out rent of £1 10s.

One farm of land with the appurtenances lying and being at Newhouse in the . . . Chapplery of Esh . . . lett by me by lease parole to William White who is in the possession thereof at the yearly rent of £23 3s. 4d.

One other farm of land with the appurtenances . . . at Newhouse . . . lett by me by lease parole to John Debord who is in the possession thereof at the yearly rent of 40s.

A farm of land with the appurtenances . . . at West Auckland . . . lett by me by lease parole to Sir Robert Eden who is in the possession thereof at the yearly rent of 40s. out of which there is a yearly rent of 6s. 8d. payable to the Bishop of Durham

A farm of land with the appurtenances . . . at Blackton lett by me by lease parole to John Gibson who is in the possession thereof at the yearly rent of £10

One other farm with the appurtenances . . . at Embleton in the parish of Sedgefield . . . lett by me by lease parole to Ninian Sheraton who is in the possession thereof at the yearly rent of £125

Another farm there now in the possession of Matthew Craggs under a lease in writing granted to him by Thomas Hind deceased for and on the behalf of my late father Sir John Smythe deceased at the yearly rent of £65

One farm of land . . . at Barmton in the parish of Haughton and . . . county of Durham now in the possession of Bryan Harrison under a lease in writing granted to him by the said Thomas Hind for and on the behalf of my said late father at the yearly rent of £215 out of which is issuing a yearly out rent of £1 2s. 4d. payable to the Dean and Chapter of Durham

I have also a fee rent of 6s. payable yearly out of certain lands there belonging to Margaret Bowes

One farm lying at Walworth in the said county of Durham now let by lease parole to John Featham who is in the possession thereof at the yearly rent of £95

Another farm there now lett by lease parole to John Smith who is in the possession thereof at the yearly rent of £80

One other farm there lett by lease parole to Michael Todd who is in the possession thereof at the yearly rent of £70

One other farm there lett by lease parole to William Forster who is in the possession thereof att the yearly rent of £1 4s. out of which said farms at Walworth I pay the yearly rent of £17 10s. for the corn tyths thereof to Doctor Offley

I allow the tenants of all and every the lands and tenements aforesaid respectively forth and out of their respective rents for the repairs of their houses and buildings and also the Land Tax

All which said farms lands tenements and premisses are lett at a Rack Rent as aforesaid and I the said Sir Edward Smythe am seized of and have an estate in fee tail generall therein

Edward Smythe

The name of the said Sir Edward Smythe was subscribed . . . by Hendry Hopper gentleman his attorney . . . in open Court at the Generall Quarter Sessions of the peace holden at the City of Durham in and for the County of Durham 7 October 1741 before . . . John Hedworth Antho. Wilkinson

Son of the next. Born 21 October 1719, succeeding his father as 4th baronet 17 September 1737. Died 2 November 1784. See G.E.C. *Baronetage* iii, 167.

148. JOHN SMYTHE 1717

(enrolled 29 April 1717)

I John Smythe of Acton Burnell in the county of Salop esq. . . . Imprimis the manors or reputed manors of Barmton and High and Low Embleton alias Embledon with their rights members and appurtenances in the parishes of Sedgefield and Haughton in the County Palatine of Durham now in the possession of me the said John Smythe

Item a chief rent of 6s. payable to me yearly out of the estate of Robert Bowes Esq in Barmton. . . . Item a messuage tenement and farm and all lands tenements and hereditaments thereunto belonging . . . in Barmton in the parish of Haughton . . . let from year to year to Jane Collins widow at . . . the yearly rent of £30, the said Jane Collins the present possessor Item a messuage tenement and farm and all lands tenements and hereditaments thereunto belonging . . . in Barmton . . . let from year to year to Christopher Dobyns at . . . the yearly rent of £20, the said Christopher . . . the present possessor Item a messuage tenement and farm and all lands tenements and hereditaments thereunto belonging . . . in Barmton . . . let to Bryan Harrison by indenture of lease dated 9 June 1711 and made by George Harvey on the behalf of Sir Edward Smythe Bart., deceased to the said Bryan . . . for 21 years under the yearly rent of £165, the said Bryan . . . the present possessor and liberty for landlord or tenant to determine the lease at the end of the first seven or fourteen years of the term Item a messuage tenement and farm and all lands tenements and hereditaments . . . in High and Low Embleton . . . in the parish of Sedgefield . . . let to George Orde and Thomas Orde by George Coxon on behalf of Sir John Smythe for three years by indenture dated 24 December 1715 at

. . . the yearly rent of £150, the said George Orde and Jane the widow of the said Thomas Orde the present possessors

Item a messuage tenement and farm and all lands tenements and hereditaments . . . in High and Low Embleton . . . let by George Harvey on behalf of Sir Edward Smythe Bart deceased to William Lamb by indenture dated 19 May 1711 for six years at . . . the yearly rent of £32 10s., the said William . . . the present possessor.

Item a messuage tenement and farm and all lands . . . in High and Low Embleton . . . let by George Harvey on behalf of the said Sir Edward Smythe to Matthew Craggs by indenture dated 19 May 1711 for six years at . . . the yearly rent of £32 10s., the said Matthew Craggs the present possessor Item a messuage tenement and farm and all lands tenements and hereditaments . . . in Walworth in the parish of Heighington . . . let from year to year to John Glenton at . . . the yearly rent of £105, the said John Glenton the present possessor Item a messuage tenement and farm and all lands . . . in Walworth . . . let from year to year to Richard Smyth at . . . the yearly rent of £87, the said Richard . . . the present possessor

Item a messuage tenement and farm and all lands tenements and hereditaments . . . in Walworth let from year to year to William Harrison at . . . the yearly rent of £65, the said William . . . the present possessor.

Item a messuage tenement and farm and all lands tenements and hereditaments . . . in Woodham in the parish of Aicliffe . . . let from year to year to Thomas Lee at . . . the yearly rent of £30, the said Thomas . . . the present possessor Item all those collieries and coal-mines and quarries of stone and slate in the parish of Lanchester . . . let to John Hunter by Thomas Conyers and Sir Edward Smythe Bart by indenture of lease dated 13 January 1713 for the several terms therein mentioned, vizt. the coalmines, quarries except the Flagg Quarry for 16 years and the said Flag Quarry for the remainder of the said 16 years that should be to come at the expiration of the lease thereof then granted to one William Taylor at . . . the yearly rent of £15 for all the premises (except the Flagg Quarry) and £1 for the Flagg Quarry at the expiration of Taylor's lease

Item a colliery and quarry of slate in the Chapelry of Ash . . . and another colliery in the said parish of Lanchester . . . all now in the possession of the said Smith but no use made thereof by me

Item another colliery called Towlaw Colliery in the said parish of Lanchester let to Lancelot Ayre by Thomas Hinde on my behalf for one year ending at Pentecost next under the yearly rent of £3 of all which manors lands tenements and hereditaments herein-before particularly described other than the collieries and quarries of stone and slate I . . . am tenant for life without impeachment of waste other than voluntary waste in the buildings with divers remainders over but there is an allowance to the said Bryan Harrison of £8 a year for lime to improve his farm and also an allowance to my said tenants George Orde and Jane Orde widow, of £5 a year for lime to improve the farm and £5 a year towards their keeping repairs and also an allowance of £3 a year to my tenant William Lamb to buy lime to improve the farm and the like allowance of £3 yearly to my said tenant Matthew Craggs for lime to improve his farm

And I am possessed of all those the said collieries and quarries for the remainder of a term of 21 years which commenced on 20 September 1711

Witness my hand 6 April 1717

John Smythe

Witness Thos Hinde

The name of the said John Smith was subscribed to this registry by Robert Spearman gent his attorney thereunto authorized by warrant of attorney under his hand and seal . . . in open court at this General Quarter Sessions of the peace held for the county of Durham 1 May 1717 before us Jno Rudd Fr. Carre.

148. SIR JOHN SMYTHE 1737

I Sir John Smythe of Acton Burnell in the County of Salop Barronett. . . .

One farm of land with the appurtenances lying and being at Nunstainton in the parish of Aycliff in the . . . county of Durham lett by me by lease parole to Ralph Smith who is in the possession thereof at the yearly rent of £128

One other parcell of land with the appurtenances lying and being at Nunstainton . . . let by me by lease parole to John Arrowsmith who is in the possession thereof at the yearly rent of £132

one water corn mill and land with the appurtenances . . . at Nunstainton . . . let by me by lease parole to John Thompson who is in the possession thereof at the yearly rent of £15

Out of which said farm lands and mill there is issueing a yearly out rent of 30s. payable to the heirs or assigns of the late Honourable John Lord Somers and I allow the repairs of the said mill and houses upon the premisses at Nunstainton out of the said rents thereof

one farm of land with the appurtenances . . . at Woodham in the said parish of Aycliff . . . let by me by lease parole to Robert Walker who is in the possession thereof at the yearly rent of £84 5s. out of which rent he hath a yearly allowance for lime of £5

One other farm of land with the appurtenances . . . at Woodham . . . let by me by lease parole to John Hutton who is in the possession thereof at the yearly rent of £25

One other farm of land with the appurtenances . . . at Woodham . . . let by me by lease parole to Michael Hedley who is in the possession thereof at the yearly rent of £42 10s. out of which rent he hath a yearly allowance from me of £4 for lime out of all which said lands and tenements at Woodham . . . there is issueing a yearly out rent of 8s. payable to the Dean and Chapter of Durham

One farm of land with the appurtenances . . . at Herrington in the parish of Houghton in the Spring . . . let by me by lease parole to Ralph Reed who is in the possession thereof at the yearly rent of £60

One other farm of land with the appurtenances . . . at Middle Herrington in the parish of Houghton in the Spring . . . let by me by lease parole to Thomas Taylor who is in the possession thereof at the yearly rent of £57 out of which said lands and tenements at Herrington and Middle Herrington there is issueing a yearly out rent of £3 3s. 11d. payable to the Lord Bishop of Durham

One farm of land with the appurtenances . . . at Low Marley in the parish of Houghton in the Spring . . . let by me by lease parole to Stephen Haddock who is in the possession thereof at the yearly rent of £10

The mansion house at Ash and yard and a little close containing about three acres of land at Ash in my own possession at the yearly value of £5 one farm of land with the appurtenances . . . at Ash in the parish of Lanchester and Chappelry of Ash . . . let by me by lease parole to Ralph Jackson who is in the possession thereof at the yearly rent of £28 10s.

One other farm of land with the appurtenances . . . at Ash . . . let by me by lease parole to William Rippin who is in the possession thereof at the yearly rent of £16

One other farm of land with the appurtenances . . . at Ash . . . let by me by lease parole to William Kay who is in the possession thereof at the yearly rent of £5

One other farm of land with the appurtenances . . . at Ash . . . let by me by lease parole to Thomas Pinckney who is in the possession thereof at the yearly rent of £8 10s.

One other farm of land with the appurtenances lying and being at Ash aforesaid let by me by lease parole to Michael Batmanson who is in the possession thereof at the yearly rent of £4

One other farm of land with the appurtenances . . . at Ash . . . let by me by lease parole to John Hixon who is in the possession thereof at the yearly rent of £80 out of which the said John Hixon hath a yearly allowance from me of £5 for lime and 2s. 6d. for keeping the Lowd wall in repair

A cottage at Ash . . . let by me by lease parole to John Harrison who is in the possession thereof at the yearly rent of 6d. out of all which lands and tenements at Ash . . . there is issuing a yearly out rent of £1 18s. 8d. payable to the Lord Bishop of Durham

One farm of land with the appurtenances . . . at Ushaw in the . . . parish of Lanchester and Chapplery of Ash . . . let by me by lease parole to Miles Pinckney who is in the possession thereof at the yearly rent of £39 10s. out of which rent 2s. 6d. yearly is payable to the Bishop of Durham

One other farm of land with the appurtenances . . . at Ushaw . . . let by me by lease parole to Michael Batmanson who is in the possession thereof at the yearly rent of £31 10s.

One other farm of land with the appurtenances . . . at Ushaw . . . let by me by lease parole to Thomas Hills who is in the possession thereof at the yearly rent of £10 19s.

The prebendary of Ash consisting of the tyths of corn and grain of severall lands and grounds in the said parish of Lanchester and Chapplery of Ash let by me by lease parole to Thomas Pinckney who is in the possession thereof at the yearly rent of £50 out of which tyths of corn and grain there is issueing a yearly out rent of £8 13s. 4d. payable to Anthony Duncomb Esquire

One farm of land with the appurtenances . . . at Heugh in the . . . Chapplery of Ash . . . let by me by lease parole to John Grainger who is in the possession thereof at the yearly rent of £30 out of which rent he hath an allowance of 20s. per annum for lime

One farm of land with the appurtenances . . . at Rowley in the . . . Chapplery of Ash . . . let by me by lease parole to George Greenwell who is in the possession thereof at the yearly rent of £32 out of which rent he hath an allowance from me for lime and I pay parish and county sesses for that farm

One other farm of land with the appurtenances . . . at Rowley . . . in the . . . Chapplery of Ash let by me by lease parole to Mary Stock who is in the possession thereof at the yearly rent of 40s.

One farm of land with the appurtenances . . . at Coxside House in the parish of Brancepeth . . . lett by me by lease parole to Michael Peet who is in the possession thereof at the yearly rent of £18 10s. out of which farm there is issueing a yearly out rent of 12s. 4d. and I allow poor sess for the same farm out of the said rent

One other farm of land with the appurtenances . . . at Coxside house aforesaid . . . let by me by lease parole to Thomas Charleton who is in possession thereof at the yearly rent of £9 out of which lands there is issueing a yearly out rent of 2s. 4d.

One farm of land with the appurtenances . . . at Underside in the . . . Chapplery of Ash . . . let by me lease parole to Thomas Pinckney who is in the possession thereof at the yearly rent of £16

One farm of land with the appurtenances . . . at Haghouse in the . . . Chapplery of Ash . . . let by me by lease parole to Ralph Jackson who is in the possession thereof at the yearly rent of £16 10s. out of which rent I allow 20s. yearly for lime

One farm of land with the appurtenances . . . at Newhouse in the . . . Chapplery of Ash . . . let by me by lease parole to William White who is in the possession thereof at the yearly rent of £23 3s. 4d.

One other farm of land with the appurtenances . . . at Newhouse . . . let by me by lease parole to Mr Robert Carnaby who is in the possession thereof at the yearly rent of 40s.

A farm of land with the appurtenances . . . at West Aukland in the . . . County of Durham lett by me by lease parole to Sir Robert Eden who is in the possession thereof at the yearly rent of

40s. out of which there is a yearly rent of 6s. 8d. payable to the Bishop of Durham

A farm of land with the appurtenances . . . at Blakiston let by me by lease parole to John Gibson who is in the possession thereof at the yearly rent of £10

I allow the tenants of all and every the lands and tenements aforesaid respectively forth and out of their respective rents for the repairs of their houses buildings and also the land tax

In all which said farms lands tenements hereditaments and premisses I the said Sir John Smythe am seized of and have an estate or interest therein for the term of my naturall life without impeachment of waste

In witness whereof I the said Sir John Smith have hereunto put my hand and signed my name this 29 day of March in the year of our Lord God 1737

John Smythe

The name of the said Sir John Smythe was subscribed . . . by Farrow Eden gentleman his Attorney . . . in open Court at the Generall Quarter Sessions of the peace holden at the City of Durham in and for the County of Durham 20 Aprill 1737 before Tho. Davison J. Johnson

Son of Sir Edward Smythe of Esh, first baronet. Succeeded his brother as third baronet December 1736 and died 17 September 1737. (G.E.C. *Baronetage* iii, 167.) Some details of his will, dated 14 January 1736, codicil 11 September 1737, proved 6 December 1737, are given in Payne, *Rec. EC*, 13.

149. SIR RICHARD SMYTHE 1717

(received in office 20 June 1717 between 9 and 10 a.m enrolled 26 June 1717)

I Sir Richard Smythe of Ash in the County of Durham Barrt. . . .

one farm of land with the appurtenances . . . at Nunstainton in the parish of Aycliffe . . . let by me by lease parole to Richard Collin who is in the possession thereof at the yearly rent of £128

One other farm of land with the appurtenances . . . at Nunstainton . . . let by me by lease parole to Francis Walker who is in the possession thereof at the yearly rent of £132

one water corn mill and land with the appurtenances . . . at Nunstainton . . . let by me by lease parole to Thomas Humble who is now in the possession thereof at the yearly rent of £15 out of which said farms lands and mill there is issuing a yearly out rent of 30s. payable to the heirs or assigns of the late Honble John Lord Somers and I allow the repairs of the said mill and houses upon the premises at Nunstainton out of the said rents . . .

one farm of land with the appurtenances . . . at Woodham in the said parish of Aycliffe . . . let by me by lease parole to Robert Walker who is in the possession thereof at the yearly rent of £84 5s. out of which rent he hath a yearly allowance (for lime) of £5

one other farm of land with the appurtenances . . . at Woodham . . . let by me by lease parole to Mr Francis Hutton, who is now in the possession thereof at the yearly rent of £25

One other farm of land with the appurtenances . . . at Woodham . . . let by me by lease parole to Michael Hedley who is now in the possession thereof at the yearly rent of £42 10s. out of which rent he has a yearly allowance from me of £4 for lime. Out of all which said lands and tenements at Woodham . . . there is issuing a yearly out rent of 8s. payable to the Dean and Chapter of Durham

One farm of land with the appurtenances . . . at Herrington in the parish of Houghton in the Spring . . . let by me by lease parole to Ralph Reed who is in the possession thereof at the yearly rent of £60

One other farm of land with the appurtenances . . . at Middle Herrington in the parish of Houghton in the Spring . . let by me by lease parole to Henry Laurence who is in the possession thereof at the yearly rent of £57, out of which said lands and tenements at Herrington and Middle Herrington there is issuing a yearly out rent of £3 3s. 11d. payable to the Lord Bishop of Durham

one farm of land with the appurtenances . . . at Low Marley in the said parish of Houghton in the Spring . . . let by me by lease parole to Mary Haddock who is in the possession thereof at the yearly rent of £10

The mansion house at Ash and garden and a little close containing about three acres of land at Ash in my own possession of the yearly value of £5

One farm of land with the appurtenances . . . at Ash in the parish of Lanchester and Chapelry of Ash . . . let by me by lease parole to Robert Smith who is in the possession thereof at the yearly . . . of £4 10s.

One other farm of land with the appurtenances . . . at Ash . . . let by me by lease parole to William Rippon who is in the possession thereof at the yearly rent of £16

One other farm of land with the appurtenances . . . at Ash . . . let by me by lease parole to Jane Griffin who is in the possession thereof at the yearly rent of £5

one other farm of land with the appurtenances . . . at Ash . . . let by me by lease parole to Ralph Jackson, who is in the possession thereof at the yearly rent of £17

One other farm of land with the appurtenances . . at Ash . . . let by me by lease parole to George White who is in the possession thereof at the yearly rent of £8 10s.

one other farm of land with the appurtenances . . at Ash . . . let by me by lease parole to Thomas Lambton who is in the possession thereof at the yearly rent of £4

One other farm of land with the appurtenances . . . at Ash . . . let by me by lease in writing without any fine for three [?] years ending at May day 1718 to John Hixon who is in the possession thereof at the yearly rent of £80 out of which rent the said John Hixon by his said lease hath a yearly allowance from me of £5 for lime and 40s. for keeping the Lood [?] wall in repair

A cottage at Ash . . . let by me by lease parole to John Harrison who is in the possession thereof at the yearly rent of . . . and tenement at Ash . . . there is issuing a yearly out rent of £1 . . . to the Lord Bishop of Durham

. . . of land with the appurtenances . . . at Ushaw in the said parish of Lanchester . . . let by me by lease parole to Miles Pinckney who is in the possession thereof at the yearly rent of £30 10s. out of which rent 2s. 6d. is yearly payable to the Lord Bishop of Durham

One other farm of land with the appurtenances . . . at Ushaw . . . let by me by lease parole to Michael Batmeson who is in the possession thereof at the yearly rent of £18

One other farm of land with the appurtenances . . . at Ushaw . . . let by me by lease parole to Ann Douglass who is in the possession thereof at the yearly rent of £14

One other farm of land with the appurtenances . . . at Ushaw . . . let by me by lease parole to Catherine Burdon who is in the possession thereof at the yearly rent of £5

One other farm of land with the appurtenances . . . at Ushaw . . . let by me by lease parole to Robert Joplin who is in the possession thereof at the yearly rent of £10 19s.

The Prebendary of Ash, consisting of the tithes of corn and grain of several lands and grounds in the said parish of Lanchester and chappelry of Ash in my own possession of the yearly value of £30 out of which tithes of corn and grain there is issuing a yearly out rent of £8 13s. 4d. payable to Anthony Duncomb Esqr.

One farm of land with the appurtenances . . . at Heugh in the said Chapelry of Ash . . . let by me by lease parole to Thos. Grainger who is in the possession thereof at the yearly rent of £30 out of which rent he hath an allowance from me of 20s. per annum for lime.

One farm of land with the appurtenances . . . at Rowley in the said chapelry of Ash . . . let by me by lease parole to George Greenwell who is in the possession thereof at the yearly rent of £32 out of which rent he hath an allowance from me of 40s. per annum for lime and I pay parish and county sesses for that farm

One other farm of land with the appurtenances . . . at Rowley aforesaid . . . let by me by lease parole to Mary Stock who is in the possession thereof at the yearly rent of 40s.

One farm of land with the appurtenances . . . at Coxside house in the parish of Brauncepeth . . . let by me by lease parole to Anthony Hedley who is in the possession thereof at the yearly rent of £19, out of which farm there is issuing a yearly out rent of 12s. 4d. and I allow the poor sess for the same farm out of the said rent.

one other farm of land with the appurtenances . . . at Coxside house . . . let by me by lease parole to Thomas Charlton who is in the possession thereof at the yearly rent of £9 out of which said land there is issuing a yearly out rent of 2s. 4d.

One farm of land with the appurtenances . . . at Underside in the said Chapelry of Ash . let by me by lease parole to George Lainge who is in the possession thereof at the yearly rent of £16

One farm of land with the appurtenances . . . at Haghouse in the said chapelry of Ash . . . let by me by lease parole to Mary

Potts who is in the possession thereof at the yearly rent of £16 10s. out of which rent I allow her 20s. yearly for lime

One farm of land with the appurtenances . . . at Newhouse in the said chapelry of Ash . . . let by me by lease parole to William White who is in the possession thereof at the yearly rent of £14

One other farm of land with the appurtenances . . at Newhouse aforesaid . . . let by me by lease parole to Robert Baxter who is in the possession thereof at the yearly rent of £9 3s. 4d.

One other farm of land with the appurtenances . . . at Newhouse aforesaid let by me by lease parole to Mr (*blank*) Simpson who is in the possession thereof at the yearly rent of 40s.

A farm of land with the appurtenances . . . at West Auckland . . . let by me by lease parole to Sir Robert Eden Barrt. who is in the possession thereof at the yearly rent of 40s. out of which there is a yearly rent of 6s. 8d. payable to the Bishop of Durham.

A farm of land with the appurtenances . . . at Blakistone let by me by lease parole to George Todd who is in the possession thereof at the yearly rent of £10

I allow the tenants of all and every the lands and tenements aforesaid respectively forth and out of their respective rents for the repairs of their houses and buildings and also the land tax

I am intituled and have an estate and interest in and to all and singular the messuages lands tenements tithes and mill aforesaid for and during my natural life without impeachment of or for any manner of waist

Given under my hand 21 May 1717

Ri: Smythe

The name of the said Sir Richard Smythe was subscribed to this Registry by Thomas Wilkinson Esqr. his attorney thereunto authorized by warrant of attorney under his hand and seal . . . in open court at the general quarter sessions of the peace held by adjournment for the County of Durham 27 June 1717 in the presence of Jno Rudd Antho: Hall

Brother of the foregoing. Succeeded his father as second baronet 1714 and died December 1736. Admin. 3 May 1737 and 17 December 1746. He married in 1688 Grace, daughter and heir of the Hon. Carrill Carrington or Smith, but had no male issue. G.E.C. *Baronetage* iii, 166.

150. WILLIAM STOCK 1723/4

I William Stock of Stockton upon Tease in the county of Durham weaver . . .

I am seized to me and my sequells in jure of and in the severall copyhold messuages and cottages following all lying within the Town and townshipp of Stockton . . . and now in the several possessions following . . .

of one messuage or cottage in my own possession the yearly value being computed at 40s. one other in the possession of Simon Wilson at and under the rent of £1 17s. one other in the possession of George Robson att and under the rent of £1 10s. one other in the possession of Christopher Harrison att and under the rent of £1 10s. one other in the possession of George Tweedyatt and under the rent of £1 10s. one other in the possession of Ralph Swainston att and under the rent of 15s. one other in the possession of Jane Mackqueen att and under the rent of 15s. one other in the possession of Mary Farrow att and under the rent of £1 5s. one other in the possession of William Carpinter att and under the rent of £1 4s. one other in the possession of John Hamlinn att and under the rent of £1 8s.

All which said messuages and houses were severally lett to my said tenants for the term of one year

Item I am intitled for my life and to my sequells in jure after the death of my sister Frances Stock of in and to a house standing within the Town of Stockton now in the possession of John Reed and now lett for the rent of £2 7s.

William Stock

The name of the said William Stock was subscribed . . . by John Mann Gent his Attorney in open Court att the Generall Quarter Sessions of the peace held att the City of Durham in and for the County of Durham by Adjournment 9 March 1723 before Jno Rudd J. Fawcet

151. THOMAS STONOR 1717

(enrolled 17 April 1717)

I Thomas Stonor of Stonor in the County of Oxon Esqr. . . .

A true particular of the several messuages lands tenements farmes and hereditaments scituate . . . in the parish manor and places within the county and Bishopricke of Durham whereof I . . . am or any other person in trust for me . . . is seized . . . or in receipt or perception of the rents or profitts that is to say

several messuages lands tenements farms and hereditaments in Westwicke within the manor or township of Bernard Castle parish of Gainford and County and Bishopricke of Durham . . . with all woods underwoods commons moors wastes wastegrounds rights members and appurtenances . . . viz

One farm called East Shaws in the occupation of Thomas Browne yeoman containing a messuage or farm house out houses barns stables meadow pasture and arable lands thereunto belonging scituate in the said parish . . . let by me and others from year to year to the said Thomas Browne att the yearly rent of £80

One farm in the several occupations of Samuell Rowlandson of West Shawes George Smales and Joseph Swainston containing one tenement or farm house barns stables outhousing stack garths field garths meadow pasture and arable lands thereunto belonging scituate in the said townshipp of Westwicke . . . let by me and others from year to year or by contract in writing to the said Samuel Rowlandson at the yearly rack rent of £54 10s.

One farme called Swainston's farm in the occupation of John Swainston sen' and John Swainston junr containing two tenements or dwelling houses two stables two garths one stackgarth meadow pasture and arable lands thereunto belonging scituate in the said parish . . . let by me and others from year to year to the said John Swainston senior at the yearly rack rent of £40 10s.

One farme called Mainhouse or Perkins farm in the occupation of Robert Perkin, yeoman and William Stevenson containing one tenement or farmhouse two barns stable meadow pasture and arable lands thereunto belonging scituate in the said parish . . . let by me and others from year to year to the said Robert Perkin at the yearly rack rent of £36.

One farm called Smales's farm in the occupation of Christopher Smales yeoman and James Wensley containing a tenement or farmhouse barn stable garth meadow pasture and arable lands thereunto belonging . . . in the said parish . . . let by articles or agreement in writing made by Henry Copland Gent to the said Christopher Smales at the yearly reserved rent of £30

One farm in the occupation of Joseph Swainston yeoman known by the name of Swainston's farm containing one tenement or dwelling house barn stable garth meadow pasture and arable land thereunto belonging . . . in the said parish . . . let by me and others from year to year to the said Joseph Swainston at the yearly rack rent of £27

A farm called Blenkinsopp's farm in the occupation of Thomas Blenkinsopp yeoman containing two tenements or dwelling houses one barn one stable two garths meadow pasture and arable lands thereunto belonging . . . in the said parish . . . let by me and others from year to year to the said Thomas Blenkinsopp at the yearly rack rent of £19 13s. 4d.

A farm known by the name of Kiplin's farm in the occupation of Richard Kiplin yeoman Anthony Peirson and Christopher Smales containing a tenement or farmhouse barn stable and garth meadow pasture and arable lands thereunto belonging . . . in the said parish . . . with two ridges of land in a field called Lee field in the parish of Bernard Castle lett by me and others from year to year to the said Richard Kiplin at the yearly rack rent of £18

A farm called Belwood's farm in the occupation of Ralph Belwood yeoman containing a tenement or farmhouse barn meadow pasture and arable lands thereunto belonging . . . in the said parish . . . let by me and others from year to year to the said Ralph Belwood at the yearly rack rent of £18

A farm called Peel's farm in the occupation of Ambrose Peele yeoman containing a tenement or farm house barn stable meadow pasture and arable lands . . . in the said parish . . . let by me and others from year to year to the said Ambrose Peele at the yearly rack rent of £17

A farm called Peirson's farm in the occupation of Anthony Peirson senior of Bernard Castle butcher and Anthony Peirson his son containing a barn two closes with diverse parcells of ground and pasture lands . . . in the said parish . . . let by me and others from year to year to the said Anthony Peirson senior at the yearly rent of £16

A farm called Hawdons farm in the severall occupations of Thomas Blenkinsopp Isaac Robley Lyonell Dowthwaite Thomas Shaw and John Iveson containing a tenement or dwelling house barn stable with diverse parcells of ground inclosures and premises thereunto belonging . . . in the said parish . . . let by me and others from year to year to John Hawdon yeoman at the yearly rack rent of £14

A farm called Scotts farm in the occupation of James Scott [*Badger?*] Thomas Blenkinsop and Richard Hill containing a tenement or dwelling house with divers closes and parcells of pasture ground . . . in the said parish . . . let by contract or agreement in writing made by Robert Daile gent to the said James Scott at the yearly reserved rent of £10

A farm called Wilson's farm in the occupation of Thomas Wilson yeoman containing a messuage dwelling house barn stable with several closes or parcels of meadow pasture and arable lands . . . in the said parish . . . let by an article indented made by the said Robert Daile to John Wilson father of the said Thomas Wilson at the yearly reserved rent of £8

A farm in the occupation of Jane Holmes widow and Ambrose Peele containing one tenement or dwelling house barn stable with several inclosures or parcells of ground . . . in the said parish . . . let by me and others from year to year to the said Jane Holmes at the yearly rack rent of £6 10s.

A farm in the occupation of Anne Newby and Christopher Newby her son containing a tenement or dwelling house barn and lodge with several closes . . . in the said parish . . . let by contract or agreement in writing made by the said Henry Copland gent to the said Anne Newby at the yearly reserved rent of £2

All the before mentioned tenants within the said parish . . . have right of common of pasture upon the moor and waste saving Thomas Browne tenant in possession of the farm aforesaid called East Shaws.

Mary Dowthwaite widow a poor woman receiving alms of the parish holds at will one small cottage in the said town of Westwick gratis

Richard Hill labourer a poor man holds another small cottage gratis

Out of which said several messuages lands tenements farms hereditaments and premises before mentioned (amongst other lands and tenements) there is issuing and payable to the most Noble Anne Dutchess and wife of his Grace the Duke of Richmond and Lenox (during her natural life) a yearly rent charge or sum of £1,000

Of all which said several messuages lands . . . I the said Thomas Stonor am seised of an estate for my life as tenant in common of and in an undivided fourth part . . . of . . . the same messuages lands and premises and residue of the rents and profitts thereof (after such deductions . . . shall be made as is before mentioned)

Thomas Stonor

The name of the said Thomas Stonor was subscribed . . . by Francis Coulston gent his attorney thereunto authorized by warrant of attorney under his hand and seal the execution whereof was proved by two witnesses at the General Quarter Sessions of the peace held for the County of Durham 1 May 1717 and the said subscription was made at the said General Quarter Sessions . . . held by adjournment 27 June 1717 in the presence of Jno Rudd Antho: Hall

Thomas Stonor of Stonor, near Henley-on-Thames, was eldest son of John Stonor of Stonor and Lady Mary Talbot, his wife. Born on 20 June 1677, he died 10 August 1724. He married on 16 March 1696 the Hon. Isabel Belasye, the youngest of the four daughters and co-heiresses of John, first Baron Belasye of Worlaby, and so acquired her share of her father's Durham estate. Secondly, on 14 July 1705, he married the Hon. Winifred Roper, daughter of Christopher, 5th Baron Teynham. An abstract of his will dated 14th January 1723, proved 13 August 1724, is printed in Payne, *Rec. E.C.*, 50.

152. FRANCIS SUTTON 1717

(enrolled 21 April 1717)

I Francis Sutton of Coundon in the parish of St Andrew Auckland . . . gentleman . . .

Imprimis one messuage tenement or farmhold with the appurtenances . . . within the parish . . . aforesaid called Rackwood hill, part freehold of which I have an estate in fee simple and part copyhold lying within the township of Redburne . . . held of the Bishop of Durham and surrendered by me to Michael Mickleton and Robert Spearman and their sequells by surrender or copy of court roll dated 28 November 13 William III, in trust for such uses and purposes as I by my last will or other deed in writing should limit and appoint. All which premises are now in possession of John Teasdaile tenant by vertue of a lease made by me to him dated 10 March 1714 for the term of three years and so from three years to three years for nine years commencing from 25 March then instant and 3 May then next after, at . . . the rent of £33 per annum payable to me at Martinmas and May day by equal portions

one other messuage tenement or farmhold with the appurtenances . . . in the said parish . . . called . . . Blackhouse all copyhold held of the Bishop of Durham and surrendered by the surrender above mentioned to the said Michael Mickleton and Robert Spearman and their sequells to the uses aforesaid now in the possession of George Gibbin tenant and demised by me to him for the term of nine years commencing from 25 March and 3 May 1714 at the yearly rent of £7 payable to me . . . at Martinmas and May day by equal portions

one freehold messuage tenement or farmhold and premises with the appurtenances . . . within the chapelry of Hamsterly and parish . . . aforesaid called Malam whereof I have an estate in fee simple (charged and incumbered as hereinafter is mentioned) and the same is now in possession of George Marshall tenant and demised by lease made by me to him for the term of 12 years commencing from Lady day and 3 May 1706 at the yearly rent of £22 payable to me at Martinmas and May day by equal portions

Several messuages lands tenements and hereditaments with the appurtenances . . . in Coundon . . part freehold, part copyhold and part customary in all which I have an estate or interest in fee to me and my heirs and sequells according to the tenure of the said respective estates; part whereof is now in my possession and other part thereof let to tenants as hereinafter is mentioned (to wit)

To Tho. Parkin several closes and parcels of ground there called Pease bank, two Smithsides, the Leazes, one acre of meadow in the Townfields of Coundon . . . Burne Crookes and a croft now in his own possession and demised by me to him for one year ending at May day next at the yearly rent of £23 5s. payable to me at Martinmas and May day by equal portions

To Ralph Shorte those closes there called Westfield and Tydey's Close now in his possession and demised by me to him for the like term at the yearly rent of £5 2s. 7d. payable to me as above

To Toby Harrison one cottage house and two garths there on the back thereof now in his possession and demised by me to him for the like term, rent £3 2s. 6d. payable as abovesaid

To Cuthbert Fawell one messuage or tenement and three closes there called East Closes the Kiln roods and Grass green close now in his possession let by me to him for the like term, rent £7 10s. payable as above

To John Nateby one close there now in his possession called Ettall let by me to him for the like term, rent £4 payable as above

To John Willy two closes there called Coundon Moores now in his possession let by me to him for the like term, rent £6 5s. payable as above

To Mrs Mary Bowser widow one close there called Markendales Moore now in the possession of Christopher Smurfoote her tenant let by me to her for the like term rent £1 10s. payable as above

To Anthony Lax one cottage and garth there now in his possession let by me to him for the like term rent 10s. payable as above

To George Rawling one close there called Melderstone park wall let by me to him for the like term, rent £1 10s. payable as above

To Robert Scott one close there calling (*sic*) Wintering Close let by me to him for the like term, rent £2 1s. payable as above

one messuage or tenement two cottages and one garth with the appurtenances . . . in Coundon . . . and several closes and parcels of ground thereunto belonging called the Lyme Kilne fields the new Close fourteen acres in the Town fields and Silvertopp garth also lying at Coundon . . . and now in my possession

Out of which rents is paid or allowed by me the several sums following . . .

To the Bishop of Durham for rent payable to him out of Backwood hill, Black House and Malam yearly (beside acquittances) £1 16s.

To the Parson of Hamsterly out of the same places a yearly rent or payment of 6s. 8d.

To the said Bishop for rent out of Coundon (besides acquittances) yearly £3 17s. 4d. Paid yearly for window tax for Coundon £1 besides all manner of sesses, taxes and repairs for all the said premises.

To the said parson of Hamsterly out of Malam a yearly rent or payment of £1 charged upon Malam by a mortgage made thereof by me to John Fawcett Esq by lease and release dated 2-3 January 1716, £300 payable to him with interest.

As witness my hand 19 April 1717

Fran: Sutton

The name of the said Francis Sutton was subscribed to this registry by Robert Spearman gent. his attorney thereunto authorized by warrant of attorney under his hand and seal . . . in open court at the Quarter Sessions of the peace held for the County of Durham 1 May 1717 before us Jno Rudd Fr. Carre

152. FRANCIS SUTTON 1724/5

I Francis Sutton of Coundon in the county of Durham gentleman . . .

A messuage and lands in Coundon and the tythes and other small tythes thereof now in the occupation of George Rawling as tennant thereof from year to year att the yearly rent of £23 10s.

Two little Closes or garths in Coundon aforesaid with the tyth hay and other small tythes thereof now in the occupation of James Fenwick as Farmer thereof from year to year att the yearly rent of £1 10s.

A Cottage in Coundon in the occupation of Margarett Morgan as tennant thereof from year to year att the yearly Rent of 10s.

The Tythe hay and other small tythes of severall lands in Coundon containing in all about 30 acres belonging to Mr Humphrey Doubleday which tythes are now unlett and the yearly value thereof uncertain but one year with another worth about 10s. per annum

All which said messuage lands and tenements were conveyed to and are now vested in Margaret Sheperdson widow and her heirs but with a Covenant and agreement on the part of the said Margarett Sheperdson comprized in the conveyance thereof by which the said premisses are agreed to be a security to the said Margaret Sheperdson for payment of £300 interest as therein mentioned and all sume and sumes to become due from me my heirs executors or administrators and assignes with Interest and to be redeemable by me upon payment thereof upon which said security there is now due from me to the said Margaret Shepherdson £300 with interest from 26 September last and I have only such estate and interest in the premisses as aforesaid

Fran. Sutton

The name of the said Francis Sutton was subscribed . . . by William Maddeson his attorney . . . in open Court at the Generall Quarter Sessions of the peace held att the City of Durham in and for the County of Durham by adjournment 12 February 1724 before Jno Rudd Tho. Rundle

The registers of St. Oswald's Church, Durham, record that on 8 January 1699 Mr. Francis Sutton, of this parish, was buried in the chapelry of St. Margaret's in Durham. He lived in Old Elvet, Durham, and had an only child, Francis Sutton, of Coundon. Admin. of the estate of Francis Sutton late of the City of Durham was granted 10 May 1728 at Durham to his son Francis Sutton of Coundon, co. Durham, armiger. Francis Sutton the younger was living at Lancaster when on 23 March 1750 he and his wife Teresa sold a capital messuage at Coundon to John Bacon of Newton Cap, co. Durham, Esq. In Greystoke Churchyard, Cumberland, there is an inscription to the memory of Francis Sutton gentleman late of the county of Durham "in life virtuous in behaviour decent in conversation courteous and engaging", died 18 November 1764 aged 83, and to Teresa his wife, died 5 November 1764 aged 77. The rest of the inscription is illegible, but it probably recorded that the monument was set up by Charles Howard of Greystoke Castle. Arms, a chevron between three annulets. Greystoke register says that Sutton died "at Graystock Parsonage a Roman Catholic" and was buried on 20 November. Teresa is also described as a Roman Catholic in her burial entry of 7 November.

153. SIR JOHN SWINBURNE 1720

I Sir John Swinburne of Capheaton . . . Barr[t] . . .

I am seized of an estate to me and the heires males of my body in tail male of and in all that capitall messuage or cheif mansion house orchards gardens and curtillages with severall other messuages lands tenements and hereditaments thereto belonging commonly called . . . Halliwell with their and every of their rights members and appurtenances . . . in the parish of Brancepeth in the county of Durham . . . which are now held and enjoyed by and are in the possession or occupation of John Akenside or his sub tenants or assignes at . . . the yearly rent of £116 but the said John Akenside is only tenant at will and holds not the same by any lease or indenture of demise which said lands and premises are subject to and charged and chargeable with the payment of £13 6s. 8d. to Philip Papillon Esq. as a fee farm rent

I am alsoe seized of an estate to me and the heires males of my body in tail male of . . . all that capitall messuage tenement or farmhold with all the lands tenements and hereditaments . . . belonging commonly called . . . New Nafferton . . . in the said parish of Brancepeth . . . all which are now held and enjoyed by and are in the possession of Frances Johnson widdow her sub tenants . . . at . . . the yearly rent of £45 . . . the said Frances . . . is only tenant at will and holds not the same by any lease or indenture of demise.

Jo Swinburne

Subscribed by George Forster gent. his attorney . . . in open Court at the Generall Quarter Sessions of the peace held at the City of Durham for the County of Durham 27 April 1720 in the presence of Jno Rudd John Hedworth.

See G.E.C. *Baronetage* iii, 124. He was eldest son of Sir William Swinburne, second baronet, and was born 8 July 1698. He succeeded to the baronetcy in 1716, and died at Bath 8 January 1744/5, m.i. Bath. His will, dated 13 September 1742, was proved at Durham by his eldest son and successor, John Swinburne, 26 March 1746. Sir John married in 1721 Mary, only daughter of Edward Bedingfeld: she died at York 7 February 1761. Will, dated 29 May 1759, codicil 30 May 1759, proved at York 20 May 1762. The registration of Sir John's mother follows.

154. LADY MARY SWINBURNE 1717

(enrolled 22 April 1717)

A yearly rental of the Lady Mary Swinburne's lands as they are let for in the year 1717 and settled by her late husband Sir William Swinburne Bart deceased as followeth

Jointure Lands

Item. Hamsterly and Hamsterly South Field } in the parish of Medomsley in the County of Durham held by Richard Dunn by lease for twelve years granted by Sir William Swinburne Bart from May Day 1708

	£	s.	d.
	51	0	0
part of South Feild in Ditto parish to Ursula Atkinson and her daughter Atkinson by verbal contract for one year ending at May day 1717 at per annum	25	0	0
Low Hamsterly in Ditto parish to Mr William Radclyffe by verbal contract for a year ending at May Day 1717 at per annum	34	0	0
Hamsterly Mill. In Ditto parish to Cuthbert Henderson by verball contract for a year ending at May Day 1717 at per annum	10	0	0
Font burn house and close In Ditto parish let a year at per annum	1	6	0
In all	£121	6	0

	£	s.	d.
Paid yearly to the Bishop of Durham out of the abovesaid lands	3	16	8
paid yearly to the seting out of a light horse	1	2	6
Allowed George Dunn for lime yearly	2	0	0
Allowed Mr Radclyffe for lime yearly	2	0	0
The Land tax	20	18	8
	£29	17	10
The Balance	£91	8	2

Capheaton April 18th 1717 These are to desire Mr Stonhewer, Clerk of the peace for the County pallatine of Durham pursuant to a late Act of Parliament for registering papist estates that I do intend (God Willing) to register the lands above mentioned at the next general quarter sessions and desires the said Clerk may enter this notice as the law directs as witness my hand

Mary Swinburne

The name of the said Mary Swinburne was subscribed to this registry by Ralph Gowland gent her attorney . . . in open court at the general quarter sessions of the peace held for the County of Durham 1 May 1717 in the presence of Jno Rudd Fr. Carre

See G.E.C. *Baronetage* iii, 124. She was daughter of Anthony Englefield of White Knights near Reading and married in 1697 Sir William Swinburne, who died 1716 and was bur. at Kirkwhelpington 17 April. She died 7 February 1761, aged 56.

155. JOHN TALBOT 1717

(enrolled 3 October 1717)

I John Talbot of Longford in the county of Salop esq. (*This register is identical with those of Thomas Stonor and Sir John Webb, q.v. with the following addition*):—

I am also seized of and in the preception and receipt of the several and respective annual fee farm rents or yearly payments issuing out of and for the several manors lands tenements and hereditaments . . . in the said county Palatine and Bishoprick of Durham . . .

That is to say

All that annual or fee farm rent of £34 5s. 3d. lawful money reserved and issuing out of or for divers lands and tenements with the appurtenances in Peirce Brigg in the said county Palatine . . . now or late in the possession of Christopher Lord Barnard or his under tenants and also all that annual or fee farm rent of £29 19s. 4d. like lawful money reserved and issuing out or for diverse lands and tenements with the appurtenances in Gainford . . . now or late in the possession of Mr Cuthbert Raines John Burrell and others or their under tenants and also all that annual fee farm rent of £35 6s. 2d. of like lawful money reserved and issuing out of and for diverse lands and tenements with the appurtenances in Elwick in the said County Palatine . . . now or late in the possession of Nicholas Hall Esq George Crow George Raine Robert Sheraton and Richard Reed gent. and others or their under tenants and also all that annual or fee farm rent of £43 11s. 9d. . . . reserved and issuing out of and for the manor and lands of Eggleston with the appurtenances in the said County Palatine . . . now or late in the possession of Mr Francis Baker or his under tenants and also all that annual or fee farm rent of £42 15s. 9½d. . . . reserved and issuing out of or for divers lands and tenements with the appurtenances in Elden in the said County Palatine . . . now or late in the possession of Mr John Stephenson or his undertenants and all and singular their rights royalties privileges immunities members and appurtenances. All which said manor lands tenements and premises charged and chargeable as aforesaid are . . . in the said county palatine and bishoprick of Durham aforesaid and the said several and respective annual or fee farm rents are payable half yearly at Lady Day and Michaelmas by even and equal portions subject to parliamentary taxes of which said several and respective annual fee farm rents or yearly payments hereinbefore set forth and expressed I am seised for the term of my natural life

John Talbot

Subscribed by Francis Goulton gent . . . at the quarter sessions at Durham 9 October 1717.

E.P. 50, say that John Talbot married one of the four daughters and co-heiresses of John, first Baron Belasye of Worlaby. See the registers of Thomas Stonor (no. 151) and Sir John Webb (no. 176).

156. ANNE TAYLOR 1717

of West Stobbilee

(enrolled 25 April 1717)

I Anne Taylor of West Stobbele in the parish of Lanchester widow . . .

Imprimis a messuage tenement or farm hold called Lane house and the moiety of another messuage tenement or farmhold called West Stobble in the parish . . . aforesaid . . . all now in my possession (save the moiety of a close called Patricks Close, part of Stobbelee), in which said messuage and tenements I have an estate and am interested for the term of my natural life and the part thereof in my possession is valued to be let at £7 10s. per annum and the moiety of Patricks Close is now in the possession of Thomas Rippon and let to him by me for a year ending at May Day next at and for the yearly rent of 50s. reserved and made payable to me for the same out of which rents and premises there is paid yearly to the Bishop of Durham 15s. for the same

As witness my hand 18 April 1717

Anne Taylor
(mark)

The mark of the said Anne Taylor was set to this registry by the said Anne Taylor in open court at the general quarter sessions of the peace held for the County of Durham 9 October 1717 in the presence of Jno Rudd, James Fynney

157. ANNE TAYLOR 1717

(enrolled 5 October 1717)

I Anne Taylor of Cornsey Rawe in the parish of Lanchester and County of Durham widdow

Imprimis all the rooms and lodgings above stairs of the seat house . . . in Cornsey raw . . . now in my possession and a third part of a tenement or farmhold in Cornsey rawe . . . wherein I am interested and have an estate during my natural life part of which farmhold is let as follows to wit three little closes and one house called Savage feild house and pasture gate to Andrew Oliver for three years commencing from May Day last under the yearly rent of £3 17s. 6d. payable at Martinmas and May Day by equal portions and a house and little close called the awards and a pasture gate there to Eliz. Tayler spinster for a year from May Day last and so from year to year under the rent of £4 per annum payable as above which estate is part freehold and part coppyhold valued at £30 per annum out of which is paid yearly a rent of 12s. 8d. to the Bishop of Durham besides all taxes sesses and repairs and allowances for lime and a clear or yearly annuity payment of £6 per annum to Eliz. Taylor for her life (who is yet living) all which said premises save such part thereof as let as above, are now in my possession for answering my thirds and maintenance and education of my eldest son William Taylor and my other two sons Thomas and George, all infants until my son William come to the age of 21 . . .

Anne Taylor

Subscribed by the said Anne Taylor in open court at the General Quarter Sessions of the peace held at the City of Durham 9 October 1717 in the presence of Jno Rudd James Fynney

157. ANNE TAYLOR 1723

I Anne Taylor of Cornsey Row in the county of Durham widdow. . . .

A parcell of land with the houses thereupon built being freehold scituate . . . at Cornsay in the parish of Lanchester and County of Durham which is now in the possession of William Dinnen as tennant thereof and was let to him with some other lands at Cornsey by John Taylor my late brother deceased and valued in the rent with the said other lands and not by itself but maybe of the yearly value of £8

In which said parcell of land . . . I claim an estate for my own life only

Anne Taylor

Subscribed by the said Anne Taylor in open Court at the General Quarter Sessions of the peace held at the City of Durham in and for the County of Durham 9 October 1723 before Jno Rudd Tho Davison G. Vane

Widow of William Taylor of Cornsaw Row in the parish of Lanchester, yeoman, who made his will 1 March 1707/8, mentioning his now wife Anne Taylor, his eldest son and heir William Taylor, a minor, and his sons Thomas and George Taylor (to whom he left "my now lately built house called Sanagfield House"). He also mentions his brother-in-law Gabriell Dayle of Ugthorp, parish of Lyth, Yorks, and his brother John Taylor. The will was proved at Durham on 22 April 1710 by his widow Anne, to whom was granted the curation of the three sons, William, Thomas and George. The testator was buried in

Lanchester Church, "at the foot of the middle ailey next the font" on 6 August 1709. The eldest son, William, was baptised at Lanchester on 16 May 1699, and the second son Thomas on 16 June 1700. There is a pedigree of the family in the printed registers of Satley.

158. JOHN TAYLOR of Dikenooke 1717

(enrolled 4 July 1717)

I John Taylor of Dikenooke in the county of Durham yeoman . . . a messuage or tenement and a parcel of land . . . at Iviston in the parish of Lanchester.

I let the same together with some other lands therewith I hold by lease from the Dean and Chapter of Durham for 21 years to Robert Wheatley by paroll, who is in the possession thereof and is worth about £7 10s. per annum, although the rent thereof is not distinguished from the said leasehold part and I do claim an estate of fee simple in the said freehold part worth £7 10s. per annum

John Taylor

Subscribed by . . . John Taylor in open court at the general quarter sessions of the peace held by adjournment 4 July 1717 in the presence of James Fynney John Bowes

159. JOHN TAYLOR 1717

(enrolled 8 October 1717)

I John Taylor of Allertongate nigh the City of Durham . . .

A cottage . . . at Cornsey in the parish of Lanchester . . . let by me by parole to James Ruckey who is now in the possession thereof at the rent of 10s. by the year

One other house and outhouses and a farm or parcel of land . . . at Cornsey . . . and at Butfeild in the said parish of Lanchester . . . let by me by parole to Thomas Ovington who is in the possession thereof at the rent of £15 by the year out of which I pay or allow all manner of taxes and sesses charged upon the same and also half the charge that he lays out for lime for the ground and that part of the said farm which lies at Butfeild . . . is copyhold held under the Bishop of Durham and is worth £4 10s. per annum though it is not distinguished in value or rent separately from the rest of the said farm and I do claim an estate of inheritance according to the custom of the manor in and to the same and other part of the said farm which lies at Cornsay . . . I hold for a remainder of a term for 60 years if I so long live only and that is worth 50s. by the year though it is not distinguished in value or rent separately from the rest of the said farm and the residue of the said farm lying at Cornsey . . . is a freehold and worth £8 per annum though it is not distinguished in value or rent from the rest of the said farm in and to which said freehold part of the said farm I claim an estate for my life only

John Taylor

Subscribed by . . . John Taylor in open Court at the general Quarter Sessions of the peace held at the City of Durham 9 October 1717 in the presence of Jno Rudd James Fynney

160. MARY TAYLOR 1717

(enrolled 24 April 1717)

I Mary Taylor of Cornsey in the parish of Lanchester . . . widow . . .

Imprimis. one messuage or tenement two cottage houses and two little garths with the appurtenances . . . in the town of Cornsey . . . two closes in Cornsey West Town field and severall riggs butts and parcels of ground lying dispersed and undivided in Cornsey East Town field and six foggates therein all lying . . . within the township of Cornsey . . . and in my possession and valued to be let at £5 per annum or thereabouts wherein I have an estate or interest for the term of my natural life out of which tithe in kind and all manner of taxes sesses and lime is paid and allowed and I am indebted to Ann Smith spinster £20

As witness my hand this 19 April 1717

Mary Taylor

Subscribed . . . in open court at the general quarter sessions of the peace held for the county of Durham 1 May 1717 in the presence of Jno Rudd Fr. Carre

161. NICHOLAS TAYLOR 1723/4

I Nicholas Taylor of Sunderland near the sea in the county of Durham gentleman

A freehold messuage tenement or dwelling house with a garden sumer-house and stables with other the appurtences thereunto belonging scituate . . . at the east end of Sunderland . . . near the Cunny Warran in the tenure or occupation of George Robinson let by me to him att and under the yearly rent of £8

Another freehold messuage tenement or dwelling house adjoyning upon the said messuage . . . on or towards the west in the severall tenures or occupations of Valentine Usher Elenor Hodshon Thomas Thompson Michael Thurlbeck Grace Scroggs Mary Henderson Marmaduke Carter Elizabeth Aninson and Anne Richardson let by me to them from year to year att and under the yearly rent in the whole of £6 10s.

Another freehold messuage tenement or dwelling house adjoyning upon the last mentioned messuage . . . on or towards the south in the severall tenures or occupations of George Liall Margt Greggs and David Side lett by me to them from year to year att and under the yearly rent in the whole of £3

Another freehold messuage tenement or dwelling house situate . . . on the west side of the High Ferry Boat Lands in Sunderland . . . in the tenure or occupation of John Holmes let by me to him att and under the yearly rent of £6

Another freehold messuage tenement or dwelling house adjoyning upon the last mentioned messuage or tenement on or towards the north in the tenure or occupation of John Weemes let by me to him att and under the yearly rent of £5

Of and in all which said severall messuages tenements or dwelling houses and other the premisses I . . . am seized to me and my heirs in fee simple and of which I pay all manner of taxes sesses and other annuall charges

Ni. Taylor

Subscribed . . . in open Court held by adjournment att the City of Durham 9 March 1723 before Jno Rudd J. Fawcet

According to Corder's MS. pedigrees, xii. 33f. in Sunderland Public Library, Nicholas Taylor was son of Elizabeth Taylor, sister of Abraham and Jacob Craster. He was perhaps son of John Taylor of Sunderland next the Sea, mariner, who made his will 2 December 1702, mentioning his loving wife Bridget, his son Nicholas Taylor (under 21), his brother Tobias Taylor and his sister Elizabeth Taylor.

Mr. Corder stated that Nicholas was elected in 1721 as a member of the first vestry to fix rate values "and I possess an indignant protest by ratepayers saying he was a Popish recusant 'and openly avoweth himself as such' ". He resigned next year. There is a Durham marriage bond for Nicholas Taylor of Sunderland gent. and Rosamond Browne of the same, 27 January 1731/2, the marriage to take place at Sunderland or St. Oswald's Durham, but it is not in either register. Their son, John Paul, was bap. at Sunderland 25 January 1731/2, as "base-born". He died 9 June 1734 aged one year and seven weeks and was buried at Bishopwearmouth on 10 June, m.i. in churchyard. A daughter Elizabeth was bap. at Sunderland 18 Dec. 1733, and is described as base-born: she married in 1759 Ralph Granger of Stockton. Other children were Michael, buried at Bishopwearmouth 31 March 1735, Bridget buried there 27 March 1737, William buried there 14 January 1737/8, Rosamund, bap. at Sunderland 20 Oct. 1738, married Matthew Furnace, and Catherine, buried at Sunderland 13 Nov. 1740. In 1757 Nicholas was a deponent in a suit (Atmar v. Greatet) in Durham Consistory Court, and was then said to be 60 years old; he was buried at Bishopwearmouth 21 January 1777 aged 86.

162. WILLIAM TAYLOR of Cornsey Raw 1720-1

I William Taylor of Cornsey Raw in the County of Durham . . .

A tenement and parcell of land . . . at Cornsey Raw in the parish of Lanchester . . . part whereof I lett to Andrew Olliver by paroll at £4 per annum other part whereof I lett to George Fillyard by paroll at £5 per annum and the rest of the lands there belonging to me is in my own possession and may be worth the yearly rent of £20 more or thereabouts part of which land is freehold and the other part copyhold which said premises are charged with the payment of £100 to my two younger brothers and with the yearly summe of £6 to my aunt Elizabeth Taylor for her naturall life and I agree with and pay to my mother Anne Taylor widdow . . . £15 per annum for her life for such estate as she may claime out of the said lands for her life and there is a yearly rent of 12s. 8d. paid out of the premisses to the Lord Bishopp of Durham

In which freehold premisses I have and claim an estate in fee simple and in the copyhold an estate of inheritance according to the custom of the mannor

William Taylor

Subscribed . . . in open court at the Generall Quarter Sessions of the peace held by adjournment 23 January 1720 before us Antho: Hall Gyles Rain Mayor.

For biographical details, see the registration of his mother Anne Taylor of Cornsey Raw (no. 157).

163. WILLIAM TAYLOR of Satley 1717

(enrolled 5 October 1717)

William Taylor of Satley in the parish of Satley and County of Durham yeoman . . .

One messuage in Satley . . . and also a cottage there with several closes and parcels of ground thereto belonging with the appurtenances all now in my own possession valued at £16 per annum to be let All freehold of which I have an estate in fee simple to me and my heirs out of which I pay an out rent of 19s. 4d. yearly to the Bishop of Durham and all taxes sesses and repairs and for lime I am indebted £60 principal money to Ralph Steele of Hough Hall payable with interest for which he has my bond and warrant of attorney for judgement

Wm. Taylor

Subscribed by the said William Taylor in open Court at the General Quarter Sessions of the peace held at the City of Durham 9 October 1717 in the presence of Jno Rudd James Fynney

164. FRANCIS THORNBURGH 1738

I Francis Thornburgh of Layburn in the County of York gentleman . . .

All that capital messuage at Stubhouse with the severall buildings outhouses gardens orchards rights of common inclosures or parcells of ground now enjoyed therewith . . . in the Mannor Grange or Hamlet of Stubhouse in the parish of Winston and all those inclosures or parcells of ground in the township of Whorlton and parish of Gainford end

All which premisses were lett by William Sudell of Wanless in the County of York gentleman deceased from year to year under the yearly rent of £40 to Ralph Waphup alias Johnson the present tenant the royalties thereunto belonging were reserved to himself by the said William Sudell deceased in his agreement with the said Ralph Waphup

All which said lands and tenements are subject to and chargeable with the payment of such debts and legacies of the said William Sudell deceased as the personall estate and other money appointed by his last will to be applyed towards the payment thereof fall short and are deficient in discharging

All which said lands and premisses with the appurtenances in the Registry before described I the said Francis Thornburgh am in the receipt and perception of the rents issues and profitts in the right of Catherine my wife who is tenant thereof for life remainder to her issue male and female

Fra. Thornburgh

The name of the said Francis Thornburgh was subscribed . . . to this Registry by Robert Hilton gentleman his attorney in open Court at the General Quarter Sessions of the peace holden at the City of Durham in and for the County of Durham by adjournment 11 May 1738 before . . . Ja. Clavering G. Vane

Son of William Thornburgh (*Catholic Rec. Soc.* vi, 152; *EP*, 283) of Selside Hall, Westmorland, and Mary Hudleston his wife. He was out in the '15, taken prisoner at Preston, but escaped in woman's clothes. His wife was Katherine, daughter of Thomas and Johanna Sudell of Wanlass Park and West Witton, Yorks. He died s.p. in 1774.

165. JOHN THORNHILL 1723/4

I John Thornhill of Stockton upon Tease in the County Palatine of Durham mariner . . .

A messuage tenement or dwelling house and garden on the backside thereof with the appurtenances thereunto belonging (in

Stockton) now in my own possession and is of the yearly value of 40s. or thereabouts after a deduction of taxes sesses and other annuall outlayes

Of which said messuage tenement or dwelling house and garden with the appurtenances . . . I the said John Thornhill am in the receipt and perception of the profitts and am seized thereof of a copyhold or customary estate to me and Elizabeth my wife and my heirs on her body lawfully begotten to be begotten and for default of such issue to me and my said wife and our heirs according to the custome of the Mannor

John Thornhill

The name of John Thornhill was subscribed . . . by Hendry Hopper Gentl his attorney . . . in open Court at the Generall Quarter Sessions of the peace held at the City of Durham for the County of Durham 16 January 1723 before . . . Jno Rudd Nich. Tempest.

166. ANNE THORNTON 1717

(enrolled 22 April 1717)

(A brief abstract of this register is printed in *SS*. cxxxi, 128. The house in Old Elvet is described as "within the suburbs of the City of Durham, but in the parish of St. Oswald's in the county of Durham". The lease of four rooms to Mrs Mary Morland, "the present possessor" was for one year ending at Whitsuntide 1717, and the remainder of the house was unlet. The register was subscribed by Edward Riddell gent., before John Rudd and Francis Carr.)

See *SS*. cxxxi, 53. She was living on 25 April 1727 (will of her sister, Mary Swinburne).

167. ELIZABETH TODD 1717

(enrolled 25 April 1717)

I Elizabeth Todd of Old Elvett in the parish of St. Oswalds in the county of Durham spinster . . .

Imprimis one leasehold burgage or tenement or garth . . . in Elvett . . . now in my possession and valued to be let at £4 10s. per annum wherein I have an estate or am interested for the remainder of a term of 40 years (granted by the Dean and Chapter of Durham and legally vested in me) commencing from 23 July 1701 under the yearly rent of 12s. 8d. payable to them and their successors yearly at Martinmas and Pentecost by equal portion.

The moiety of the tithe of corn and grain yearly growing and renewing in and upon all the lands and grounds of Stillington in the parish of Red Marshall and County aforesaid held by lease of the Master and Brethren of Christ's Hospital in Sherburne in the said county wherein I have an estate or am interested for the remainder of a term of 21 years granted by them and legally vested in me, commencing from 30 April 1711, under the yearly rent of 53s. 4d. payable to them at two days in the year by equal portions which said tithes were let by me by lease paroll to John and George Carlisle, John Denham, Robert Buckle, Ralph Starlock, William Wilson and Ralph Sparke for a term ending at May day 1718 at . . . the yearly rent of £16 5s. reserved and payable to me . . . and the said tenants are now in possession thereof

one freehold cottage croft and toft and ten riggs of ground . . . in Stillington . . . known by the name of the Westhouse and garth and two beast gates on Stillington Moore wherein I have an estate in fee simple to me and my heirs for ever and which were by lease paroll demised by me to John Denham for one year ending at May day next who is now in possession thereof under the yearly rent of £3 reserved and payable to me for the same.

Out of which rents and premises the payments and allowances following are yearly made or paid by me, to wit to the said Dean and Chapter for their rent and acquittances 14s.

	£	s.	d.
For the said tithe rent to the Hospital besides acquittances	2	13	4
Land tax and all other assessments	2	13	4*

* *(These figures are struck out)*

Besides repairs

As witness my hand 18 April 1717

Eliz. Todd

The name of the said Elizabeth Todd was subscribed to this registry by Robert Spearman gent authorized by letter of attorney under her hand and seal . . . in open court at this general Quarter Sessions of the peace held for the County of Durham 1 May 1717 in the presence of Jno Rudd Fr. Carre

Elizabeth Todd of Elvet, Durham, spinster, obtained a lease from the Dean and Chapter of Durham on 13 July 1721 of a burgage or tenement and garth, together with brewlead and steaplead in the burgage, which was in Elvet and late in the tenure of Francis Sutton gent. The rent was 12s. 8d. (Reg. Montague 1720-4, ff. 37-38). Her will, dated 9 August 1728, was enrolled at the general Quarter Sessions for the County of Durham on 15 January 1728/9. Describing herself as "very aged and infirm", she left to her niece Winefred Todd her house in Old Elvet, held by lease of the Dean and Chapter, and her messuages, cottages, lands, beastgates, tithes, tenements and hereditaments in Stillington in the County of Durham. She left to her nephew Anthony Todd an annuity of £5, to be paid out of the Stillington property, and to her niece Agnes Colling and nephew John Todd she left 20s. for rings. Forgiving her nephew John Todd a debt of £11, the testatrix laid it down that this gift and the annuity to Anthony Todd were made only on condition that they released to Winefred all their rights to the testatrix's property. Winefred was residuary legatee and executrix with John Rudd of the City of Durham esq. and Katherine his wife. The witnesses were William Howard, John Maire and Margaret Robinson. It seems likely that Elizabeth Todd was daughter of Winefred Todd, of Stillington, widow, whose will is dated 16 April 1671, inventory 3 October 1671. She mentions her son George Todd, her eldest daughter Mary, wife of William Kendaile, and her loving daughters Elizabeth and Margaret Todd. She makes these two joint residuary legatees, and executrices with Richard Wasse of Yafford, Yorks. Mrs Elizabeth Todd, papist, was buried at St. Oswald's, Durham, 2 September 1728.

168. WINEFRED TODD 1728-9

To the Clerk of the peace of and for the County of Durham or his lawfull Deputy

I Winefred Todd of Old Elvet in the County of Durham spinster . . .

I am seised to me and my heirs of and in a house and garth in

Stillington in the said County of Durham in the possession of George Carlisle I am also intitled to a moiety of the tyths of corne in Stillington . . . for the residue of a term of 21 years thereof granted by the Master and Brethren of Sherburne Hospitall by indenture bearing date 30 Aprill now last past commencing from the day of the date of the same indenture. All which said freehold and leasehold premises are let from year to year to the said George Carlisle at the yearly rent of £21, the freehold being reputed to be £4 per annum and the leasehold £17 per annum and there is payable for the said leasehold premisses a yearly rent of 53s. to the said Master and brethren and a yearly rent of £5 out of the said freehold and leasehold premisses to Anthony Todd for his life.

Winefred Todd

Signed by the said Winefred Todd in open court at the general Quarter Sessions of the peace held at the City of Durham for the County of Durham by adjournment 30 January 1728 before us Jno Rudd Ra: Robinson

Niece of the foregoing. On 3 June 1736 she obtained a lease from the Dean and Chapter of Durham (Reg. Bland 1734-37, f. 200) of the burgage in Elvet, which was bequeathed to her by her aunt. The rent was increased to 14s. because included in it were two walls "upon which or the one of them have lately been erected and built a new house and stable".

169. GEORGE TROTTER 1717

(enrolled 24 April 1717)

I George Trotter of Byers Green in the parish of St. Andrew Auckland gentleman . . .

Imprimis one messuage tenement or farmhold with the appurtenances in Byers Green . . . now in my possession valued to be let at £20 per annum wherein I have an estate in fee simple

one other messuage tenement or farmhold and several closes or parcels of ground thereunto belonging with the appurtenances . . . in Byers Green . . . now in possession of Joseph Scott my tenant and let by me to him for three years from Lady day last and May

Day next at the yearly rent of £30 . . . payable to me at Martinmas and May day by equal portions, of which last mentioned farmhold I have . . . an estate in fee simple

one cophold (sic) messuage tenement and farmhold with the appurtenances . . . in the parish of Stanhope . . . now in possession of Robert Anderson (incumbered as undermentioned) which are surrendered to the use of me and my wife and to her sequells in right to hold according to the custom of the manor wherein the same lie and demised by me to the said Robert Anderson for a term ending at May day next under the reserved yearly rent of £23 15s. and now let by me to John Raine for seven years from May day next under the yearly rent of £22 for the first year and £23 for the rest of the said term payable to me at Martinmas and May day by equal portions and I am to be at the charge of building him a wall upon part of the said premises and of repairing the hedges thereof for the advancement of the said farm which charge will amount to about £14 or £15 and I am to pay or allow out of the said premises and yearly rents the yearly payments following (to wit) A crown rent for Byers Green payable yearly £6

A rent payable yearly to the Bishop of Durham for the said copyhold farm (besides acquittances) £1 1s. 10d. besides sesses, taxes and repairs

Which said copyhold premises are mortgaged to Mr Richard Stonehewer for securing the payment of £100 to him with interest and I am indebted to Isabell Trotter spinster upon bond £20 payable with interest

As witness my hand 19 April 1717

George Trotter

Subscribed . . . in open court at this General Quarter Sessions of the peace held for the county of Durham 1 May 1717 in the presence of Jno Rudd Fr. Carre.

Said in *EP*, 53 to have been probably a son of James Trotter, who on 19 May 1672 married Margaret, daughter of John Walton of Shildon, and died in 1721. By will dated 24 August 1720, proved 21 July 1721 by John Trotter of Bishop Auckland, merchant, one James Trotter, a dyer, of Bishop Auckland, left to his son George a close called Punder Acre. There is a Durham marriage bond of 15 May 1714 for George Trotter, of Byers Green, gent. and Mary Stobbs, of Stanhope, spinster. On March 30 1727 the registers of St. Andrew Auckland record that George

Trotter "a Papist de Byers Green" was buried, he having died on 28 March, and Mary, his widow, died 10 January 1751 aged 63. Admin. of the estate of George Trotter, late of Byers Green, was granted at Durham to Mary his widow on 15 April 1727.

170. GEORGE TROTTER 1743/4

I George Trotter of Byers Green in the parish of St. Andrew Auckland in the county of Durham gentleman . . .

In the first place one messuage tenement or farmhold with the appurtenances . . . in Byersgreen and parish aforesaid now in my possession valued to be lett at £35 a year and wherein I have an estate in fee simple

one other messuage tenement or farmhold and severall closes . . thereunto belonging with the appurtenances . . . in Byersgreen . . . now in the possession of William Wright my tenant and lett by me to him for three years from May day 1741 at the yearly rent of £36 . . . payable to me at Martinmas and May day by equall portions of which said last mentioned farmhold I have likewise an estate in fee simple

Two other closes . . . in Byers Green . . . now in the possession of George Farrow my tenant and lett by me to him for three years from May day 1741 at the yearly rent of £11 11s. . . . payable to me at Martinmas and May day by equall portions wherein I have also an estate in fee simple

One other close . . . in Byers green . . . now in the possession of Thomas Wright my tenant and lett by me to him for three years from May day 1741 at the yearly rent of £5 . . . payable to me at Martinmas and May day by equall portions and wherein I have likewise an estate in fee simple a crown rent for Byers Green payable yearly £6

George Trotter

Subscribed by the said George Trotter in open Court at the Generall Quarter Sessions of the peace holden at the City of Durham in and for the County Palatine of Durham 11 January 1743 before us Tho. Davison Robt. Eden

171. CUTHBERT TUNSTALL 1717

(enrolled 23 April 1717)

I Cuthbert Tunstall of Lower Silton alias Nether Silton in the County of Yorke esq. . . .

In the parish of Whorleton in the County Palatine of Durham

A messuage or dwelling house garth and curtelage, a fulling mill and fish locke in the River Teese and one half of the fish to be taken therein with their and every of their appurtenances let by my father Fran: Tunstall Esq deceased to Ralph Ronetree and Elizabeth his wife both since deceased by lease for 21 years and now in the possession of Mary Ronetree his daughter at . . . the yearly rent of £2 The other half part of the fish to be gotten in the said fish locke in my own possession

A ferry boat over the River Teese with free liberty of landing the same ferry boat on either side of the said river of Teese with all other priviledges and appurtenances thereunto belonging let by me from year to year to James Baron and now in the possession of the said James Baron or his assigns without any rent paid . . . in regard of his poverty and necessity. Of all which said messuage or dwelling house fulling mill fish locke ferry boat lands tenements and hereditaments . . . I . . . am in the receipt perception of the rents and profits and am seized thereof to me and my heirs in fee simple and I am also seised to me and my heirs in fee simple of a burrow stead or front stead in Barnard Castle . . . let by me from year to year to [*blank*] now possessor thereof at the yearly rent of 6s.

Cuth: Tonstall

The name of the said Cuthbert Tonstall was subscribed to this registry by Francis Goulton gent his attorney thereunto authorized by warrant of attorney under his hand and seal, execution whereof was proved by two witnesses in open court at the general quarter sessions of the peace held for the County of Durham 1 May 1717 and the said subscription was made at the said general quarter sessions held for the said county by adjournment 27 June 1717 in the presence of Jno Rudd Antho: Hall.

See *DNB*. Grandson of William Tunstall of Scargill, Yorks., who married Mary, daughter of Sir Edward Radcliffe, second baronet of Dilston. His father, Francis Tunstall, of Scargill and Wycliffe, Yorks., married Cecily, daughter of John Constable, second Viscount Dunbar. Cuthbert went to Douay in 1700 and studied medicine at Montpellier, where he graduated M.D. On the death of his uncle William Constable, fourth Viscount Dunbar, in 1718, he succeeded to the Constable estates and assumed the surname of Constable.

He was residuary legatee and executor of the will of his cousin Lady Mary Radcliffe of Durham (see her register, no. 124), dated 22 November 1722, and proved by him at Durham 25 March 1725. His aunt, Dorothy Lady Dunbar, in her will of 28 December 1734, left him the picture of Lord Dunbar, and that of the Duchess of Feria, to be kept as heirlooms in his family. The *DNB* says that he was known as the "Catholic Maecenas of his age". He collected books and manuscripts, and was the friend and correspondent of many eminent literary men.

He died 27 March 1746. Extracts from his will, dated 14 March 1746, proved 27 May 1747, are given in Payne's *Rec. EC*, 81. See his register sub Cuthbert Constable (no. 31), and also the register of Thomas Mitchell (no. 111). He married firstly Amy, third daughter of Hugh, second Baron Clifford of Chudleigh, and sister of Elizabeth, wife of his uncle William Viscount Dunbar. She died 25 July 1731 in her 26th year, and was buried in St. Pancras Churchyard, London, m.i. Secondly he married Elizabeth, daughter of George Heneage of Hainton, Lincs.

172. CHARLES AND MARGARET TURVILE 1717

(enrolled 7 October 1717)

We Charles Turvile of Whitehaven in the parish of St Bees in the County of Cumberland Doctor of Physick and Margaret my wife . . .

A true particular of the messuages lands tenements and hereditaments . . . within the County Palatine of Durham . . .

All that messuage farmhold or tenement . . . within the manor of (*sic*) Lordship or reputed manor or lordship of Claxton in the parish of Greatham . . . now in the possession or occupation of Robert Johnson of Claxton . . . yeoman as tenant or farmer thereof together with all and singular the appurtenances . . . under the annual . . . rent of £18 . . . payable at Pentecost and St Martin the Bishop in Winter by even and equal portions by vertue of an indenture of lease under the hand and seal of the said Margaret my now wife then by the name and style of Margaret Johnson of Elvet in the county of Durham widdow of the one part and the said Robert Johnson by the name and style of Robert Johnson of Claxton in the said county yeoman of the other part bearing date 29 November 11th year of the reign of her late Majesty Queen Anne . . . 1712, whereby the said premises were by the said Margaret let and demised unto the said Robert Johnson his executors administrators and assigns in manner following

the Pasture Grounds from 26 March then next ensuing and the rest of the said premises from 3 May next ensuing unto the full end and term of six years from thence next ensuing and the said Margaret was thereby to allow twenty shillings to the said tenant towards the repairs of the hedges the first year and to pay or allow all taxes or assessments whatsoever which should be laid upon the said premises during the term aforesaid as by the said indenture of lease may more fully appear.

Item All that other messuage farmhold or tenement . . . within the said manor of Claxton now in the possession or occupation of Thomas Reed of Claxton . . . yeoman as tenant or farmer thereof together with all and singular houses outhouses barns byars stable folds fold garths lands meadows feedings pasture ways easements and appurtenances . . . under the annual . . . rent of £45 . . . payable at Pentecost and St Martin the Bishop in Winter by even portions, by vertue of an indenture of lease under the hand and seal of the said Margaret Johnson of Elvet . . . widow of the one part and the said Thomas Reed of the name and style of Thomas Reed of Claxton . . . yeoman of the other part bearing date 3 January in the 11 year of the reign of her late Majesty Queen Anne . . . 1712. whereby the said premises were by the said Margaret let and demised unto the said Thomas Reed his executors administrators and assigns in manner following . . .

the pasture ground (except one close called Oliver Close) from 25 March next ensuing unto the full end and term of six years from thence next ensuing and the said Margaret was by the said lease to pay or allow £3 for lime and thirty shillings towards the charge of building a byar upon the said premise, and to find wood for the building thereof and also paying or allowing yearly all taxes and assessments whatsoever except the window sess as by the said last mentioned indenture of lease relation thereunto being had may appear

Item All that other messuage farmhold or tenement . . . within the said manor of Claxton late in the possession of William Harrison yeoman as tenant or farmer thereof together with all and singular houses outhouses edifices buildings barns byars stables folds fold garths land meadow feedings pasture ways . . . under the annual . . . rent of £36 payable at twelve several kalendar monthly payments (that is to say) £2 3s. 4d. upon every first day of every month in every year the first payment to begin . . . upon 1 June 1716 by vertue of an indenture of lease 8 September in the second year of his now Majesty's reign 1715 under the hands and seales of the said Charles Turvile and Margaret said wife by the names of Charles Turvile of Old Elvet in the County of Durham Doctor of Physick and Margaret his wife of the one part and the said William Harrison by the name of William Harrison of Hart Warren house in the said county yeoman of the other part whereby the said premises were by me and the said Margaret my said wife let and demised unto the said William Harrison in manner following (that is to say) the pasture ground from 25 March 1716 and all other the premises from 3 May then next ensuing unto the full end and term of three years from the said respective days of entry severally to be completed ended and run we the said lessors to pay all assessments taxes and duties . . . and to maintain and uphold the said premises with thatch and the said lessee to be at the charge of thatching as by the said last mentioned indenture of lease relation thereunto being had may more fully appear

To all and every which said messuages farmholds or tenements lands and premises I the said Charles Turvile . . . am entitled in right of Margaret my wife for her life during the coverture and she . . . is intitled thereunto for and during her natural life as her jointure estate and in lieu and full satisfaction of her dower and thirds out of any the messuages lands tenements and hereditaments of David Johnson of the City of Durham Esqr. deceased her late husband by force and vertue of an indenture or deed of marriage settlement tripartite 17 October in the third year of her late Majesty Queen Anne made or mentioned to be made between the said David Johnson of the first part Anthony Salvin of Old Elvet in or near the said City of Durham esq. and Thomas Burlison of Sheerburn in the said county of Durham Gent of the second part and Margaret Salvin one of the younger daughters of the said Anthony Salvin of the third part before the intermarriage of the said David Johnson and the said Margaret Salvin now wife of the said Charles Turvile as by the said deed of settlement more fully appears

In witness whereof we have hereunto set our hands 30 September 1717

Charles Turville Margt Turville

The names of the said Charles Turville and Margt Turville were subscribed to this registry by David Dixon gent their attorney . . . in open court at the General Quarter Sessions of the peace held at the City of Durham 9 October 1717 in the presence of Jno Rudd James Fynney

Charles Turville married (bond Durham 8 August 1713) Margaret, daughter of Anthony Salvin and widow of David Johnson, Esq. of Old Elvet, Durham, whose will dated 31 March 1708 was proved at Durham 20 February 1709 by Margaret, to whom he left his messuages and lands at Claxton for life, with remainder to his son George Johnson and his heirs and failing them to his (the testator's) daughter Mary Johnson.

173. ELIZABETH VAREY [*not dated*]

I Elizabeth Varey of Gateshead in the County of Durham . . . .

I am legally intitled to and have an estate in fee to me and my heirs of and in one moiety or half part of a parcell of copyhold or customary land called [*blank*] with the appurtenances within the mannor or lordshipp of [*blank*] in the said County of Durham but of what yearly value the same now is I do not certainly know having never been in the possession thereof but I believe it to of the yearly value of £3 or thereabouts

I am also legally intitled to a moiety or halfe part of a leasehold messuage or Tenement and Gardens with the appurtenances scituate in or near the City of Durham in a place or street there called the Old Bailey held by lease under the Dean and Chapter of Durham and now in the possession of Mrs [*blank*] Wright but of what yearly value the same now is I know not having never been in the possession thereof, but the same now being in the possession of a mortgage by vertue of a forfeited mortgage from the person under whom I claim the moiety of the said Leasehold messuage

I am intitled to the reversion of a messuage or tenement with the appurtences in Gateshead aforesaid expectant on the death of Elizabeth Varey my daughter, part of it lett to James Burrell from year to year at £4 per annum other part thereof lett to Eleanor Heslop from year to year at 29s. per annum and the remaining part thereof in my own possession at the yearly rent of £3 per annum

174. ELIZABETH WALKER 1723/4

I Elizabeth Walker of Old Elvett in the County of Durham widdow . . .

Severall copyhold lands and tenements lying . . . att Stockton upon Tease in the said County of Durham lett to and in the possession of William Richardson att and under the yearly rent of £30 or thereabouts after a deduction of taxes sesses and other annuall outlayes of all which said premises . . .

I the said Elizabeth Walker am in the receipt of the rents and profitts and have an estate therein for and during the term of my naturall life

I am alsoe entitled to and in the receipt and perception of an annuall sume or yearly rent charge of £10 issuing and payable to me during my naturall life forth and out of certain lands called Middleton in the parish of Hart in the said county of Durham

Elizabeth Walker

Subscribed . . . in open Court at the General Quarter Sessions of the peace held at the City of Durham by adjournment 31 January 1723 before Jno Rudd Fr. Cornforth

175. JOHN WALTON 1717

(enrolled 8 April 1717)

I John Walton of Crosgate in or near the city of Durham yeoman and Elizabeth the wife of the said John Walton . . .

one messuage or tenement and little garth with the appurtenances . . . in Crosgate aforesaid, part of which messuage or tenement is now in the occupation of Catherine Salkeld spinster, who holds the same of us by paroll under the rent of 15s. per annum and the rest of the said messuage tenement and garth is now in our own possession or occupation and is of about the yearly rent of 25s. more in which messuage or tenement and garth the said John Walton hath an estate for the life of the said Elizabeth and the said Elizabeth hath the fee simple and inheritance thereof

John Walton
Elizabeth Walton

The names of the said John Walton and Elizabeth Walton were subscribed to this registry by Anthony Wilkinson gent their attorney . . . in open court at the quarter sessions held for the county of Durham 1 May 1717 in the presence of Jno Rudd Wm Ettricke

The will of John Walton of Crossgate, Durham, dated 27 October 1718, was proved at Durham by his widow Elizabeth Walton on 31 March 1720. He leaves 20s. to George Speed of Malton, Yorks., 2s. 6d. to "my sister Anne Speed", to Francis Moore of Coxhoe the £9 "which I lent him and 2s. 6d. more", to Robert Wilson of Low Stobbalee the 40s "I lent him and 2s. 6d. more". He leaves to his sister Elizabeth Taylor of Cornsey widow and her two children one shilling apiece, to Mary Best of Hart his trunk, a shilling to Mary Smirk widow, and to her three children George Smirk, Catherine Smirk and Mary Young one shilling each. The residue is bequeathed to his beloved wife Elizabeth Walton, whom he appoints executrix. The witnesses were John Taylor, Edward Mewborn (?) and John Smith.

176. SIR JOHN WEBB 1717

(enrolled 2 October 1717)

I Sir John Webb of Great Canford in the County of Dorset baronet . . .

(This register is identical with that of Thomas Stonor [no. 151], q.v.

The name of Sir John was subscribed at the quarter sessions in Durham 9 October 1717 by Francis Goulton gent., his attorney)

Third baronet, of Odstock, Wilts, Great Canford, Dorset, and

Hatherop, Gloucestershire. Succeeded his father 29 October 1700, died at Aix la Chapelle in October 1745. He married first, c. 1700, Barbara, daughter and co-heiress—eventually sole heiress—of John, first Baron Belasye of Worlaby. Through his marriage Sir John succeeded to the estate at Westwick in the parish of Gainford. Lady Webb died 28 March 1740 and was buried at St. Pancras, London, m.i. Sir John married secondly Helen, daughter of Sir Richard Moore, Bart.

177. SIR THOMAS WEBB 1746

A Register or true particular . . . of the name of me Sir Thomas Webb of Odstock in the county of Wilts Baronet

And as far as in me lies of all such mannors messuages farmholds lands tenements and hereditaments scituate . . . in the county palatine of Durham . . .

The Mannor or Lordship of Westwick . . .

one messuage farmhold or tenement with the appurtenances called East Shaws and severall closes and parcells of arable meadow and pasture ground therewith held in the possession or occupation of Anthony Hutton as tenant at will at and under the yearly Rent of £116 5s.

one other messuage farmhold or tenement with the appurtenances called West Shaws and several Closes or parcells of arable meadow and pasture ground therewith held in the possession or occupation of Samuel Rowlandson as tenant at will and under the yearly rent of £57

one other messuage farmhold or tenement with the appurtenances and severall closes or parcells of arable meadow and pasture ground therewith held now in the possession or occupation of John Swainston as tenant at will at and under the yearly rent of £40 10s.

one other messuage farmhold or tenement with the appurtenances and severall Closes or parcells of arable meadow and pasture ground therewith held and enjoyed and now in the possession or occupation of Robert Perkins (and called . . the Demesnes house or Perkins Farm) together with a piece or parcell of ground containing by estimation one day's work of land lying and being in a certain Inter Common field belonging to Barnard castle in the . . . County of Durham (called the Lowfield) as tenant at will at and under the yearly rent of £361

One other messuage farmhold or tenement with the appurtenances and severall Closes or parcells of arable meadow and pasture ground therewith held and enjoyed now in the possession or occupation of Christopher Smales as tenant at will at and under the yearly rent of £19

One other messuage farmhold or tenement with the appurtenances and severall closes or parcells of arable meadow and pasture ground therewith held and enjoyed now in the possession or occupation of Mr William Lodge as tenant at will at . . . the yearly rent of £24 10s.

One other messuage farmhold or tenement with the appurtenances and severall closes or parcells of arable meadow and pasture ground therewith held . . . together with a piece or parcell of ground containing by estimation one day's work lying and being in the said inter common field belonging to Barnard Castle . . . now in the possession . . . of Anthony Pearson as tenant at will at . . . the yearly rent of £20

one other messuage farmhold or tenement with the appurtenances and severall closes or parcells of arable meadow and pasture ground therewith held . . . in the possession . . . of Francis Blenkinsop as tenant at will at . . . the yearly rent of £53 10s.

one other messuage farmhold or tenement with the appurtenances and severall closes . . . of arable meadow and pasture ground therewith held . . . now in the possession . . . of Thomas Wilson as tenant at will at . . . the yearly rent of £10 5s.

one other messuage farmhold or tenement with the appurtenances and severall closes . . . of arable meadow and pasture ground therewith held . . . with one other days work of land lying in the said fields called the Lowfield belonging to Barnard Castle . . . now in the possession . . . of George Smales as tenant at will at . . . the yearly rent of £43

one other messuage farmhold or tenement with the appurtenances and severall closes of arable meadow and pasture ground therewith held . . . now in the possession . . . of William Carter as tenant at will at . . . the yearly rent of £21

one other messuage farmhold or tenement with the appurtenances and severall closes . . . of arable meadow and pasture ground therewith held . . . now in the possession . . . of James Scott as tenant at will at . . . the yearly rent of £11

Two other messuages with their appurtenances and several closes

. . . of arable meadow and pasture ground therewith held . . . now in the possession . . . of Christopher Newby the elder and Christopher Newby the younger as tenants at will at . . . the yearly rent of £8 15s.

And also all that piece . . . of Waste Ground moor or common called Westwick Moor whereon the said severall tenants have each a number of gates and a right of common adjoined to their said farms except the said Anthony Hutton and Robert Perkin

One other tenement or Cottage in the possession or occupation of Mary Douthwaite (a poor person) as tenant at will gratis of and in all every which said mannor messuages farms lands . . . I . . . claim to have an estate for and during the term of my naturall life . . . 6 September 1746

Thomas Webb

The name of the said Sir Thomas Webb was subscribed to this Registry by Adam Dale gentleman his attorney . . in open Court at the Generall Quarter Sessions of the peace holden at the City of Durham in and for the County Palatine of Durham by adjournment 19 December 1746 before us G. Vane Antho. Wilkinson

Fourth baronet, eldest surviving son of the last named, and brother of the Countess of Derwentwater. He died 29 June 1763 aged 60 and was buried in St. Pancras Churchyard, London, m.i. He married *circa* 1738 Anne daughter and co-heiress of William Gibson, of Welford, Northants. She died 7 October 1777 aged 73, buried St. Pancras, m.i. (G.E.C. *Baronetage* ii, 221)

178. THE HON. ANN WIDDRINGTON 1717

(enrolled 22 April 1717)

I the Honourable Ann Widdrington of Cheesburne Grange in the County of Northumberland widow and relict of William Widdrington late of the same place Esq. deceased . . .

I . . . am in possession and in the receipt of an annual sum or yearly rent charge of £400 secured to me by indenture tripartite bearing date 14 June 1693 made or mentioned to be made between (1) Ralph Widdrington of Cheeseburne Grange . . . Esq., and William Widdrington gent., his then son and heir apparent (both since deceased) (2) The Right Honourable Sir Caryl Mollineux

Bart., Lord Viscount Mollineux of Maryburg in the Kingdom of Ireland and me the said Ann Widdrington by the name of the Honourable Ann Mollineux daughter of the said Lord Viscount Mollineux (3) the Honourable William Mollineux Esquire son and heir apparent of the said Lord Viscount Mollineux Thomas Cholmondley of Vale Royall in the County of Chester Esq. Edward Horsly Widdrington of Horsly in the County of Northumberland esquire and William Ogle of Cassey Park in the same county esq.

In consideration of a marriage intended and since had and solemnized between the said William Widdrington and me the said Ann, they the said Ralph Widdrington and William Widdrington did grant and convey unto the said William Mollineux Thomas Cholmondley Edward Horsly Widdrington and William Ogle and their heirs (together with several lands therein also particularly mentioned . . . to lie in the said County of Northumberland) all the tithes of corn and grain lamb wool and hay and all other tithes whatsoever of them the said Ralph Widdrington and William Widdrington or either of them yearly happening arising or renewing in the parish or tythable places of Lanchester in the said county palatine of Durham, to the intent and purpose that the said Anne after the death of the said William Widdringon should have and receive out of the said tithes of Lanchester and the said lands mentioned to lie in the . . . county of Northumberland (and by the said indenture therewith also charged) the yearly rent . . . of £400 for . . . the term of my natural life in full recompence of my dower or thirds at common law to be paid on 2 February and 2 August by even and equal portions without any defalcation diminution or abatement for or by reason of any tax or assessment already laid or imposed or hereafter to be laid or imposed upon the said premises therewith charged or any part thereof or upon the said yearly rent by verute of any Act of Parliament or otherwise howsoever, the first payment thereof to commence at such of the said feasts days or times of payment as such first happen next after the death of the said William Widdrington with power of distress on nonpayment thereof by vertue of which said indenture and the death of the said William Widdrington my late husband I am intituled to and in the possession of the said rent charge of £400 a year for the term of my natural life which is all my real estate in the said County of Durham

Ann Widdrington

The name of the said Ann Widdrington was subscribed to this Registry by Edward Riddell gent her attorney . . . in open court at this general quarter sessions of the peace held for the County of Durham 1 May 1717 in the presence of Jno Rudd Fr. Carre

See *SS*. cxxxi, 16.

179. RALPH WIDDRINGTON 1718

I Ralph Widdrington of Cheese:burne Grainge in the County of Northumberland Esqr. . . .

A true particular of the severall tythes and hereditaments risen and being in the parish of Lanchester . . . whereof I . . . am or any other person in trust for me or for my benefitt . . . is seized . . . Robert Baliffe holds all the tythes of corne grain hay lamb wool geese pigg hemp and flax and all other tythes . . . within the parish of Lanchester together with all oblations obventions Easter reckonings prescriptions prescript rents and all other tythes . . . as well great as small mixt or petty . . . tythes whether the same be personall . . . now in the possession of . . . the said Robert Baliffe under me . . . att and under the yearly rent of £170 as tennant att will In which said premises I . . . am seized of an estate in fee simple to me my heires and assigns for ever subject . . . to the severall incumbrances following: to the executor of Mrs. Anne Radcliffe on mortgage and severall years arrear of interest £100 to Mr. John Hodgshons one annuity for his life £15 . . .

Ralph Widdrington

Subscribed by Edward Riddell gent his attorney . . . in open court at the Generall Quarter Sessions held at the City of Durham for the County of Durham 23 Aprill 1718 in the presence of Jno Rudd Jon. Eden

Only son and heir of William Widdrington and Anne his wife (no. 178). Under age 25 January 1715, but of full age 1 Sept. 1718. Died s.p. "respected by all ranks of people", and buried at Stamfordham 21 December 1752, the last of his family. He married Anne, daughter of Martin Woolascott of Woolhampton; she died at Hammersmith September 1764 (ex inf. Mr W. P. Hedley, F.S.A.).

180. WILLIAM LORD WIDDRINGTON 1742

A register or true particular (in obedience to an Act of Parliament Intitled an Act to oblige papists to register their names and reall estates) of the name of me William Widdrington late Lord Widdrington of Nunnington in the county of York . . .

The severall messuages lands tenements and hereditaments hereinafter mentioned scituate lying and being in Stanley in the parish of Chester in the Street in the County of Durham to witt one messuage with the appurtenances and severall closes of arable meadow and pasture ground therewith held in the possession of William Davison at tenant at will under the yearly rent of £70

One other messuage with the appurtenances and severall closes of arable meadow and pasture ground therewith held in the possession of William Jackson as tenant at will under the yearly rent of £66

One other messuage with the appurtenances and severall closes of arable meadow and pasture ground therewith held in the possession of Ralph Cumming and William Cumming as tenants at will under the yearly rent of £34

One other messuage with the appurtenances and severall closes of arable meadow and pasture ground therewith held in the possession of Ann Smith and John Emmerson as tennants at will under the yearly rent of £111

One other messuage with the appurtenances and severall closes of arable meadow and pasture ground therewith held in the possession of William Forster as tenant at will under the yearly rent of £2 10s.

One other messuage with the appurtenances and severall closes of arable meadow and pasture ground therewith held in the possession of John Pearson as tenant at will under the yearly rent of £30

In witness whereof I the said William Widdrington have hereunto set my hand 4 October 1742

William Widdrington

The name of the said William Widdrington was subscribed . . . by George Silvertop gentleman his Attorney . . . in open Court at the Generall Quarter Sessions of the peace holden at the City of Durham in and for the County Palatine of Durham by adjournment 29 October 1742 before Antho. Wilkinson J. Fawcett

See G.E.C. *Peerage* xii, pt. ii, 629-630.

181. WILLIAM TEMPEST WIDDRINGTON 1743

A register . . . or true particular . . . of the name of me William Tempest Widdrington of Stanley in the county of Durham Esquire . . .

The severall messuages lands tenements and hereditaments . . . scituate . . . in Stanley in the parish of Chester in the Street . . . (to witt) One messuage or tenement with the appurtenances and severall closes of arable meadow and pasture ground therewith held in the possession of William Davison as tenant at Will under the yearly rent of £70

One other messuage or tenement with the appurtenances and severall closes of arable meadow and pasture ground therewith held in the possession of William Jackson as tenant at will under the yearly rent of £70

One other messuage or tenement with the appurtenances and severall closes of arable meadow and pasture ground therewith held in the possession of Ralph Cumming and William Cumming as tenants at will under the yearly rent of £47

One other messuage or tenement with the appurtenances and severall closes of arable meadow and pasture ground therewith held in the possession of Ann Smith as tenant at will under the yearly rent of £40

One other messuage or tenement with the appurtenances and severall closes of arable meadow and pasture ground therewith held in the possession of John Emmerson as tenant at will under the yearly rent of £60

One other messuage or tenement with the appurtenances and severall closes of arable meadow and pasture ground therewith held in the possession of William Forster as tenant at will under the yearly rent of £2 10s.

One other messuage or tenement with the appurtenances and severall closes of arable meadow and pasture ground therewith held in the possession of John Pearson as tenant at will under the yearly rent of £50

And in all and every which said messuages lands tenements and hereditaments herein before particularly mentioned and set forth I . . . have an estate of inheritance in fee simple to me and my heirs . . . 1 July 1743

Wm. Tempest Widdrington

The name of the said William Tempest Widdrington was subscribed to this Registry by Hendry Hopper gentleman his attorney . . . in open Court at the Generall Quarter Sessions of the peace holden at the City of Durham in and for the County Palatine of Durham by adjournment 9 September 1743 before us Dormer Parkhurst John Hedworth

Third son of no. 180. Of Stanley, Co. Durham and Easton Grey, Wilts. Will dated 22 January 1753, proved P.C.C. 28 February 1753. See J. W. Clay, *Extinct and Dormant Peerages of the Northern Counties*, 252.

182. WILLIAM WILLIAMSON 1717

(received in office 11 September 1717 between five and six p.m. Enrolled same day)

A register . . . of the name of me William Williamson of Newton Morrell in the county of York yeom. . . .

All that messuage or tenement with the garth gardens and appurtenances thereunto belonging situate . . . at Blackwell in the parish of Darlington . . . one part of which said tenement and premises is in the possession of Margaret Carter as tenant at will or from year to year at the yearly rent of 40s., the other part of which said tenement and premises is in the possession of John Wharton as tenant at will or from year to year at the yearly rent of 20s.

Of and in which said messuage or tenement and premises hereinbefore mentioned I . . . have an estate or inheritance in fee simple to me and my heirs.

In witness whereof I . . . have hereunto set my hand 7 September 1717

William Williamson

Subscribed . . . in open court at the General Quarter Sessions of the peace held for the county of Durham 9 October 1717 in the presence of Jno Rudd James Fynney

183. WILLIAM WINSHIP 1723/4

I William Winship of Chester co Durham gent. . . .

A moiety of the tyths of corn and grain of severall lands within the townpps or villages of Chester Tanfield Birtley Pelton Urpeth Lumley East Edmondsley, West Edmondsley Twisell Picktree and Pelaw, all within the parish of Chester now in my own possession and of the yearly value of £80

There are severall prescripts in lieu of tyth corn issuing and payable out of severall of the lands above mentioned amounting in the whole to about £5 per annum which is included in and taken as part of the said £80 per annum

I am intitled to the said tyths onely during the terme of my naturall life and the same are charged with the payment of £50 yearly to my son Wm. Winshipp by vertue of a settlement made upon his marriage with Mary his now wife and he is in the receipt thereof There is likewise issuing and payable out of the said Tyths a yearly fee farm rent of £13 1s. 4½d. to Edward Noel Esqr. besides all taxes and sesses I am seized to me and sequells according to the custom of the mannor of and in one copyhold house and Garth with the appurtenances in Chester aforesaid now in my own possession of the yearly value of £5

Wm. Winshipp

Sworn 24 March 1723 before Fr. Cornforth Mayor, J. Fawcett at Generall Quarter Sessions of the peace held at the City of Durham in and for the County of Durham

Mr William Winshipp senr. was buried at Chester-le-Street 7 July 1738. In his will dated 16 October 1737 (in which he describes himself as of Chester in the Street gentleman) he mentions his copyhold messuages and tenements in Chester, and his leasehold houses in Sadler Street, Durham, which he leaves to his friend Mr Thomas Mascall, with all his personal estate "which I have in my own right or as administrator to my late son Wellbury Winshipp deceased", in trust to pay £100 each to his grandsons John and Robert Williams, £50 to his friend Mr Edward White, £50 to Mr John Hutton of Durham, £20 to "my kinswoman and servant Elizabeth Simpson" and £5 to Ferdinando Hendry. In a codicil of 18 November 1737, he mentions an indenture of release of 2 October 1716, and "a covenant therein from William Winshipp the younger my son". A second codicil is dated 17 April 1738, and the will was proved at Durham by Thomas Mascall on 1 December 1738.

184. CATHERINE WITHAM 1717

(enrolled 23 April 1717)

I Catherine Witham of Preston upon Tease . . . widow . . .

I the said Catherine Witham am possessed of and entituled to one annuity yearly sum or rent charge of £100 a year for my life secured to me by indentures of lease and release bearing date . . . 19-20 May 1701, the release being tripartite . . . between Marmaduke Witham of Preston upon Tease . . . Doctor of Phisick (my late husband deceased) of the first part William Tanckred of Branton in the County of Yorke Bart., Waldgrave Tankard of Branton aforesaid esq. son of the said Sir William . . . and Thomas Tankard of . . . nd in the county of York esq. eldest son of the said Sir William . . . and Edward Trotter of Skelton Castle in the County of York esq of the third part whereby the said Marmaduke Witham did grant and convey unto the said Sir William Tanckred and Waldgrave Tanckred and their heirs all that capital messuage or mansion house called Preston Hall with the appurtenances thereunto belonging . . . in the County Palatine of Durham . . . and all those closes . . . commonly called . . . Great Pasture and one close taken or divided, from the Great Pasture containing about 12 acres Blakely Hill Norman Feild taken of the West mire the West Long Lands and East Long Lands lately divided the Cow Pasture Annams the meadow Annams the Tillage Annams the Fish Stake Annams the Meadow Long Lands South Brewers pasture Sandy lands divided into two feilds Lishills and Poole holme with North Brewers Pasture Beanfield Thisley Field South West moore mire [?] plain and a house and a garth in the tenure of Eliz. Davison and one other house barn stable and garth containing about three acres called Sixconn [?] office all . . . in Preston upon Tease . . . and all other lands tenements and hereditaments whatsoever of him the said Marmaduke . . . in Preston . . . or elsewhere in the County of Durham (a farm called Red house Farm exclusive of the Close called Moore plain only excepted) with their and every of their rights members and appurtenances to hold the same except before and therein excepted unto the said Sir William Tanckred and Waldgrave Tanckred their heirs and assigns to for and upon the several uses intents and purposes therein after limited expressed and declared (and amongst others) to the intent and purpose that I . . . should and might after the decease of Marmaduke Witham my late husband out of the messuages cottages lands tenements hereditaments and premises (except before excepted) have receive and take the clear yearly rent . . . of £100 without any deduction for taxes or other matter or things whatsoever imposed or to be imposed by Act of Parliament or any other power or authority . . . at four times in the year (vizt.) on the second day of February on the second day of May on the second day of August and on the second day of November by equal portions for and during the term of my natural life and that when and so often as the said yearly rent or any part thereof should be behind and unpaid by the space of 20 days next after any of the said days of payment that then and so often it should and might be lawful to and for me the said Catherine Witham my executors administrators and assigns upon the said premises or any part or parcel of the same (except as before excepted) to enter and distrain and such distress and distresses to detain and keep until I should be satisfied and paid the said rent and arrearages thereof with reasonable costs and damages as in and by the said indentures of lease and release relation being thereunto had it doth and may more fully and at large appear by virtue of which said indentures of lease and release and the uses and provisions therein and thereby limited made and expressed and the death of the said Marmaduke Witham my late husband I . . . am intituled to the said annuity . . . of £100 for my life and am in possession and perception of the said rent charge . . .

Catherine Witham

The name of the said Catherine Witham was subscribed to this registry by Francis Goulton gent her attorney thereunto authorized by warrant of attorney under her hand and seal, the execution whereof was proved by two witnesses in open court at the general quarter sessions of the peace held for the County of Durham 1 May 1717 and the said subscription was made at the said general quarter sessions of the peace held by adjournment 27 June 1717 in the presence of Jno Rudd Antho: Hall.

Daughter of Sir William Tancred, Bart., and widow of Marmaduke Witham, whose second wife she was. She was living at Stockton on 23 May 1749 (enrolled deed, Durham Quarter Sessions records).

185. GEORGE WITHAM 1717

(enrolled 23 April 1717)

I George Witham of Cliffe in the County of Yorke gent . . . I . . . am possessed of and intituled unto one annuity yearly sum or rent charge of £105 a year during the term of my natural life, secured to me by the last will and testament of my late father George Witham of Cliffe aforesaid Esq deceased whereby . . . [*he*] did give and bequeath unto his grandson William Witham all his lands in Preston upon Tease in the County Palatine of Durham with the free fishery in the River of Tease . . . for ever paying yearly . . . out of the rents and profits of the said Preston upon Tease to me . . . £105 during my natural life . . . in equal portions at the feast of Pentecost and St. Martin in Winter subject to a proportionable abatement for taxes as in and by the said last will relation being thereunto had it may and doth more fully and at large appear . . .

Geo: Witham

The name of the said George Witham was subscribed to this registry by Francis Goulton gent his attorney thereunto authorized by warrant of attorney under his hand and seal the execution whereof was proved by two witnesses in open court at the general quarter sessions of the peace held for the County of Durham 1 May 1717 and the said subscription was made at the said general quarter sessions of the peace held by adjournment 27 June 1717 in the presence of Jno Rudd Anth: Hall

See *DNB* lxii, 258. Born in 1655, the third son of George Witham (bur. at Manfield 27 October 1703) by his wife Grace Wyvill. Vicar-Apostolic of the North district and Bishop of Marcopolis. Died 1725. Uncle of no. 187.

186. THOMAS WITHAM 1717

(enrolled 24 April 1717)

I Thomas Wytham of New Elvett in or near the city of Durham gent . .

All that my manor or lordship of Preston upon Skern in the parish of Great Aycliffe . . . and all the messuages lands tenements and hereditaments whatsoever thereunto belonging or therewith held or enjoyed or reputed to be parcel thereof, part of which said manor lands and premises to wit one pasture and two meadow closes are now in the possession of John Stephenson and now let by me to him by note or memorandum in writing for a term of six years part whereof is yet to come and unexpired at . . . the yearly rent of £11 and one cottage house and one garth other part thereof are now in the possession of John Hixon and Mary Hixon and now let by me to the said John Hixon by paroll agreement from year to year at . . . the yearly rent of 12s. and all the said residue of the said manor lordship messuages lands tenements hereditaments and premises aforesaid with the appurtenances are now in the possession of George Graham and were let by me to him at . . . the yearly rent of £120 by a lease in writing for a term of nine years part whereof is yet to come and unexpired with a proviso that the same shall be void at the end of any three years of the said term upon giving six months' notice in writing; of which said yearly rent the said George Graham is to have . . . £3 4s. 6d. allowed yearly for lime and all taxes assessments and repairs.

In which said manor lordship messuages lands tenements hereditaments and premises I . . . have an estate in fee tail speciall with remainder in fee to me and my heirs for ever and that no fine or sum of money was paid to me by the said John Stephenson and George Graham . . . for making of the said several leases.

and also all that my message or tenement with the appurtenances . . . in New Elvett . . . which I hold by lease of the Dean and Chapter of Durham for the term of 40 years under the yearly rent of 16s. part whereof is now in my own possession and the residue thereof in the possession of Catherine Smith widow and Jane Carnaby spinster and was let by me to them by paroll agreement for a term of seven years not yet expired at . . . the yearly rent of £6; out of which I pay or allow them the land tax

Of which said message or tenement I . . . have only the equity of redemption for the residue of the said term of 40 years, the same being mortgaged to John Pickering of Hedley hill in the county of Durham for securing the payment of £100 with interest, which is due and owing from me to the said John Pickering and I . . .

am owing and indebted to several other persons several other sums of money upon bond for which I pay interest

Tho: Wytham

The name of . . . Thomas Wytham was subscribed to this registry by Hendry Hopper gent his attorney thereunto authorized by warrant of attorney under his hand and seal . . . in open court at this quarter sessions of the peace held for the County of Durham 1 May 1717 in the presence of Jno Rudd James Fynney

Son of Anthony Witham of Preston-le-Skerne and Elizabeth his wife. Of Preston-le-Skerne 1709. Leased the house in New Elvet, Durham, described as at "the east corner of the old Barr[ony] of Elvet next the River Weare descending towards the Bridge" on 5 September 1715 (his daughter Elizabeth Ord obtained a lease of this house on 5 September 1744). Twice married, his first wife being Ann, daughter of Thomas Gibson, gent., of Stagshaw House, Northumberland (enrolled deed, Durham Quarter Sessions records). She was living in 1709 (deed concerning Catholic chapel in Durham). His second wife Jane was buried at St. Oswald's, Durham on 27 July 1742. He was buried at St. Oswald's 15 May 1739. His will, as of Elvet, Durham, infirm of body, is dated 5 May 1739, and mentions his dear wife, his daughter Elizabeth Ord, his grandchildren Elizabeth Ord and William Ord and his son-in-law Michael Tunstall. He leaves to his daughter Elizabeth Ord, "the house I now dwell in with garden behind and adjoining upon the River Weare." The will was proved at Durham on 7 June 1739.

His daughter Elizabeth married (settlement 26 November 1729) Richard Ord of Sturton Grange, Northumberland, who was buried at Warkworth on 2 August 1733. On 15 April 1735 an indenture was entered into between Thomas Witham of New Elvet and his daughters Elizabeth Ord, widow, and Bridget Witham, spinster (Durham Quarter Sessions records).

Elizabeth Ord lived on in the house in New Elvet and made her will on 28 October 1742, proved at Durham 20 July 1747 by her uncle Jasper Gibson, Esq., of Stonecroft, Northumberland and Michael Tunstall. She names her daughter Elizabeth Ord and her son, William Ord. She was buried at St. Oswald's on 17 April 1747. See *SS.* cxxxi, 91 and *N.C.H.N.* v, 247.

Bridget, the younger daughter, married (bond 1737/8) Michael Tunstall gent., of Wycliffe, Yorks., and died 4 May 1745 aged 33 years 11 months and 12 days (m.i. Wycliffe Church).

187. WILLIAM WITHAM 1717

(enrolled 22 April 1717)

I William Witham of Cliff in the county of York Esq . . .

In Sledwish in the parish of Whorlton and Gainforth in the County Palatine of Durham

The manor or lordship of Sledwish with its rights members and appurtenances together with Court Leet View of franck pledge Court Baron Waifs estreats felons goods deodands and escheats thereunto belonging now in my own possession

One part of the capital messuage or chief mansion house garden and curtilage with the appurtenances let by me from year to year to Mrs Elizabeth Wawbank the present possessor thereof at and under the yearly rent of £2 10s.

The residue of the said capital messuage or chief mansion house with all houses, outhouses, buildings, barns, stables, farm garden orchard and curtelage with several lands tenements and hereditaments thereunto belonging let by me to Charles Hodgson the present possessor thereof by note or memorandum of agreement in writing for the term of seven years at . . . the yearly rent of £60

A farm and several closes or parcels of ground with the appurtenances let by me to John Ovington the present possessor thereof by note or memorandum of agreement in writing for the term of five years at . . . the yearly rent of £60

A farm and several closes or parcels of ground with the appurtenances let by me from year to year to George Peacock the present possessor thereof at . . . the yearly rent of £42

A close or parcel of ground about the value of £1 10s. and let by me from year to year to Thomas Johnson the present possessor . . . without any rent other than looking after the other grounds

In Preston upon Teese in the parish of Stockton . . . the manor or lordship of Preston with its rights members and appurtenances together with Courts Leete view of frank pledge Court baron waifs estrays felon goods deodands and escheats . . . now in my own possession.

A messuage or tenement farm garden and curtilage with several lands tenements and hereditaments thereunto belonging let by me to Robert Stoopes the present possessor thereof by note or memorandum of agreement in writing for the term of seven years at . . . the yearly rent of £68

A messuage or tenement farm garden or curtelage with several lands tenements and hereditaments thereunto belonging let by me to John and Mary Walton the present possessors . . . by parole lease and agreement for the term of seven years at . . . the yearly rent of £55

A cottage and several closes or parcels of ground with the appurtenances let by me from year to year to Richard Garbutt the present possessor thereof at . . . the yearly rent of £4

A free fishery in the River Teese let by me from year to year to Robert Harrison the present possessor thereof at . . . the yearly rent of £1 10s.

In Old Elvett in the parish of St. Oswalds in the County Palatine of Durham two messuages burgages or dwelling houses (now converted into one) a garden and curtelage with the appurtenances thereunto belonging let by me from year to year to Mrs Elizabeth Johnson the present possessor . . . at . . . the yearly rent of £6

of all which said manors or lordships capital and other messuages farms lands tenements tithes and hereditaments . . . I . . . am in the receipt and perception of the rents and profits and am seised hereof to my (*sic*) and my heirs in fee simple. But the said manor or lordship of Sledwish and the lands tenements in Sledwish . . . are subject to several debts or sums of money secured out of the same amounting together to . . . £1,040 and to a yearly free rent of 1s. 11d. and to a modus or prescript rent of 6s. 8d. yearly paid for hay tithes. And the said manor or lordship of Preston upon Tees and the lands tenements and hereditaments in Preston upon Tees . . . are subject to several debts and sums of money charged thereupon amounting to £1,016 and to one annuity or yearly rent charge of £105 . . . payable to my uncle George Witham during his life and to a fee farm rent of £1 5s. payable to the Bishop of Durham and the said messuages or premises in Durham aforesaid to a free rent of 8d. to the Chapter of Durham

Wm. Witham

The name of the said William Wytham was subscribed to this Registry by Francis Goulton gent his attorney thereunto authorized by warrant of attorney under his hand and seal the execution whereof was proved by two witnesses in open court at the general quarter sessions of the peace held for the County of Durham 1 May 1717 and the said subscription was made in open court at the said general quarter sessions of the peace held by adjournment 27 June 1717 in the presence of Jno Rudd Antho: Hall.

Son and heir to John Witham of Cliffe and Elizabeth (Standish) his wife. Nephew of nos. 132 and 185. Married Anne daughter of Sir Henry Lawson, Bart. Will dated 8 July 1723, proved York 14 September 1723. His sons were Henry, George, William and Thomas. The last named, M.D., was of the city of Durham and married Elizabeth daughter of George Meynell, for whom see below, Appendix, no. 109a.

188. WILLIAM WITHAM 1723/4

I William Witham of Preston upon Tease in the County Palatine of Durham gent . . .

The messuages or tenements farms lands tenements and hereditaments . . . scituate in Preston upon Tease in the parish of Stockton

A Capitall messuage called Preston Hall and several closes or parcells of ground commonly called . . . The House pasture containing by estimation nine acres or thereabouts, the Brewhouse pasture containing by estimation 24 acres or thereabouts, the Avenew containing by estimation 8 acres or thereabouts and the little Avenew containing by estimation 3 acres or thereabouts with their and every of their appurtenances all in my own possession and are of the yearly value of £12 thereabouts after a deduction of taxes sesses and other annuall outlays

A messuage or tenement and farme garden and curtilage with several lands tenements and hereditaments thereunto belonging lett by Mrs Catherine Witham my mother to Samuell Grimshaw the present possessor thereof by lease for the term of 3 years till the expiration of 12 years att and under the yearly rent of £73 9s. or thereabouts after a deduction of taxes sesses and other annuall outlayes

A messuage tenements and farm garden and curtilage with severall lands tenements and hereditaments thereunto belonging lett by the said Catherine Witham my mother to Christopher Harrison the present possessor thereof by lease for the terme of

3 years att and under the yearly rent of £34 10s. after a deduction of taxes sesses and other annuall outlayes

A cottage with the appurtenances thereunto belonging lett by me from year to year to John Watson the present possessor thereof att and under the yearly rent of 10s.

Of all which said messuages or tenements cottage closes or parcells of ground and premisses I the said William Witham am in the receipt and perception of the Rents and profitts and am seized thereof of an estate of inheritance in fee tail to me and the heirs male of my body with remainder after severall others to me and my heirs in fee simple the which said premisses are subject to one clear annuity without deduction for taxes or other matter or thing of £100 per annum payable to the said Catherine Witham my mother for her life and severall incumbrances

William Witham

The name of William Witham was subscribed . . . by Hendry Hopper his Attorney . . . in open Court at the Generall Quarter Sessions of the peace held at the City of Durham for the County of Durham 16 January 1723 before . . . Jno Rudd Nich. Tempest.

Born 1702, son and heir of Marmaduke Witham by Catherine his wife (no. 184). On 15 October 1724 when of Preston upon Tease, he granted to Hendry Hopper his capital messuage called Preston Hall. On 23 May 1749 described as late of Preston Hall in the parish of Stockton and now of Stockton (enrolled deeds, Durham Quarter Sessions records).

In 1751 said by his cousin Henry Witham of Cliffe to be "near 50 and at Stockton". He married in 1725 Dorothy Sturdy and had issue Catharine, a nun at Lisbon, Dorothy who married . . . Langdale, distiller in Holborn, Ann, above 20 and at Stockton, Marmaduke, near 20 at Paris, William, "I fancy about 15 at Doway, and Margaret younger than him at Stockton" (Henry Witham's letter of 9 August 1751 in Hutton John, Cumberland, archives). William Witham died in 1777 and his widow in 1787, aged 87 (*Chetham Soc.* NS. lxxxix, 394).

189. FRANCIS WREY 1723/4

I Francis Wrey of North Thorn in the county of Durham yeom.

An estate of coppyhold land called North Thorn lying and being at Shield Row in the . . . parish of Tanfield and county of Durham now in my own possession of the yearly value of £5

Francis Wray

Subscribed by the said Francis Wray in the open General Quarter Sessions of the peace 16 January 1723 Jno Rudd Nich. Tempest

The will of Francis Wray, yeoman, of Shield Row in the parish of Chester-le-Street and chapelry of Tanfield, is dated 6 February 1753. He leaves to his son John Wray his estate in a messuage, lands and tenement at Shield Row alias Northhorn in the chapelry of Tanfield, one mansion or dwelling house excepted. He leaves to his said son's children Margaret, Eleanor, Francis and George £5 each at 21. To his grandson William Foreman, son of his daughter Elizabeth Foreman, he leaves all his right "to that freehold mansion so above excepted", situate at Shield Row alias Northhorn. He leaves to Francis, John and Dorothy, children of Laurance Wray, one shilling each. The residue is bequeathed to his grandchildren, the sons and daughters of his daughter Elizabeth Foreman, equally at 21, his household goods to go to his grandchildren Elizabeth and Dorothy Foreman. He appoints his daughter executrix and desires Francis Bradshaw gent., of Esh, John Fawell of Hilton Bridge and John Mill of Tanfield, to assist her and be tutors or guardians for his grandchildren. The witnesses were Peter Scorrer, John Waugh, and William Newton. Administration was granted at Durham to John Foreman, yeoman, of Witton Gilbert, husband of Elizabeth Foreman, daughter of deceased, on 17 November 1753.

APPENDIX

The following registrations have come to light since the publication of part I (*SS*. clxxiii). They have been numbered to indicate their place in the alphabetical sequence.

8a. THOMAS BIGGINS 1721

I Thomas Biggins of Sunderland near the bridge . . . yeoman . . .

A messuage or tenement with severall lands tenements and hereditaments . . . belonging . . . in Sunderland near the bridge in the parish of St. Oswald's in the County of Durham now in my own possession.

A cottage or dwelling house in Sunderland near the bridge . . . the possession of Richard Hutchinson as tenant . . . lett by me from year to year . . . at the yearly rent of 2s.

Of all which said premises I . . . am seized to me and my heirs of the equity of redemption only the same being mortgaged to David Dixon of New Elvett in or near the City of Durham gentleman for securing the payment of £1500 with interest which is all resting due and unpaid

Thomas Biggins

Subscribed in open Court at the Generall Quarter Sessions of the peace held att the City of Durham for the County of Durham by adjournment . . . 15 June 1721 before us Geo: Wheler Antho. Hall.

41a. THOMAS VISCOUNT FAUCONBERG 1720/1

Thomas, third Viscount Fauconberg died in Brussels 26 November 1718, and was succeeded by his son Thomas, who, on 11 January

1720/1, registered his estate which was identical with his father's (no. 41) except that Ralph Shaw is described as holding Thorngate and not Thorgates Mills. The subscription was made by Lord Fauconberg's attorney Robert Hilton junior before T. Williamson and Geo. Liddell.

54a. SIR CARNABY HAGGERSTON 1719-20

(Received in office 26 December 1719 enrolled 2 January 1719-20)

The preamble of this registration corresponds word for word with that of his son Sir Thomas Haggerston, printed in *SS*. clxxiii, 83-84, except that the date 1 March 1757 in the first paragraph on p. 84 should read 1 March 1657.

On p. 83, line 32, *for* Nowraw *read* Newraw.

p. 84 line 21: the illegible words are communibus annis.

p. 84 lines 25 and 26: *for* John Strother *read* Roger Abernathy *and for* £4 10s. *read* £4.

p. 84 line 29: *for* John Leedle *read* Elizabeth Thompson.

p. 84 lines 32 and 33: *for* Adam Dryden *read* George Purves *and for* 15s. *read* 13s.

p. 84 line 35: *read* the smith's shop in the possession of Oswald Dodds, at the yearly rent of 6s. 8d. and a salmon.

p. 85 after line 8: *insert* A moyety . . . of a messuage tenements and farm called Easter Milkington and of the garden curtelage and of severall lands tenements and hereditaments thereunto belonging lett by me from year to year to James Young the present possessor . . . at the yearly rent of £13 10s.

p. 85 line 13: *for* Francis Blake *read* Robert Blake.

p. 85 line 16; *for* Robert Fenwick *read* William Ord Esq.

p. 85 line 18: *for* Ralph Clavering *read* John Clavering.

p. 85 line 21: *for* Henry Ogle *read* William Ord.

p. 85 line 27: *for* George Orde *read* Alexander Hird.

p. 85 line 28: *for* Francis Orde *read* George Ord.

p. 85 line 31: *for* John Orde *read* William Ord, Esq.

p. 85: *substitute for the last two lines:* In Ancroft a castle ward rent of £1 5s. per annum paid by Henry Grey Esqre A messuage tenement or dwelling house a water corne mill and drying Kilne with a garden and curtelage and severall lands tenements and hereditaments lett by me from year to year to Edward Sibbett at . . . the yearly rent of £15.

p. 86 lines 5 and 6: There is no mention of Greenwich Hospital in Sir Carnaby's registration.

p. 86 line 13: *read* Five parts of a sixth part of the tithe of corn and grain arising . . . within the townshipp of Cheswicke lett by me to Christopher Sibbitt Elizabeth Strangeways and Ralph Heslop . . . att . . . the yearly rent of £50.

A cottage house and garth . . . with common right on the moor for cattle . . . lett by me from year to year to James Burne . . . att . . . the yearly rent of 5s. A parcell of ground lett by me . . . to Edward Haggerston Esqr . . . att . . . the yearly rent of £3.

(There is no mention of the messuage let to John Strangeways.)

p. 86 line 28: Bitchfield Hall . . . in the possession of Bryan Grey Esq. for the residue of a term of 21 years to him . . . granted by Sir Thomas Haggerston my late grandfather deceased by indenture of lease att . . . the yearly reserved rent of £31

A Capitall messuage or tenement and severall other messuages or dwelling houses orchards gardens and curtelages and severall lands tenements and hereditaments and a fifth part of the same colliery being another fifth part of the township of Kylo and Bitchfield Hall . . . lett by me . . . to Mr Francis Reed . . . but without any rent reserved in regard of his indigent circumstances.

p. 86 line 37: The freehold rents are paid by George Morrison and John Lee.

p. 87 line 10: *for* in possession of William Jackson *read* lett by me to James Rose at the yearly rent of £52 10s.

In place of the next three paragraphs the following is in Sir Carnaby's registration:

One close or parcel of meadow ground . . . and the tyths of corn hay wooll and lamb and all other tyths great and small and oblations . . . let by me . . . to Thomas Beednell Roger Main and William Heslop . . . at the yearly rent of £27.

One close or parcel of meadow ground . . . and the tyths . . . let to Stephen Porterfield and George Walker . . . at the yearly rent of £8.

One close or parcel of meadow ground . . . and the tyths . . . let to Edward Cooke Thomas Bonna Robert Steward and Ralph Collard . . . at the yearly rent of £10 10s.

One close or parcel of meadow ground . . . and the tyths . . . let to Anne Selbye widow and Thomas Ord . . . at the yearly rent of £8

One close or parcel of meadow ground . . . and the tyths . . . let to Thomas Dodds . . . at the yearly rent of £11 10s.

p. 87 lines 37 and 38. The quit or fee farm rent is paid by Edward Haggerston. *Add* the tyths of corn hay wooll and lamb and all other tyths great and small and oblations . . . in Smeefield . . . lett by me . . . to Thomas Wake . . . at the yearly rent of £5

p. 87 line 40: *read* the capital messuage let by me to Andrew Piercy at the yearly rent of £210

p. 88 line 9: *read* In Fenwick and Mounthully . . .

The capital messuage is let by Sir Carnaby to Matthew Bell at a yearly rent of £100

p. 88 line 21. The several messuages are let to Thomas Robinson and Charles Davison at a yearly rent of £80

p. 88 line 27. The several messuages are let to George William and Robert Davison at a yearly rent of £80

p. 88 line 33. The messuage or dwelling house with water corn mill etc. is let to Richard Hall at a yearly rent of £10

p. 88 line 38: *for* two messuages *read* one messuage or dwelling house maltkin coat yards etc. let by Sir Carnaby to Henry Hudspeth at a yearly rent of £5

p. 89 line 3. This messuage is "let by my grandfather Sir Thomas Haggerston to Andrew Fish by lease for 21 years and now in the possession of the said Andrew Fish at the yearly reserved rent of £2"

p. 89 line 8. This messuage is let by Sir Carnaby to Thomas Wilson at yearly rent of £1

p. 89 line 12: *for* two messuages etc *read* one messuage or dwelling house and coat land with the curtelage let by Sir Carnaby to Thomas Todd at the yearly rent of £1 17s. *Add* messuages let by Sir Carnaby to John Wright, yearly rent £1; to Clement Cheesam, yearly rent £1 13s.; to Richard Day, yearly rent £1 10s., which is remitted to him "for looking after the woods".

p. 89 line 20. This, and the following paragraph are not given in Sir Carnaby's register.

p 89 line 30. The quit rents are paid by John Luckly and John Taylor.

p. 89 line 34. The fishery was in Sir Carnaby's possession.

p. 89 line 39. The messuage was in the possession of Stephen Porterfield at a yearly rent of £4.

p. 90. For the first paragraph substitute "two cottages let to George Walker and Thomas Luckly without any reserved rent or other consideration than that of their assistance in the management of the said fishery".

p. 90 lines 10-15: *for* closes . . . possession *read* on the south side of the town of Haggerston containing 125 acres a parcel of land called the Moor outfield ground and containing 390 acres a close called the Stony Flatt lying on the north side of the said town containing 41 acres a parcel of ground called the Flowes containing 20 acres a parcel of ground called the Haugh pool containing 17 acres a parcel of pasture ground in the Fenna containing 25 acres a close called the Allarey meadow containing 25 acres a close of pasture ground called the Short Long flatt containing 17 acres several parcells of ground on the north side of the town containing 72 acres two closes of meadow ground called the calfe closes containing two acres a parcel of meadow ground called the Bridge Close alias Archbald containing three acres and a parcell of arable land called the Foulside Lee containing 28 acres in my own possession.

p. 90 line 16 to bottom of page and p. 91 lines 1-36: *read* A messuage or tenement farme garden and curtelage with severall lands tenements and hereditaments . . . and the tyths . . . lett by me from year to year to Thomas Beadnell at . . . the yearly rent of £37 3s. 4d.

A messuage or tenement [*as before*] lett by me from year to year to William Heslop . . . yearly rent . . . £20

A messuage or tenement [*as before*] lett by me from year to year to Roger Main . . . yearly rent . . . £14

A messuage or tenement [*as before*] lett by me from year to year to Ignatius Main . . . yearly rent . . . £21

A messuage or tenement [*as before*] lett by me from year to year to James Harne . . . yearly rent . . . £10 13s. 4d.

A messuage or tenement garden and curtelage and the third part of a close . . . lett to Robert Fenwicke . . . yearly rent . . . £5 13s. 4.

A messuage [*as before*] . . . lett to Alexander Dash . . . yearly rent . . . £5 13s. 4d.

A messuage [*as before*] . . . lett to William Thompson . . . yearly rent . . . £5 13s. 4d.

A messuage or tenement farm garden and curtelage with several lands tenements and hereditaments and the tyths . . . lett by me to John Ivison . . . at the yearly rent of £22 3s. 4d.

A messuage [*as before*] . . . lett . . . to Thomas Hogg . . . yearly rent . . . £7 13s. 4d.

A messuage or tenement and water corn mill garden and curtelage lett to Elener Smith . . . yearly rent . . . £70

A parcel of pasture ground and the tyths . . . let . . . to Adam Sibbett . . . at the yearly rent of £5

One close or parcell of meadow ground and the tyths let . . . to James Purdy . . . yearly rent . . . £4

A cottage or dwelling house garth and curtelage and the sixth part of a close called the Wester Close . . . and the tyths . . . let to Robert Dickenson . . . yearly rent £2 3s. 4d.

A cottage [*as before*] . . . let to Henry Browne . . . yearly rent . . . £2 3s. 4d.

A cottage [*as before*] . . . let to Elizabeth Bell without any rent reserved in regard to her poverty.

A cottage and garth with the curtelage and tyths let to Barbara Bard without any rent reserved in respect of her poverty.

A cottage [*as before*] . . . let to James Thompson without any rent reserved in regard of his indigent circumstances

A cottage [*as before*] . . . let to Anne Trotter without receiving any rent in regard of her indigent circumstances

A cottage [*as before*] . . . let to Stephen Bide without any rent reserved in regard of his poverty

A cottage [*as before*] . . . let to Anthony Peacock without any rent reserved in regard of his poverty

A cottage [*as before*] . . . let to Alexander Blaikey without any rent reserved in regard of his needy circumstances

A cottage [*as before*] . . . let to William Kellett without any rent reserved in regard of his needy circumstances

A cottage [*as before*] . . . let to Henry Jackson without any rent reserved in regard of his needy circumstances

A cottage [*as before*] . . . let to James Cockrum without any rent reserved in regard of his needy circumstances

A close . . . called the Flattening Close and the tyths . . . let by me . . . to Edmund Dodds . . . at . . . the yearly rent of £12

A cottage let to Margaret Ruttlige without any rent reserved in regard of her poverty

A small cottage wherein I permitt a schoolmaster to teach the children of the town without any rent.

p. 91 lines 37 and 38 are the same in Sir Carnaby's registration

p. 91, last two lines, and p. 92. *Read* I am seized of the mannors or lordshipps of Fenwick and Buckton and tyths of Cheswicke and the two rent charges of £18 and £12 per annum issuing out of Lowlinn to me and the heires males of my body in taile male subject to a terme of 99 years (if my mother Anne Haggerston soe long live) thereof limitted in and by my father William Haggerston Esqr his marriage settlement to trustees therein named and to the trust of the said terme thereby declared for raiseing and paying out of the rents issues and profitts thereof one annuity or yearly rent . . . of £400 unto the said Anne Haggerston or her assignes for . . . soe many years of the said terme of 99 years as she shall happen to live with remainder (in default of heires male of the body of my uncle Edward Haggerston Esqr) to me and my heirs in fee simple as heir at law to Sir Thomas Haggerston Barrt. my grandfather deceased save that my estate in the said two rent charges of £18 and £12 is defeazable on payment of the severall summes of money in the respective grants thereof mentioned pursuant to severall provisoes therein . . . contained And in all and singular other the Lordshipps mannors messuages cottages farms lands tenements advowsons tyths rents and hereditaments in this Register or particular above written mentioned (the Manor or township of Haggerston and all messuages cottages demesne and other lands grounds and mills in Haggerston aforesaid a moyety . . . of a messuage tenement and farm called Easter Milkington within the Chappelry of Cornhill . . . of the yearly value of £13 10s. two fifth parts of Kyloe and Bitchfield Hall and colliery there. a messuage or tenement and water corn mill with severall lands tenements and hereditaments thereunto belonging within the Chappelry of Ancroft of the yearly value of £15 and a rent charge of 24s. per annum out of certain lands in Beale (above mentioned only excepted) I . . . have in remainder expectant on the determination of a terme of 500 years thereof (and of certain lands tenements and hereditaments in the county of Northumberland) limitted by my said father's marriage settlement to trustees therein named an estate to me and the heires males of my body in taile male with remainder (on default of issue male of the body of my said uncle Edward Haggerston Esqr) to me and my heires in fee simple as heir at law to my said grandfather Sir Thomas Haggerston . . . subject . . . to the said terme of 500 years and to the trusts thereof declared in and by my . . . father's marriage settlement and amongst others to the trust thereby declared for the levying and raiseing out of the rents issues and profitts thereof and of the said other lands tenements and hereditaments in the . . . county of Northumberland or by mortgage lease or other disposition thereof as to them shall seem meet the summe of £4000 for the portions of my sisters and interest for the same for their . . . maintenances after the rate of £6 per cent per annum and of and in the one moiety of the manor or townshipp of Haggerston and a moyety of all messuages cottages lands and grounds and windmill in Haggerston . . . and of and in all those two water corne mills in Haggerston called Brock Mill and Bridge Mill and the rent charge of 24s. issueing out of Beale . . . I . . . am seised of an estate to me and the heires males of my body in taile maile with remainder (after severall others) to the heires males of the body of my said uncle Edward Haggerston Esqr and for default of such to the respective heirs females of the respective bodys of my said father and uncle severally respectively and successively to me and my heirs in fee simple as heir at law to my said grandfather . . . save that my estate in the rent charge of 24s. per annum out of Beale . . . is defeazable on payment of the money in the grant thereof mentioned pursuant to a provisoe therein in that behalfe contained And as for and concerning the other moyety of the mannor or townshipp of Haggerston and of all messuages cottages lands closes and grounds with the appurtenances in Haggerston . . . and as for and concerning a moiety of the said farme called Easter Milkington . . . I . . . am seised thereof of an estate to me and my heirs in fee simple and in the said messuage or tenement and water corn mill with severall lands tenements and hereditaments thereunto belonging within the Chappelry of Ancroft . . . of the yearly value of £15 I have a trust or equitable estate to me and my heires defeazable nevertheless on payment of severall summes of money in the severall grants . . . thereof mentioned pursuant to the severall provisoes in that behalfe therein contained But the said manor or townshipp of Haggerston and all messuages cottages mills closes lands and grounds in Haggerston . . . are subject to and charged and chargeable by the . . .

will . . . of Sir Thomas Haggerston my said late grandfather with an annuity of £20 . . . payable without any deductions for taxes or other matter or thing to my uncle John Haggerston Esqr for . . . the terme of his naturall life and to and with one annuity . . . of £190 10s. granted by indenture of settlement by the said Sir Thomas . . . on my . . . father's marriage to trustees . . . for the term of 500 years upon trust for the better raising of my said sisters' portions and maintenances and after the determination of the said terme of 500 years, the same annuity . . . of £190 10s. is thereby limitted to me and the heires males of my body with remainder (on default of heires males of the body of my said uncle Edward Haggerston) to me and my heires as heir at law to my said grandfather Sir Thomas Haggerston and the said premisses in this register . . . are further . . . subject to and charged with the yearly payments hereinafter mentioned . . . Haggerston with the payment of a yearly free rent of £5 Milkhouse field within Goswicke with the payment of a yearly free rent of 8s. 9d. Lowlin Mill with the like yearly payment of a free rent of £4 and Kyloe with the payment of a quitt rent of 3s. per annum and the Milkhouse field and other lands within Goswicke and the said tyths with the yearly payments of £10 a peice per annum to the severall curates of Holy Island Tweedmouth Ancroft Kyloe and Lowicke

Carnaby Haggerston

The name of the said Sir Carnaby Haggerston was subscribed to this Registry by Robert Bulman of Morpeth gentleman his attorney thereunto authorized by warrant of attorney under his hand and seal the execution whereof was proved by two witnesses and the said subscription and proof was made in open Court at the Generall Quarter Sessions of the peace held att the City of Durham for the County of Durham . . . 13 January 1719 in the presence of Jno Rudd Geo Liddell

G.E.C. *Baronetage* ii, 245. Son and heir of William Haggerston. Succeeded his grandfather, Sir Thomas Haggerston, as third baronet. Father of no. 58.

97a. FRANCIS MAIRE 1718

(received in office 23 December, enrolled same day 1718)

I Francis Maire of Lartington in the county of Yorke gentleman who have lately attained the age of 21 years . . .

I am intitled to me and my heirs of and in all that close . . . of ground in Hutton Henry . . . now in the possesson of Richard Cowle as tenant from year to year att the yearly rent of £3 out of which he has an allowance of 20s. yearly for lime

One house or cottage in Hutton Henry . . . with a malt milne and other buildings and appurtenances thereto belonging and a yard or garth thereunto adjoining with the appurtenances which . . . premises were lett and demised by Thomas Maire Esqr my late father in my infancy together with other lands and tenements of the said Thomas Maire to John Smith by indenture . . . 6 March 12 Anne [1713-14] for nine years commencing from Lady day and May day then next following att the yearly rent of £77 of which the yearly summe or rent of £12 was and is intended and agreed to be the yearly rent and proportion for the said premises belonging to me . . . and the said premisses are now in the possession of the said John Smith or his undertenants or assignes and there is an allowance to be made to the said tenant out of the said rent of all taxes and assessments except window money and for such repairs as in the said lease is mentioned

All that cottage or tenement and garth in Hutton Henry aforesaid now in the possession of William Winshipp his undertenants or assignes att the yearly rent of 7s., the said William Winshipp being tenant thereof from year to year

Of all which premises I am seized to me and my heirs in fee simple

Francis Maire

Subscribed by David Dixon gent his attorney . . . att the generall quarter sessions held by adjournment att the City of Durham for the County of Durham 4 February 1718 in the presence of Cuth: Morland Wm Cotesworth.

See *SS*. clxxiii, 143-144.

109a. GEORGE MEYNELL 1722

I George Meynell of Aldbrough in the County of York Esqr. . . .

In Colpighill in the parish of Lanchester . . . two messuages or dwelling houses and severall other houses outhouses barns byars stables farme gardens orchards and curtelage with severall lands tenements and hereditaments thereunto belonging lett by Mr George Coxon to Michael Willy and John Willy the present possessors thereof by lease for a terme of about sixteen yeares att and under the yearly reserved rent of £60

A messuage or tenement farme garden orchard and curtelage with severall lands tenements and hereditaments thereunto belonging lett by Mrs. Anne Coxon to George Darnell the present proprietor thereof by word of mouth for the terme of three yeares att and under the reserved yearly rent of £20

Two messuages or dwelling houses a water corn mill and a fulling mill garden orchard and curtelage and severall peices or parcells of ground with the appurtenances thereunto respectively belonging lett by me from year to year to Robert Fulthorp the present proprietor . . . at . . . the yearly rent of £12

Of which said premises one messuage and about fifty acres . . . are copyhold the rest freehold but the said copyhold lands lye soe adjoyning to and intermixed with the freehold lands that I cannot particularly describe the same and of all the said messuages mills farmes lands tenements hereditaments and premises as well freehold as copyhold . . . I . . . am in the receipt and perception of the rents and profitts and have therein a trust estate to me and my heires all the said premises . . . being vested in Solomon Wycliffe Esqr and Thomas Metcalfe gentleman and their heires for the securing of all such summe and summes of money as then were or thereafter should be due and owing from me . . . to the said Solomon Wycliffe and Thomas Metcalfe . . .

George Meynell

. . . Subscribed by Robert Spearman gent his attorney . . . and proof . . . made in open court at the Generall Quarter Sessions of the peace held at the City of Durham for the County of Durham . . . 1 October 1722 in the presence of Jno Rudd Jo: Mountagu

See *SS.* clxxiii, 32-34. Two deeds enrolled in the 1717-22 book of registrations throw some light on the Cockson and Meynell families. The first, dated 17 April 1722, is between (1) the above George Meynell, (2) Elizabeth Cockson of Old Elvett spinster, (3) Thomas Cockson of the City of London gent., and recites that the said Thomas is entitled to £5 a year for life chargeable upon lands in Lanchester late the estate of George Cockson deceased, Elizabeth's father. Thomas at Elizabeth's request has joined in a conveyance of the premises to or in trust for Meynell and his heirs and Meynell, at Elizabeth's request, has entered in to a bond of even date in the penal sum of £100 conditioned for payment of £5 yearly to Thomas Cockson. Meynell grants to Thomas the annuity of £5, chargeable upon a messuage in West Dalton alias Dalton Ryall, Yorks., in the possession of William Heslup at £17 per annum.

The second deed dated 19 April 1722 is between (1) Ann Cockson of Old Elvett widow and relict of George Cockson, and Elizabeth Cockson spinster daughter and heiress of the said George Cockson by the said Anne his wife, Thomas Cockson of the city of London gent., brother of the said George Cockson and James Wass of Romanby, Yorks., gent., (2) George Meynell of Aldbrough esq., (3) Solomon Wycliffe of Gales Yorks., esq. and Thomas Metcalfe of Richmond, Yorks., gent. This deed, after reciting Thomas Cockson's right to £5 a year, goes on to say that a marriage is agreed upon and intended by God's permission to be shortly had between the said George Meynell and Elizabeth Cockson. It also states that Meynell owes Wycliffe £100 and Metcalfe £50, and that in consideration of the intended marriage and of a settlement made by Meynell of his lands and tenements at Aldbrough and West Dalton whereby a provision is made for Ann Cockson for life and for the jointure of Elizabeth Cockson and for her issue to be begotten by Meynell and in consideration that Meynell has secured to Thomas Cockson £5, Ann and Elizabeth Cockson grant to Wycliffe and Metcalfe the premises at Colpighill, and a messuage called Binkhouse in Romaldkirk, Yorks., to the use of Ann and Elizabeth Cockson, until Elizabeth's marriage takes place. After that event, the premises to Wycliffe and Metcalfe in trust for securing the money due to them from Meynell and then in trust for Meynell and his heirs and assigns.

114a. JOHN OWEN 1719

(received in office 2 October 1719, enrolled 3 October 1719)

I John Owen of Sunderland near the sea gentleman . . .

One copyhold messuage or tenement with the garth yard outhouses and buildings and appurtenances . . . in Chester in the Street . . . now unlett and lately in the possession of Thomas Pickering . . . of the yearly value of £6

One other messuage or house . . . in Chester aforesaid . . . in the possession of William Owen gentleman as tenant . . . from year to year att the yearly rent of £10 out of which I pay or allow all manner of taxes and assessments parliamentary and parochiall and repaires both which . . . messuages . . . are held by copy of Court Roll of the Lord Bishopp of Durham as parcell of his mannor of Chester in the Street . . . att . . . several yearly rents which together with the other copyhold premises . . . in Chester . . . amount to the yearly rent of 7s. . . .

One other messuage and parcell of ground . . . called . . . Blaydon Staiths . . . in the parish of Ryton . . . in the possession of Edward Cowey as tenant . . . from year to year att . . . the yearly rent of £7 out of which I pay or allow all taxes and assessments . . .

a copyhold close . . . lyeing in Chester . . . called Kelsy well hill in the possession of Peter Smurfield as tenant . . . from year to year att . . . the yearly rent of £6

All that copyhold close . . . called Great Kelsy . . . in the possession of John Rogerson as tenant . . . from year to year att . . . the yearly rent of £7

All that other copyhold close . . called Middle Kelsy . . . in Chester . . . in the possession of Robert Ridley as tenant . . . from year to year att . . . the yearly rent of £7 the same being vested in Richard Owen gent. in trust for me and my sequells in right

All that other copyhold close . . . called Little Kelsy . . . in Chester . . . in the possession of Robert Ridley as tenant . . . from year to year att . . . the yearly rent of £4

A beastgate in the Holmhill in Chester . . . in the possession of William Owen as tenant . . . from year to year at the yearly rent of 10s. out of which I pay or allow all manner of taxes and assessments and I am seized of the . . . last mentioned closes and beastgate to me and my sequells in right the same being held by copy of Court Roll of the . . . Lord Bishopp of Durham as Lord of the . . . manor of Chester . . . and there are issueing and payable out of all the said copyhold premisses in Chester the yearly summe of 7s. . . . and for all the said copyhold premisses there are fynes payable to the Lord Bishopp . . . upon the death of the tenant or alienations

A messuage and four other copyhold closes containing together by estimation 12 acres of ground . . . in Waldridge . . . now in the possession of George Winter as tenant . . . from year to year att the yearly rent of £8 10s. out of which I pay or allow all taxes and assessments . . . of which last mentioned copyhold premisses I am seized to me and my sequells in right and I hold the same by copy of Court Roll of John Hedworth Esqr as of his Mannor of Walridge . . . and there are issueing and payable to the said John Hedworth out of the said last mentioned premisses the yearly rent . . . of 1s. 4d.

A freehold close . . . containing . . . three acres . . . in Walridge . . . now in the possession of Margarett Jackson as tenant . . . from year to year att the yearly rent of £3 10s. out of which I pay or allow all manner of taxes and assessments

One other freehold close . . . containing . . . four acres . . . in Walridge . . . in the possession of John Jopling as tenant . . . from year to year at the yearly rent of £4 out of which I pay all manner of taxes and assessments . . .

Severall closes . . . called . . . the Coleway closes . . . in Chester in the Street . . . in the possession . . . of Robert Robinson and William Cleugh as tenants . . who hold the same . . . with the leasehold lands and tenements hereinafter mentioned to be in their possessions from year to year at . . . the yearly rent of £30 out of which I pay or allow all taxes and assessments and am seized of the said Coleway Closes to me and my sequells in right the same being held by copy of Court Roll of the said Lord Bishopp . . . at . . . severall yearly rents amounting in the whole together with other copyhold premises in Chester to the said yearly rent of 7s.

All those lands called a Cavill of land being a parcel of undivided ground . . . in the North field and in the Demains of Chester . . . of which . . . I am seized to me and my heirs for the lives of

William Owen Thomas Pickering and of me . . . and the longest liver . . . by . . . a lease made . . . by Nathanael Lord Crewe Lord Bishopp of Durham to John Owen late of Chester . . . my late grandfather whose heir att law I am . . . and the same are . . . lett together with . . . Coleway Closes to . . . Robert Robinson and William Cleugh from year to year at . . . such yearly rent (payable to me) as aforesaid and there is reserved and payable for the same by the said lease to the said Lord Bishopp . . . the yearly rent of £1 8s. 8d.

John Owen

Subscribed by John Rudd the younger gent thereunto authorized by warrant of attorney . . . in open court at the generall quarter sessions of the peace held att the City of Durham for the County of Durham by adjournment 30 November 1719 in the presence of Geo: Bowes Jno Rudd

See *SS*. clxxiii, 122-123, 174.

ADDENDUM

Barbara Haines (no. 59; see *SS*. clxxiii, 93-4) became the wife of Joseph Porter of Elvet (marriage bond Durham 6 January 1718/9). He is the Joseph Porter, gentleman, mentioned *ibid*. p. 41, and she is the Mrs. Barbara Porter, the friend to whom Lady Mary Radcliffe left her house in Old Elvet (*ibid*. p. 189). Administration of the estate of Barbara Porter was granted at Durham on 12 January 1729/30 to her husband Joseph Porter of Old Elvet, gentleman. She was buried at St. Oswald's on 23 November 1729. A few days earlier, on 19 November, Mrs. Mary Haynes, widow, had been buried there.

II

DURHAM ENTRIES on the RECUSANTS' ROLL 1636-7

extracted and annotated by

A. M. C. FORSTER

INTRODUCTION

The RECUSANTS' ROLLS are a series of documents which record revenue accruing to the Crown from forfeitures exacted for the offence of *recusancy*. By this term was understood the *refusal* (*recusare,* to refuse) to attend "the parish church or any other church, chapel or usual place of common prayer". Such attendance was made compulsory by the Act of Uniformity of 1 Elizabeth, the penalty for abstention under that Act being 12d. for every Sunday missed. These fines were assigned to the poor of the parish, and were not the concern of the Exchequer.

In 1581 was passed "An Act to retain the Queen's Majesty's subjects in their due obedience". Under this statute recusancy was made an indictable offence, triable in the criminal courts, and the penalty for non-attendance at divine service was increased to £20 a month, payable to the Crown. This was an enormous sum,[1] which only a very few (none in co. Durham) ever attempted to pay. Accordingly, an alternative penalty was provided under the next statute, that of 1586 (28 and 29 Eliz., Cap. 6): "An Act for the more speedy execution of the statute entitled An Act to retain the Queen's Majesty's subjects in their due obedience." The recusant who failed to pay the £20 a month might forfeit to the Crown, by process out of the Exchequer, two-thirds of his lands and all his goods and chattels.

For the years 1581-1591 records of convictions and forfeitures under both the above statutes appear, among other items of revenue, on the Pipe Rolls. At Michaelmas 1592 was initiated a separate series of Rolls, the *Rotuli Recusantium*, dealing with this source of revenue only. They were continued, with certain intermissions, down to 1691.

The procedure was laid down under the Act of 1586. The recusant would be indicted at one of the criminal courts—assizes, gaol deliveries, quarter sessions—and there *proclaimed*. He would then be convicted, *in absentia* if necessary, at the following sessions. A

[1] All these sums of money should be multiplied twenty to thirty times, in order to form a conception of their value in modern currency.

commission would inquire into his estate, and estimate the annual value of his lands and tenements. Two-thirds of this amount the recusant, now termed "tenant" to the Crown, would be required to pay as rent. His goods and chattels would be valued, and an estimate of their worth returned to the Exchequer. After this he must either forfeit his goods or find money to redeem them. There was no sliding scale. Rich and poor were charged at the same rate.

Usually the next stage was the leasing by the Crown of the two-thirds of the lands to a third person, whose name now appears on the Roll as the person responsible for the rent. Sometimes this would be a relative or friend of the recusant, himself conformable, who stood in and made the tenancy secure.[1] Frequently, however, it was someone who took on the lease as a speculation, in which case it would go to the highest bidder, and the amount bid would depend upon the risk the lessee took in collecting it from the recusant. Sometimes, in a bad risk, it would go for as little as one third of the two-thirds annual value. The lessee was now in a position to squeeze what money he could out of the recusant, or alternatively to take possession of the best portions of his estate and farm them to his own profit. This system of payment through a third person, either friend or speculator, was the common one during the reign of James I. Needless to say, in unscrupulous hands, it could inflict very great hardship.

During the later years of the reign, from 1616 to 1624, there appear to have been few or no convictions in county Durham, and payments also gradually lapsed. In the latter year there was a revival of measures against recusants. Over eleven hundred persons were convicted in Durham in 1624. The first years of the new reign saw more: 845 in 1625, and 502 in 1626; many of the same names occur in all three lists.

With the accession of Charles I and his urgent need for money, and despite his protestation "We desire much rather the Conversion of these our subjects to the true Religion professed by the Church of England, than to gain by their punishment,"[2] we surmise that, for the Crown at all events, recusancy was coming to be regarded as a matter of revenue rather than religion. In a letter addressed to the

[1] This procedure of farming an estate "for the use of, or in trust for" a recusant, was illegal. Nevertheless, it seems to have been winked at.

[2] P.R.O., S.P.39/26/57: 'Instructions and directions to our Commissioners for our Revenue arising by the forfeitures of Recusants convict'; 4 Car. I, precise date not given.

Archbishop of Canterbury, 15 December 1625, the King expresses his intention of putting into execution the laws concerning recusants.[1] The proceedings of 1625 and 1626, above referred to, were followed up by a series of inquisitions into the value of recusants' lands and goods. In Durham, commissions under Sir John Calverley and others in 1626 seized and valued the lands of sixty recusants; many more not possessing landed property had their goods seized, and nearly as many inquisitions were taken the following year. Early in 1627 the Privy Council discussed suggestions for the more effectual collecting of recusants' monies, for it was recommended that all such monies should be applied towards the provision, arming and maintenance of six ships of war, to protect the eastern coast of England and safeguard London's coal supplies. To this end a special commission, dated 23 June 1627, was issued under the Great Seal and directed to the Archbishop of York, the Earl of Sunderland, President of the Council of the North, Sir John Savile and others, authorizing them to carry out a new policy with regard to recusants. They were to permit and encourage them to "compound", i.e. to take out leases for their own forfeited lands (a proceeding hitherto forbidden by law), at reasonable rents to be agreed upon between the commissioners and the recusant himself. Arrears were to be compounded for. Recusants possessing personal estate only might, in lieu of total forfeiture, compound to pay an annual rent for the same. The old procedure of forfeiture of two-thirds of lands and all goods was to be applied in the case of recusants who neglected to compound, or who, having compounded, failed to pay their rents. Sir John Savile was appointed Receiver General of recusants' monies in the counties north of the Trent: including the counties of Stafford, Derby, Cheshire, Lancashire, York, Lincoln, Westmorland, Cumberland, Northumberland and Durham, and the cities of York, Lincoln, Newcastle upon Tyne and Kingston upon Hull.

In July 1628 1000 marks (£666 13s. 4d.) of the first monies received from recusants upon composition were assigned to Savile for the use of shipping. He had already had £3,000 from other revenue, and estimated for over £12,000 for the coming year.[2] The diversion of recusants' monies towards the cost of shipping was therefore continued for another year.

[1] S.P.16/522/66.

[2] Calendar of Acts of the Privy Council, 7 July 1628.

In June 1629 another special commission was issued, directed to the Archbishop of York, Thomas Viscount Wentworth, now President of the Council of the North, and others, and this, while continuing the system of compounding, omits all reference to shipping, and directs that money received from recusants shall be paid to the Exchequer. Henceforth we find Wentworth superseding Savile as chief Commissioner for Compounding, though he was not appointed to replace him as Receiver General until June 1631.

Wentworth seems to have been an efficient agent, and more relentless in dealing with recusants than his predecessor had been. (It was alleged that Savile took bribes.)[1] His rents were consistently higher, sometimes double as much. He dated his leases as from Pentecost 1629, rent for the first half-year being payable at Martinmas 1629. Recusants who compounded in subsequent years were charged from the same date, the payment due for the years previous to compounding being termed "arrearages". Thus, a recusant who compounded, say, in August 1632, would be required to pay his first rent at Martinmas 1632, and would also be debited with 3 years' arrearages, 1629-1632, which he would pay off subsequently in half-yearly instalments. The exception was when his liability to pay had not existed in 1629, i.e. he had not then been convicted, or was not then seized of the property. Persons whose wives were recusants convicted, though themselves conformable, had to compound for them.

Wentworth's accounts, which survive, show that the system was effective. During the financial year Martinmas 1635 to Martinmas 1636, the rents received for recusancy in the countries north of the Trent amounted in all to £10,924 1s. 9d. Of these rents, Yorkshire topped the list with £4,469 10s. 5d. Lancashire came next with £2,317 5s. 7d. Durham paid in £1,015 3s. 4d., and Northumberland £989 19s. 0d. In addition arrearages were paid, to the sum of £11,121 11s. 10½d. making a total for the year of £22,046 3s. 7½d. The following year, Durham rentals rose to £1,043 16s. 8d.

About 1636, the year of the roll under consideration, we find indications of distress on the part of recusants. Some were petitioning that the fees charged them for the making and engrossing of

[1] Wentworth received a commission of 6d., having been refused 1/-, in the pound on recusant monies collected, the actual work being done by a deputy. See J. Cooper, 'The fortune of Thomas Wentworth', *Econ. Hist. Rev.* 2nd series XI (1958), 233-4.

their leases were excessive; others that, having compounded, they were now being troubled for the 12d. a week fine. At the same time instructions were being issued by the Lord Treasurer to exert pressure for payment of rent, and to "levy by distress" or commit to gaol until payment was made.[1] In many cases bonds were taken for payment at the appointed term.

Perhaps the supreme instance of the systematic way in which recusancy was being exploited in the interests of revenue may be found in the special printed receipt form used by Wentworth: a man paid his money and got a receipt for his recusancy much as today he might take out a licence to put a car on the road.[2]

Description of the Recusant Rolls

The rolls are composed of a number of strips of parchment, about 6′ long by 18″ wide, each rotulet consisting of two membranes threaded together. They are written, on both sides, in legal abbreviated Latin. The counties are separately returned, with the exception of Durham, which is nearly always included under Yorkshire (*Ebor.*). The Durham entries are found in sections and groupings of their own, and are not difficult to pick out.

A roll may contain any or all of the following types of entry:

(*a*) Preamble: the year, the name of the sheriff (or in the case of Durham, the bishop or his sheriff).

(*b*) Rental entries. These give the name and description of the recusant, the rent due to the Crown, the nature and annual value of the lands seized, the date of the seizure and the name of the head commissioner. There is also a reference to the Memoranda Roll in the Lord Treasurer's office, on which the findings of the commission are recorded. If the lease has been granted to a Crown lessee, his name appears, together with the date at which the lease was granted. If payment has been made, the note "Quietus est" signifies that the debt has been discharged for the year. The same entry, in shortened form, appears in each successive year, until "the King's hands are removed" from the property.

Often the entry, as originally written, is followed by a note which

[1] S.P. 16/329/50.

[2] For a comprehensive account of the anti-Recusant legislation and, in particular, of the working of the composition system, see *Documents relating to the Northern Commission for compounding with Recusants, 1627-1642,* with an introduction by Dom Hugh Aveling, O.S.B., published in *Publications of the Catholic Record Society* LIII (1961), pp. 291 ff.

has been added subsequently. This may indicate that the lease has been transferred, or that the whole business has been wound up and discharged, "by consideration of the Barons of the Exchequer". In this case there will be found a reference to the Memoranda Roll of the Lord Treasurer's Remembrancer which records the final *Quietus est* and the date it was granted; which may be years after the recusant's death.

(*c*) Value of recusants' goods and chattels seized by the same commissions. These are usually debited to the head commissioner as the person responsible for the seizure.

(*d*) The sheriff's charge, being arrears of payment which the sheriff has been charged to collect, and for which he is held responsible.

(*e*) Estreats of convictions. The indictment was in the following form: "A. B. of C. in the parish of D. gentleman (*yeoman, widow, etc.*) (*blank*)[1] £20 (multiplied by) M. in that being of the age of sixteen years and over, he did not repair to the parish church or to any other church chapel or usual place of common prayer within the M. months immediately following (*date*), but voluntarily and obstinately hath forborn the same contrary to the form of the statute in such a case provided . . . convicted on (*date*)."

Recusant Roll 12 Charles I. 1636-1637: (preserved in the Public Record Office, index no. E.377/44).

This roll contains eight rotulets devoted to Yorkshire, with Durham entries occurring on five of them. These portions only have been extracted and are here reproduced. Three more rotulets record Wentworth's accounts for the year, covering all the counties for which he was Receiver General. The parts of these which relate to Durham will be found, in shortened form, in Appendix A.

There are no estreats of convictions among the Durham entries of this roll. The relevant convictions are nearly all to be found in rolls E. 377/32, 33, 36 (22 James I, 1 and 4 Charles I). In a few cases the record of conviction has not been traced.

This roll, coming at the peak period of Wentworth's administration, shows the compounding system fully developed. In entry no. 1 (Richard Forster), the lands, partly in Durham and partly in Yorkshire, have been seized on 30 April and 5 May 1636 respectively; yet the lease is reckoned to run from 25 June 1629. The rent is £5 p.a.

[1] The word "*deb'*" (owes) was added only when the account was discharged.

This is charged for one year ending Martinmas 1636, *plus* £37 10s. arrearages for the previous 7½ years, £42 10s in all. It appears from a State Paper (S.P. 16/308/62) that Richard Forster had petitioned the King that, whilst employed in France on His Majesty's service in 1632, he had been called upon to make composition, and in his absence his servants had compounded on his behalf for £40 p.a. Having been obliged to sell part of his inheritance to pay his debts, he was no longer able to maintain this payment. By order of the King, the commissioners fixed the lease at £5 p.a., as here shown.

No. 4 is interesting as recording the final settlement of a very long-standing account. Thomas Forcer's name had appeared on the first Recusant Roll, and probably on every roll since. He died in 1622. Now, on the petition of his grandson, the *Quietus est* is granted, and "the hands of the King removed" from the estate. He had paid every penny the law could demand from him.

Beginning with no. 7 we have a review of a number of persons whose estates were seized and valued in 1626 and 1627, preparatory to the setting up of the new system. The original lists, found in rolls 2 and 3 Charles I, were considerably longer. Many of the persons there named have already compounded, or have obtained a *Quietus*, or are dead. The fifty-odd persons forming the residue remain here to be dealt with.

Next comes the main part of the roll, which records the findings of a commission of inquiry held at Bishop Auckland, 28 March 1636, under the presidency of Bishop Thomas Morton, in his civil capacity as chief magistrate of the Palatinate. The other commissioners were Sir John Conyers of Horden, bart., Thomas Burwell, Chancellor of the diocese of Durham, and Hugh Wright Esq. sometime Mayor of Durham. The commissioners sat with a jury, composed of George Downes, Christopher Gaynes, George Crosyer, Henry Fallonsbye, Henry Bayles, Thomas Ayslye, gentlemen: Martin Richmond, Richard Robinson, Christopher Rayne, James Clement, James Trotter, George Garth, Thomas Ferry, Richard Hopper and Ambrose Highington, yeomen.[1]

Many of the entries towards the beginning of the list have the note "*Quietus*" attached to them, together with a reference to the Memoranda roll of the Lord Treasurer's Remembrancer. Most of these are dated 13 and 14 Charles I. Further down come entries with

[1] Names on Memoranda Roll, E. 368/649.

a marginal note *C scri* (and variants), of which the precise significance is uncertain. These are persons selected for immediate action, and it will be found that the majority of them compounded within the next few months. Those who did so before Martinmas 1637 are entered up on the *Comp.* (Computatio) rotulets of the present roll, and these entries are here given in Appendix A. Those who compounded between Martinmas 1637 and Martinmas 1638, have been extracted from the following roll, E.377/45, and appear in Appendix B.

This long list contains the names of persons who are in all stages of their recusant career. Some appear for the first time, so recently convicted that the details of conviction have not yet been entered up. Others are recusants of long standing, brought to the fore in all probability because their payments are in arrear. Some, like the Hodgsons of Manor House and the Halls of Greencroft, seem to evade the payment issue time after time, and only under distraint can anything be got out of them.

It is not possible to draw conclusions regarding the outcome of this detailed investigation, partly because the ensuing rolls have not been properly examined, but also because events were stirring upon the political horizon which would alter the nature of recusancy as an indictable offence. Under the Puritan regime, attendance at the parish church will cease to be a test of orthodoxy. A new test will be devised, that of subscribing to the Oath of Abjuration (see *Surtees Society*, vol. 111, p. 411), and this will drive into the ranks of recusancy some of the Anglican party.

It has been generally accepted that, up to the period with which we are dealing, the terms "Recusant" and "Papist" were synonymous. It is always possible that previous Rolls may have included a small number of Dissenters; but the Acts of 1581 and 1586, on which the Rolls were based, were directed exclusively against the Papists. The Recusant Rolls of the post-Restoration period record the convictions of a certain number of persons who are readily recognizable as Dissenters and Quakers: but it is very doubtful whether any such were ever included at this earlier period. Certainly, whenever it has been possible to trace the individual or the family, these have been found to be Papist.

Perhaps it should be emphasized that the rolls can never be taken as an index of the extent of recusancy. They record only such persons as came within the arm of the law. Regarding these however, they give considerable information, and quite apart from the religious issue, this is often of great interest. This roll presents us with a cross-section of the people of county Durham as they were just as the shadow of civil war was about to fall upon them. Afterwards, as we know from our own day, things would never be quite the same again. Never again, perhaps, would 18 sheep be priced at 60 shillings. The computations here set down, of the livelihood of the small man, are not the least interesting part of the whole. They were probably made in somewhat perfunctory fashion, indeed they must have been or how could the commission have dealt with so many? And in fact, "the insufficiency and incertitude of the Inquisition" was to provide a convenient loophole for many subsequent actions.

We note some omissions: there is, for example, no mention of the donkey, the pig, or the poultry. Possibly the commissioners considered these beneath their notice. Nor is there, as a rule, mention of ready money among goods and chattels, the probable explanation being that money was a commodity easily concealed. There are two exceptions, and in each case the amount was considerable.

In the notes which accompany these entries, whenever possible, individual payments made for recusancy have been recorded. They are necessarily incomplete; but there is sufficient evidence to show that the penalties, if not exacted in full, could and frequently did bear heavily upon the recusant. Moreover, a comparison of this roll of 1636 with the contemporary records of the Court of High Commission at Durham (*Surtees Society*, vol. 34), reveals that in many instances he was being simultaneously prosecuted, chiefly in the matter of his marriage and the baptism of his children, by the ecclesiastical court also. His inability to accept the supremacy of the sovereign in matters spiritual, had landed him in trouble with Church and State alike. Both looked upon him as an alien and disloyal influence, hence their efforts to suppress him. But setting aside these two main forces, what was his standing among the common people? Is it possible to form an opinion as to their verdict upon him?

Here we have a record of men and women of all states and conditions of life, knights, gentlemen, merchants, yeomen, artisans, living their lives side by side with their fellow men, an integral part of the nation. These rolls and other contemporary documents, dry and formal as they are, yet give evidence of the many links which bound Catholic and Protestant together, and of the friendship and esteem in which, often enough, the recusant was held by his neighbours, who best of any, were in a position to judge of his true character. Take, for instance, the Forcer family. We find the friends of Thomas Forcer, themselves conformable, petitioning for and getting the lease of his forfeited lands, settling them in the hands of trustees; when the lands had been seized a second time, bidding up the rent and recovering possession, collecting and forwarding payments, up to the day of his death. We find Bishop Neile intervening and writing up to London to know what he is to do with the sick old man, then in custody at Durham. We find friends of the family pulling wires, so that Peter Forcer's young widow shall not be deprived of the custody of her son; and with many other families the same kindly and helpful spirit prevails.[1]

It is a state of affairs full of strange anomalies. Take the position of that singular lady, Dame Margaret Swinburne, the recusant wife of the sheriff of Northumberland, and mother of the sheriff of Durham. The two gentlemen were much of an age; we imagine that she would have something to say to both of them, where recusants were concerned. We may speculate, too, as to whether Sir William Bellasis really distrained upon his mother for the goods he was charged to collect from her, or whether he pocketed the writ and found the money himself. Then there is the charming story of Elizabeth Hedley.

We meet her in these pages, an old lady now, long widowed, recusant still. Half a century earlier, as a young wife, she had spent several years in the prison at Sadberg—for a married woman the only alternative to the £20 a month fine was, at that time, imprisonment. Her husband at length procured her release, going bail for her re-appearance when called for; but when the summons came, he would not let her go, "fearing lest she should be imprisoned to her utter undoing, as heretofore she had been for the space of four or five years." Stout Protestant as he was, he broke his bail and went to gaol himself. Nicholas Hedley is mentioned, with affection, in many wills of the period. He must have been a thoroughly decent fellow, and one would like, across the centuries, to shake him by the hand.[2]

[1] See Greenwell Deeds, nos. 340, 353, 381, calendared in *Archaeologia Aeliana*, 4th Series, III (1927); R. Surtees, *Hist. of Durham* IV, ii, 158.

[2] *Acts of the Privy Council,* 24 May 1591.

Sources

I am indebted to the Controller of H.M. Stationery Office for permission to reproduce this unpublished Crown Copyright material, which is preserved in the Public Record Office at London. Recusant Roll No. 1 (1592-3) was published in full by the Catholic Record Society, with an Introduction by the late Miss M. M. C. Calthrop, in 1916. Roll No. 2 is shortly to appear, under the auspices of the same Society, edited by Dom Hugh Bowler, O.S.B., to whom I am greatly indebted for much kind help in interpreting the technicalities of the rolls, and whose article, "Some Notes on the Recusant Rolls of the Exchequer" (*Recusant History*, vol. 4, no. 5, April 1958) I have quoted largely in the foregoing account. Citations from other rolls have been made from the originals.

The Pells Receipts (P.R.O. Index no. E.401/—) are the authority for payments made for recusancy during the reigns of Elizabeth (latter years) and James I. Wentworth's accounts for 1629 are to be found in Declared Accounts, Pipe Office (P.R.O. E.351/26): those for 1629-30, 1631-32 and 1635-36, in Land Revenue Records, Receiver's Accounts, ser. 2, bundle 87 (P.R.O. L.R.7/87). The figures for the financial year previously quoted are taken from the *Comp.* rotulets of Recusant Roll 11 Car. (E.377/43). The Special Commissions for Compounding are included among the Patent Rolls (P.R.O. C.66/2441 and 2504). The Memoranda Rolls (P.R.O. E.368/—) often give valuable information regarding the individual recusant and his circumstances, such as detailed inventories of goods etc., omitted in the Recusant Rolls. Some items regarding the Ecclesiastical Court of High Commission at Durham in 1607 were found in K.R. Exchequer (P.R.O. E.135/12/8). Details have been gathered from many State Papers, Domestic.

The biographical and other notes have been taken from a variety of sources. Printed sources include R. Surtees, *History of Durham*, with its wealth of genealogical and topographical information: the publications of the Surtees Society, in particular volumes 112 and 142 (wills), 34 (Acts of the Court of High Commission at Durham), 111 (Royalist Compositions), and 135 (Durham Protestations): the new History of Northumberland, and *Archaeologia Aeliana*, 4th ser. volumes I and III. Other local sources include a list of convictions for recusancy at Durham in 1615, printed privately for Sir C. Sharp, original quoted in *Greenwell Deeds*, *Arch. Ael.* 4th ser. III (1927), no. 356; it corresponds to the list of estreats found in Recusant Roll 11 James I.

Local unprinted sources include Raine MS. no. 108, which is a list of persons convicted at Durham, 7 Jan. 4 Jac. 1606/7 (the corresponding list, considerably longer, is to be found in Recusant Roll 5 Jac. and the original Sessions record is preserved at the County Record Office, Durham). Sharp MS. no. 110 is a list of persons presented, or indicted, at Durham assizes, 11 August 1628. This last is of particular interest because, up to the present, no counterpart has been found in the Recusant Rolls. These MSS. are preserved in the Chapter Library at Durham, and I quote them by the courtesy of the Librarian.

Two other MSS. may be mentioned: Mickleton and Spearman, MS. 2, fol. 412, 413, which is a list of 339 recusants stated in 1626 to have either died, removed or conformed within the past eight years: and Halmote Court Miscellaneous Books, no. 64, which gives the names of nine recusants who were in Durham Gaol on 26 August 1612. The former I quote by kind permission of the Curators of the University Library, Durham, the latter by that of Mr. J. E. Fagg, of the Prior's Kitchen, Durham.

My grateful acknowledgements are due also to the Rev. W. Vincent Smith, of Lanchester, for unfailing help and criticism.

A.M.C.F.

EXTRACTS FROM RECUSANT ROLL 12 CHARLES I (1636-7)

P.R.O. E 377/44
rot. *Ebor.*

Ricardus Foster generosus recusans et Henricus Foster filius eius debent C. s. per annum de firma duarum partium octo messuagiorum et octo tenementorum sive firmarum cum pertinentibus apud Rutford alias Rudford infra villam et territorium de Southbedburne in parochia de Hamsterley in comitatu Dunelmensi adtunc vel nuper in separali tenura sive occupacione Willielmi Maddison Willielmi Preston Elizabeth Garthwaite vidue Tunstall Toes Johannis Dowson Janette Mattrice Willielmi Walton et Willielmi Dowson vel assignatorum suorum annui valoris ultra reprisas XL s. Ac duarum partium unius alius messuagii et unius alius tenementi sive firme cum pertinentibus vocati West Shipley scituati iacentis et existentis infra villam et territorium de Southbedburne predicta in dicta parochia de Hamsterley in dicto comitatu Dunelmensi adtunc vel nuper in tenura vel occupatione Henrici Atkinson vel assignatorum suorum annui valoris ultra reprisas X s. — parcellarum terrarum et possessionum prefati Ricardi Foster generosi recusantis unde seisitus fuit pro termino vite sue remaner' inde post eius decessum Henrico Foster generoso filio et heredi suo apparenti pro vita sua in manus domini Regis nunc Caroli xxx^{mo} die Aprilis anno regni sui xii^{mo} [30 April 1636] per Willielmum Bellasis militem vicecomitem comitatus Dunelmensis captarum et seisitarum. Ac duarum partium manerii de Stokesley in comitatu Eboracensi . . . annui valoris C s. ultra reprisas in manus dicti domini Regis nunc v^{to} die Maii anno regni sui xii^{mo} [5 May 1636] per Willielmum Pennyman baronettum vicecomitem comitatus predicti . . .

Quam firmam Rex xxvii^{o} die Februarii anno regni sui xii^{mo} [27 February 1637] concessit et ad firmam dimisit prefatis Ricardo et Henrico habend' et tenend' omnia et singula premissa . . . a festo sancti Johannis Baptiste quod fuit in anno domini mdcxxix pro termino xli annorum extunc proxime sequentium et plenarie complend' si premissa predicta tamdiu reman' in manibus domini Regis heredum vel successorum suorum reddendo inde annuatim Regi heredibus et successoribus suis V li. legalis monete Anglie ad festa sancti Martini episcopi in hieme et Pent' per equales porciones solvend' ad Receptam Scaccari vel ad manus talis receptoris qualem dominus Rex heredes et successores sui sub magno sigillo suo Anglie de tempore in tempus pro receptione tal' redd' appunctuaverint vel appunctuabunt. In parte original' de anno xii^{mo} rotulo. Et in memorand' ex parte Rememoratoris Thesaurarii de termino Pasche anno xiii^{tio} Regis huius rotulo.

Et XXXVII li. X s. de annis preteritis. Summa XLII li. X s.

RICHARD FOSTER (1) gentleman, recusant, and Henry Foster his son owe 100 s. yearly for the farm of two parts of eight messuages and eight tenements or farms with appurtenances at Rutford otherwise Rudford within the vill and district of Southbedburne in the parish of Hamsterley in the county of Durham now or late in the several tenure or occupation of Wm. Maddison Wm. Preston Elizabeth Garthwaite widow Tunstall Toes John Dowson Janet Mattrice Wm. Walton and Wm. Dowson or their assigns of the annual value over and above outgoings of 40 s. And of two parts of one other messuage and one other tenement or farm with appurtenances called West Shipley situated lying and being within the vill and territory of Southbedburne aforesaid in the said parish of Hamsterley in the said county of Durham now or late in the tenure and occupation of Henry Atkinson or his assigns of the annual value over and above outgoings of 10 s. — parcels of the lands and possessions of the aforesaid Richard Foster gentleman, recusant, of which he was seised for the term of his life with remainder after his death to Henry Foster gentleman his son and heir apparent for his life, taken and seized into the hands of the now lord King Charles on 30 April in the twelfth year of his reign [30 April 1636] by Wm. Bellasis knight sheriff of the county of Durham. And of two parts of the manor of Stokesley in the county of York . . . of the annual value of 100 s. taken and seized into the hands of the now lord King on 5 May in the twelfth year of his reign [5 April 1636] by Wm. Pennyman bart. sheriff of the aforesaid county.

Which farm the King granted and demised to farm on 27 February in the twelfth year of his reign [27 February 1637] to the aforesaid Richard and Henry to have and hold all and singular the premises . . . from the feast of St. John the Baptist which was in the year of Our Lord 1629 for the term of 41 years immediately following and to be fully completed if the aforesaid premises shall remain for so long in the hands of the lord King, his heirs and successors, by the payment annually for the same to the King his heirs and successors of £5 of lawful English money at the feasts of St Martin the bishop in winter and of Whitsun in equal portions, to be paid to the Receipt of the Exchequer or into the hands of such receiver as the lord King his heirs and successors shall have from time to time appointed or shall appoint under their great seal of England to receive such rents. In the *originalia* of the roll for the twelfth year. And in the *memoranda* roll of the Treasurer's Remembrancer for the Easter term of the thirteenth year of this King's reign.

And £37 10s. for past years. Total £42 10s.

1. Son of Wm. Forster of Earswick and Osbaldwick, co. York, by his 2nd wife, Isabel da. of Richard Langley; Chief Treasurer to Qu. Henrietta Maria; created Bart. of Stokesley, 1649; died at Pontoise, bur. in St. Martin's Abbey there, Jan. 1661; mar. Anne Middleton of Leighton, Lancs.; issue, Henry o.v.p., Richard 2nd bart., Anne-Christina, O.S.B. at Pontoise, Abbess 1656-61.

The tenants of the two parts of the lands of ELLENORA BATMANSON (2) of Broomehall ought to pay 100s. p.a. under a composition made 21 Aug. 1632 for the farm of two parts of a moiety of a messuage called Broomehall in Durham and a moiety of 240 acres of land appertaining . . . found by Inquisition 1 Sept. 2 Car. [1626] at £10 p.a.

To pay 100s. p.a. as is contained in Roll 10 in [rot.] *Item Adhuc Item Item Item Res Ebor.*

And £10 for past years. Total £15.

But they ought not to pay the £7 10s. from the feast of Pentecost 1636, because the said Ellenora died before the month of August that same year . . . order 13 Car. Easter term. But they should pay £7 10s.

2. Da. of Sir Ralph Hedworth of Harraton and Katherine da. of Marmaduke Constable of Holme, co. York; m. Christopher Batmanson of Broom Hall, Durham (d. 1625). She was bur. 14 Oct. 1635, "aiged", St Oswald's, Durham. No issue.

Convicted with her husband 1606/7, 1615, 1624; "registered her abode" at Broom Hall 1616; as widow, convicted 1626, 1630. Seizure of land and goods, 1627; compounded in 1632 to pay 100s. p.a. with arrearages as from 1629.

The £7 10s. charged represents the amount owing at the time of her death; the £7 10s. cancelled, the further sum which had accumulated by Martinmas 1637.

Tenants . . . of REBECCA SALVIN (3) of Thornton ought to pay £15 p.a. under a composition made 13 Oct. 1629 for the lease of two parts of a capital messuage called Heworth in the parish of Aickley, a close called The longe close, another called Driclose, another called Heworth great close, another called Wynn pasture, two closes called the ould closes there. And of two closes called Pinkey nooke . . . found by Inquisition 14 Oct. 9 Jac. at 60s. p.a.

And also of two parts of Thornton not found by Inquisition;

To be held from the feast of St John the Baptist 1629 for the term of 21 years, paying to the King £15 p.a. As is contained in Roll 10 in [rot.] *Item Adhuc Item Item Res Ebor*.

And £112 10s. from previous years. Total £127 10s. Of which Thomas Wentworth . . . for the years 5, 6, 7, 8, 9, 10, 11, 12 Car. has received £105, as appears by several acquittances.

And they do not owe £15, paid to Richard Elmehirst 19 Nov. 1636. But they ought to pay £7 10s.

3. Da. of Sir Cuthbert Collingwood of Eslington, Northumberland and Eppleton, Durham; aged "90 or thereabouts" in 1652; m. Thomas Salvin of Thornton Hall and Heworth (d. 1609); issue, John, Robert, Thomas, Peter O.S.B., Dorothy, Mary. Bur. St Oswald's, Durham 10 Jan. 1655/6.

Convicted as Rebecca Collingwood 1597, as wife of Thomas Salvin 1609, as widow 1615, 1624, 1625, 1626, 1630. Lands leased to Gabriel Redman (one of over 40 such properties) 1611, rent paid up to 1622. For rent on other property, see no. 249. Cf. *SS* 111, pp. 328 ff.

rot. *Adhuc Res Ebor*.

John Welbery owes £40 p.a. . . of two parts of two parts of the manor of Gt. Kelloe in three parts divided . . . Harberhouse . . . North Waistes.

And for two parts of the third part late in the tenure of Margaret Forcer widow deceased.

Possessions of THOMAS FORCER (4) seized into the hands of the King 11 Apr. 3 Jac. by George Freville knt. & other Commissioners. Leased for a term of 21 years from 30 Sept. 3 Jac. As is contained in Roll 3 Jac. in *Adhuc Item Ebor* and in Roll 3 of the now King in *Ebor*.

And £580 for past years. Total £620.

But he ought not to be so charged, by a decision of the Barons noted in a memorandum on the part of the Remembrancer of the Treasurer for the year 13 of the now King Charles, viz. among the records for Michaelmas term. And he is Quit.

4. S. & h. of John Forcer of Harber House, par. St. Margaret's, Durham, & Kelloe, and Margaret da. of Chr. Carr of Sherburn; aged 18 years in 1575; d. 23-4 March 1621/2. Will 16 Nov. 1621, pr. 1636. Inq. p.m. 27 Apr. 1622. M. Margaret da. of Francis Trollopp of Eden, issue, John, S.J., Francis, S.J., Anthony, Peter (heir), Eleanor, Barbara wife of Rich. Hartburn, Ursula w. of Cuthb. Collingwood, Margaret.

Conv. 1590, with Margaret his wife 1594, 1600, 1604, 1605/6, 1615. Lands first seized 1593, lease to Franc. Trollopp. 1605, lease to John Welbery at £40 p.a., rent paid till 1622. The *Quietus* above records Welbery's discharge from liability for the years following Tho. Forcer's death. Tho. Forcer paid, through one agent or another, from 1593 to 1622, £761 16s. 2d. in all. He was also fined £40 in the Eccles. Court of High Commission in 1607 for contempt in non-appearance. In 1620 he was in gaol at Durham, liberated at the instance of Bp. Neile.

Tenants . . . of ANNE HIXON (5) widow owe £11 2s. 2⅔d. p.a. . . . of a moiety of three messuages, a dove-cote, 100 acres of meadow, 60 acres of land & 50 of pasture in Preston-le-Skerne for the term of her life, of a moiety of 2 messuages, 2 cottages, 2 tofts, 2 gardens, 2 orchards, 100 acres of land, 100 of meadow, 100 of pasture, 10 of woodland & 100 of moor in Morton *als.* East Morton *als. Murton super moram*; of a messuage, a cottage, 20 acres of land, 20 of meadow, 20 of pasture & 40 of moor, lately acquired through Richard Read her brother. As is contained in Roll 15 Jac. in *Res Ebor.* & Roll 3 Car. in *Item Ebor.*

And £88 17s. 9⅓d. from past years. Total £100.

But they ought not to be charged, by reason of the conformity of Richard Hixon, son & heir of Anne Hixon deceased . . . memor. . . 13 Car. Easter term. And they are Quit.

5. Sister of Rich. Read of Lumley & wid. of Edw. Hixon of Preston-le-Skerne (d. 1613), issue, Richard, William, Margaret, Eleanor.

Conv. (wife of Edw. Hixon) 1606/7, 1609; as widow registered her abode 1613, conv. 1615. Compounded 1632 to pay 40s. p.a. *plus* 3 yrs. arrearages; owed 40s. in 1636.

The entry above refers to rent due under a seizure of 17 Jan. 1619/20.

The debt appears to be for the 9 years 1620-29, accumulating on the Rolls until the formal discharge was granted.

William Mallory owes £10 p.a. . . . of Bradley, of a third part of the messuage or grange of Condon in the co. of Durh. & land in Barnard Castle & the grass of parks there, parcel of the possessions of WILLIAM EURE knt. (6) . . . from 22 Nov. 11 Jac. . . . term of 21 years to pay p.a. £10 at . . . Annunciation b.m.v. & St. Michael in equal portions. . . . Roll 11 Jac. in *It. Adh. Res Ebor.*

Total £155.

But he ought not . . . mem. 13 Car. Trin. term in a process touching George Bowes knt. & in another touching Tho. Eure Esq. son & heir of the aforesaid William Eure. . . . Quit.

6. S. of Wm. 2nd lord Eure (d. 1593/4) & Margaret da. of Sir Edw. Dymocke of Stokesley, co. York; of Bradley; d. circa 1629. M. Katherine da. of Sir Wm. Bowes of Streatlam, & Mary da. of Henry 9th lord Scrope; issue, Thomas, William, Henry, Margaret w. of Col. Tho. Howard, Mary w. of John Markindale, Elizabeth w. of . . . Leighton.

Conv. with Kath. his wife 1613, 1616. Lands leased to Mallory (bro.-in-law) 1613, rent paid till 1622.

Tenants . . . of WILLIAM HIXON (7) owe 40s. p.a. . . . of the reversion after 2 years still to come of a message in Morden annual value 60s. of which he is seized in fee . . . into the hands of the King 1 Sept. 2 Car. by John Calverley knt. and other . . . by reason of the recusancy of the said Wm. Hixon. . . . Roll 3 Car. in *It. Adh. It. (2) Res Ebor.*

And £17. . . . Total £19.

7. S. of Edw. Hixon & Anne Read (no. 5); settled his estates 1635; inq. p.m. 1636/7. M. Anne . . . , issue, Augustine.

Conv. 1615; with Anne his w. 1624, 1625, 1626, 1630.

Prosecuted in Court of High Commission in 1629 for misbehaviour in Durh. Cathedral (*SS* 34, p. 16).

Tenants . . . of GEORGE SWALWELL (8) owe 40s. p.a. . . . of a messuage in Wolveston of which he is seized in freehold for the term of the natural life of Anne his wife by lease from the Dean & Chapter of Durham; . . . into the King's hands the same day. . . .

And £21. . . . Total £23.

8. Conv. with Anne his wife & Cecily Swalwell widow, 1624, 1625, with Anne 1626. See nos. 45, 212.

Goods also were seized in 1626, at 40s. In 1634 the Sheriff paid in a sum, unspecified, collected under a writ of *fieri facias*, for goods.

Tenants . . . of RALPH CATHERICK (9) owe 13s. 4d. p.a. . . . of a messuage in Fishburn annual value 20s. freehold . . . same day.

And £7. Total £7 13s. 4d.

Look in the great Roll for 1654 in *Item Lanc.* regarding this rent & arrears.

9. Probably the Ralph Cattericke who married Anne Hickson at Aycliffe, 26 Nov. 1598.

Conv. with Anne his w. 1624, 1625, indicted 1628.

See no. 172.

Tenants . . . of ALICE GARRIE (10) owe 3s. 4d. p.a. . . . of a cottage in Sadburie a.v. 5s. for the term of her life . . . same day. . . .

And 35s. . . . Total 38s. 4d.

10. Widow, of Long Newton, conv. 1624, 1625, 1626, indicted 1628.

Tenants . . . of DOROTHY HODGSON widow (11) owe 31s. 1⅓d. p.a. . . . of an annuity of 46s. 8d. for the term of her life out of a messuage called Readhall in Middleton George . . . same day . . .

And £16 6s. 8d. . . . Total £17 17s. 9⅓d.

But they ought not . . . by reason that the aforesaid Dorothy was never seized of the aforesaid annuity . . . mem. 14 Car. Trin. term, in a process touching William Killinghall Esq. holding the premises. . . . Quit.

11. Conv. 1624 (wid.), 1625, 1626.

Tenants . . . of WILLIAM EURIE knt. (12) owe £6 13s. 4d. p.a. . . . of Bradley . . . held in fee . . . same day. . . .

And £70. . . . Total £76 13s. 4d.

But they ought not . . . mem. 13 Car. Trin. term . . . Quit.

12. See no. 6.

Tenants . . . of WILLIAM BALEY (13) owe 4s. 5⅓d. p.a. of a messuage and garden in Whorleton a.v. 6s. 8d. . . . term of his life; . . . same day . . .

And 46s. 8d. . . . Total 51s. 1⅓d.

13. Of Sledwish, carpenter, conv. with Isabella his w. 1615.

Tenants . . . of PETER WALBANKE (14) owe £4 p.a. . . . of a messuage and garden at Pearcebridge a.v. £6, held for the lives of three persons still living.

And £42. . . . Total £46.

14. Conv. with Florence his w. 1606/7, 1624, 1625, 1626, indicted 1628, conv. 1630.

Tenants . . . of JOHN HODGSON (15) of Mannorhouse in the par. of Lanchester gentleman owe £4 p.a. . . . of a capital messuage called Maidensteadhall *als*. Mannorhouse, 40 acres of land, 40 of meadow and 60 of pasture, a.v. £6 freehold, . . . same day . . .

And £42. . . . Total £46.

Tenants . . . of the aforesaid John Hodgson owe £33 6s. 8d. p.a. . . . of the Vicarage of Lanchester and all and singular tithes of grain lambs and wool . . . and of the tithes of grain of the late prebend of Langley in the par. of Lanchester; of which premises Robert Hilliard and John Willie gentlemen are possessed for the term of their lives, for their own use and the use of the said John Hodgson; which John receives an annual charge and profit of the same Vicarage and prebend of Langley for the support and maintenance of himself and his family a.v. £50 . . . same day.

And £350. . . . Total £383 6s. 8d.

15. S. & h. of Wm. Hodgson of Mannorhouse, & Jane da. of Chr. Hildyard & sister of John Hildyard of Fulforth; also of Greencroft and Hedleyhope. Dead before Feb. 1637/8. M. Jane da. of Hen. Lawson of Nesham, issue, John, William & a da. who was w. to Cuthb. Collingwood of Dalden.

Said to be in hiding Jan. 1592/3; "a special recusant" (Bp. Matthew) 1598. Conv. 1596, 1597, 1598/9, 1600, 1604, 1605. Seizures 1601, 1603. In 1607 fined £40 for contempt in Eccles. Court; in 1609 "confined himself" to Mannorhouse. Lease to Alex. Stratton 1611, rent paid till 1622. Further convictions with Jane his w. 1615, 1625, 1626, 1630.

Tenants . . . of DOROTHY CONSTABLE of North Biddick in the par. of Washington widow (16) owe £25 6s. 8d. p.a. . . . of a messuage in Gt. Kelloe, 100 acres of land, 100 of meadow and 100 of pasture there, a.v. £10; . . . of the third part of a messuage with 20 acres of land, 20 of meadow and 20 of pasture in West Auckland, a.v.

60s. of which she is seized in freehold for the term of her life in dower of Robert Dalton her husband deceased; . . . of a capital messuage, 100 acres of land, 100 of meadow and 200 of pasture in North Biddick for the term of 30 years still to come by lease from William Hilton knt. annual value £25 . . . same day . . .

And £266. . . . Total £291 6s. 8d.

But they should not be charged with £25 6s. 8d. rent for 1 year ending at the feast of the Annunciation 2 Car. But they owe £266. See the same tenants in *It. Adh. Res Ebor.*

But they should not pay the sum of £70 nor be charged the rent of £6 13s. 4d. for the messuage & lands in Magna Kelloe, by a decision of the Barons noted in a memorandum on the part of the Remembrancer of the Treasurer for the year 13 of the present King, viz. among the records of Mich. term in a process touching John Forcer. But they owe £196.

Look in the following Roll in *Ebor.* regarding this rent and arrears.

16. Da. of William Hilton of Biddick Esq. & Margaret da. of Sir Jas. Metcalf of Nappa, co. York; m. (1) Robert Dalton (d. 1567/8), (2) Michael Constable Esq. Died 1627.

Bound over to appear, Jan. 1592/3 (w. of Mich. Constable); conv. 1596, 1597, 1599/1600; as widow had lands seized in 1605; lease to Sir Wm. Constable at £15 p.a., rent paid till 1622. Further convictions, 1615, 1624, 1626.

Tenants . . . of DOROTHY MILLOTT (17) now wife of Robert Eden gentleman owe 53s. 4d. p.a. . . . of a third part of the manor of Whittell in the par. of Chester, the capital messuage of Whittell with 60 acres of land, 40 of meadow, 60 of pasture and 200 of moor, in Whittle a.v. £4, for the term of her life . . . same day . . .

And £28. . . . Total £30 13s. 4d.

But they ought not to be summoned for the same nor ought the said rent to be charged hereafter (because of the insufficiency and incertitude of the inquisition, and because the aforesaid Dorothy died in or about the month of August 1634), by a decision of the Barons . . . mem. 13. Car. Hilary term, in a process touching Thomas Wray. . . . Quit.

17. Da. of Sir Wm. Wray of Beamish & Jane da. of Wm. Selby of Whitehouse; m. (1) Robt. Millott of Whithill (d. 1622/3), issue, Ralph, William, Elizabeth w. of Albt. Hodgson of Lintz, Joan w. of Wm.

Postgate, Dorothy, Margaret, Winifred Millott; m. (2) Robt. Eden of West Auckland, issue, Alexius, Katherine Eden.

Conv. with her husb. Robt. Millott, 1616; as wid. 1624. Goods distrained by Sheriff, under writ of *fieri fac'* 1634.

Tenants . . . of THOMAS PATTESON (18) of the city of Durham owe 6s. 8d. p.a. . . . of a message and garden in Geligate in the said city a.v. 10s. . . . same day . . .

And 70s. . . . Total 76s. 8d.

18. Conv. with Jane his wife, 1624, 1625, 1626, ind. 1628. His petition, undated, but from internal evidence between 1632 & 1640, states: he was aged 50 & had been "many years" in prison at Durham for inability to pay his recusancy fines. The King, at the instance of Qu. Henrietta Maria, had given order for his release; but the Justice of Assize, Crawley, had made such release conditional upon his taking the Oaths of Supremacy and Allegiance; and on his refusing, committed him close prisoner. He, with others, makes petition anew to the Queen.

(S.P. 16/255/34, 34.i)

Tenants . . . of CHRISTOPHER DIXON of the par. of Esh (19) owe 6s 8d. p.a. . . . of a message and garden in Geligate a.v. 10s. . . . same day . . .

And 70s. . . . Total 76s. 8d.

19. Conv. with Isabel his w. as of Witton Gilbert, 1624, 1625; of Esh, 1626, ind. 1628.

Tenants . . . of CHARLES RUDDERFORD gentleman (20) owe 66s. 8d. p.a. . . . of a message called Blackhall, 40 acres of land, 20 of meadow and 40 of pasture, a.v. 100s. . . . same day . . .

And £35. . . . Total £38 6s. 8d.

20. Possibly a son of the John Rudderford of Blackhall whose wife Elizabeth was conv. 1597, 1600. Outlawed in 1615 for his part in an affray (Surtees, *Durham* II, 282). M. Margaret da. of Tho. Swinburne of Capheaton. Bur. 15 Sept. 1640, Ryton.

Conv. with his wife, 1625, 1626, 1630; land and goods seized 1626. 30s. accounted for in Sheriff's account for 1636, £4 as part of arrears of rent, 1639-1640.

Tenants . . . of ROBERT BRIGHOUSE gentleman (21) owe 20s. p.a. . . . of a message with 40 acres of land, 20 of meadow and 40 of pasture in the par. of Gateside, a.v. 30s. . . . same day . . .

And £10 10s. . . . Total £11 10s.

21. Conv. 1624, 1625, 1626.

Tenants . . . of WILLIAM NEWTON (22) owe 53s. 8d. p.a. . . . of a moiety of the manor of Bradley in the par. of Medomsley, of a moiety of 40 acres of land, 40 of meadow and 60 of pasture . . . same day. . . .

And £28. . . . Total £30 13s. 4d.

22. Conv. with Isabel his wife 1624, 1625, 1626, ind. 1628; presented at Archbishop's Court 1632; goods seized 1626, 1627.

Tenants of the lands and tenements of William Hall in Greenecroft now in the tenure of Ralph Hall gentleman owe £6 13s. 4d. p.a. for two parts of an annuity of £10 out of the said land and tenements of which CHARLES HALL (23) is seized for the term of his life . . . same day. . . .

And £70. . . . Total £76 13s. 4d.

23. 2nd s. of Wm. Hall of Greencroft (d. 1596) & Alice da. of Tho. Tempest of Stanley; apprenticed 1604 to Jn. Lambton of Durham, draper; m. at Easington 19 Dec. 1610, Isabel da. of Christopher Conyers of Horden, issue Christopher, Thomas, Robert, Charles, William, Mary, (all bapt. St. Oswald's, Durh. 1613-1621). The £10 annuity was left under his father's will.

No conviction traced except in 1624, with *Mary* his wife; ind. (no wife) 1628.

The Wm. Hall above mentioned was his nephew, upon whom Ralph Hall (see no. 55) settled the Greencroft estate.

Tenants . . . of JOHN HUTCHINSON (24) owe 13s. 4d. p.a. . . . of a messuage called Burnhouse by lease from John Hall for the term of 10 years still to come, a.v. 20s. . . . same day. . . .

And £7. . . . Total £7 13s. 4d.

24. Conv. with Alice his wife 1624, 1625, indicted 1628; compounded for goods, 21 Apr. 1635, to pay 40s. p.a. *plus* 6 years' arrearages.

Tenants . . . of MARGARET BROWNE (25) of the city of Durham widow owe 6s. 8d. p.a. . . . of a burgage in Silver Street in the said city for the term of her life, a.v. 10s. . . . same day. . . .

And 70s. . . . Total 76s. 8d.

But they ought not . . . for that the said Margaret Browne died about the last day of December 1637; nor ought they to be charged with the same rent hereafter (because of the insufficiency and incertitude of the inquisition) . . . mem. 13 Car. Hil. term in a process touching Cuthbert Bainbridge holding the premises. . . . Quit.

25. Conv. 1624, 1625, 1626.

Tenants . . . of DOROTHY GARGRAVE of Hetton in le Hole (26) owe 13s. 4d. p.a. . . . of a messuage in Hetton for the term of her life a.v. 20s. . . . same day. . . .

And £7. . . . Total £7 13s. 4d.

But they ought not . . . by reason of the conformity of the same Dorothy Gargrave . . . mem. 15 Car. Mich. term. . . . Quit.

26. John Gargrave of Hetton died 1619, leaving a s. & h. John. Dorothy was presumably widow of the former.

Conv. 1624, 1625, 1626, ind. 1628; seizures 1626, 1627.

Tenants . . . of WILLIAM CLOPTON Esq. (27) owe £4 17s. 9⅓d. p.a. being portion of a rent of £10 8s. 10⅔d. p.a. for the two parts of a water mill in Thornegate foote milne in Barnard Castle of which he is seized in fee, annual value £4, and of another mill in Barnard Castle a.v. 66s. 8d. taken and seized into the hands of the King *27 Sept. 2 Car.* by Thomas Riddell knt. and other Commissioners, as is contained in Roll 3 in *Item Adhuc Item (3) Res Ebor.*

And £48 17s. 9⅓d. . . . Total £53 15s. 6⅔d.

But they ought not . . . Mem. 1650 Hilary term in a process touching Matthew Stoddert holding the premises. . . . Quit.

27. S. of John Clopton of Clopton, Warwicks. & Elizabeth da. of Ralph Ashton of Gt. Lever, Lancs; m. his cousin Anne Clopton, issue William, John, Thomas, Cuthbert (secular priest), Mary, Joyce, Jane, Katherine (Augustinian Canonesses at Louvain), Elizabeth, Anne, Ursula.

Conv. with Anne his wife, 1606/7, 1615, with w. & sons 1624, 1625, 1626; lands seized 4 June 1608, two-thirds valued at £10 8s. 10⅔d. p.a. leased July to Robt. Walker & Rich. Brasse at 69s. 8d. p.a., rent paid till 1625.

Tenants . . . of JOHN SALVAYN (28) owe £11 2s. 2⅔d. p.a. . . . of 10 acres of land, 20 of meadow and 20 of pasture in Heworth of which he is seized in fee, a.v. £16 13s. 4d. . . . into the hands of the King *9 Aug. 3 Car.* by John Calverley knt. . . .

And £105 11s. 1⅓d. . . . Total £116 13s. 4d.

But they ought not . . . by reason of the conformity of the same John Salvayn . . . mem. 14 Car. Hil. term. . . . Quit.

28. Eld. s. of Tho. Salvin of Thornton Hall & Heworth, and Rebecca Collingwood (no. 3); aged 13 in 1610; m. Anne . . . issue, John, Thomas, Dorothy w. of Gilb. Crouch, Elizabeth, Anne, Gerard.

Conv. 1624, 1625, 1626, ind. 1628, with Anne his wife; comp. for goods 1629, to pay 60s. p.a. paid up to 1637, when *Quietus* was granted. 1641 petitioned Parliament for payment of £21 10s. contributed towards the support of the Scottish army. In 1652 after forming a trust to secure his property to his children, he refused the Oath of Abjuration & thereby suffered sequestration of two-thirds of his £56 annuity.

Tenants . . . of GEORGE CONYERS knt. (29) owe £20 p.a. rent for two parts of the Reversion of the manor of Sockburn with the appurtenances in the county of Durham. Which premises the same George Conyers by Indenture dated 6 June 15th year of the late King Jas. made between the same George on the one part and Bartram Bulmer knt. Ralph Conyers knt. and Tobias Tunstall gentleman on the other part and in consideration of the sum of £300 and for other considerations mentioned in the said Indenture demised and granted the said manor with appurtenances to the aforesaid Bartram Bulmer and Tobias Tunstall to have and to hold from the day of the said Indenture for the term of 41 years if the Lady Katherine Conyers then wife of the said George should live so long; and if the same Katherine should die before the end of the aforesaid 41 years then to have and to hold certain closes, parcel of the said manor called or known by the names of Somerholme and Winterholme, le Bancks, Trossendell and Oxclose, for and during the term of 41 years after the date of the same Indenture in full. The said Katherine is still living and the said manor during the said term is worth and after the said term will be worth by the year £30 to the said George.

. . . into the hands of the King *18 Sept. 2 Car.* by Thomas Tempest bart. . . . as is contained in Roll 3 in *Item Adhuc Item (3) Res Ebor.*

And £210. . . . Total £230.

But they ought not . . . incertitude and insufficiency of the inquisition . . . mem. 14 Car. Mich. term. . . . Quit.

29. S. & h. of Sir John Conyers (d. 1610) & Agnes da. of Sir John Bowes of Streatlam, bapt. at Witton-le-Wear 18 Mar. 1576/7; m. Katherine da. of Anthony Bulmer of Tursdale, issue, George, o.v.p., William. Dead before 1632.

Papist of Girsby 1604 (Peacock *Yorkshire Catholics of 1604*); conv. with Katherine his wife 1624, 1625.

Tenants . . . of MARGARET WANDLES widow (30) owe 40s. p.a. . . . of a moiety of the tithes of grain in Hewton Henry a.v. 40s., of the third part of a messuage in Geligate in the city of Durham a.v. 4s., of the third part of a messuage in Elvett in a suburb of the said city of Durham and a messuage with appurtenances in Sadlergate and another messuage called a Workhouse and another messuage in Clapurth in the said city of Durham a.v. 10s. And of the third part of a messuage with appurtenances in the par. of St. Giles in the city of Durham a.v. 6s. Seized in freehold for the term of her life . . . into the hands of the King *9 Aug. 3 Car.* by John Calverley knt. . . .

And £19. . . . Total £21.

30. Conv. 1624, 1626 (St. Nicholas, Durh.), 1630 (Bp. Wearmouth).

Tenants . . . of THOMAS PATTISON (31) owe 13s. 4d. p.a. . . . of a messuage and garden in Geligate a.v. 20s. seized the same day and year.

And £6 6s. 8d. from past years. Total £7.

31. See no. 18.

Tenants . . . of MARGARET BROWNE widow (32) owe 26s. 8d. p.a. . . . of a burgage in Silverstreet in the city of Durham a.v. 40s. freehold, . . . same day. . . .

And £12 13s. 4d. . . . Total £14.

But they ought not . . . for that the said Margaret died about the last day in December 1637 and also because of the insufficiency . . . mem. 13 Car. Hil. term in a process touching Cuthbert Bainbridge. . . . Quit.

32. See no. 25.

Tenants . . . of JOHN FRIZELL (33) owe 13s. 4d. p.a. . . . of a messuage and garden in Geligate for the term of his life, a.v. 20s. . . . same day. . . .

And £6 6s. 8d. . . . Total £7.

33. Conv. with Anne his wife 1624, 1625, 1626, ind. 1628, conv. 1630. Dead before 1632.

Tenants . . . of ANNE CONYERS (34) owe 13s. 4d. p.a. . . . of a messuage and garden in Hallgarth street in the city of Durham for divers years yet to come a.v. 20s. . . . same day. . . .

And £6 6s. 8d. . . . Total £7.

34. Probably the Anne da. of Sir John and sister of Sir George Conyers (no. 29); bur. St. Oswald's, 29 Apr. 1666.

Conv. 1624, 1632.

Tenants . . . of JOHN HEDWORTH knt. (35) owe £16 13s. 4d. p.a. . . . of the manor of Harverton a.v. £25 . . . into the King's hands *18 Sept. 3 Car.*

And £158 6s. 8d. . . . Total £175.

Look in Roll 23 in *Item Adhuc Item Ebor* regarding this rent and arrears.

35. S. of Ralph Hedworth & Jane Rutland, & h. to his grandfather John Hedworth of Harraton: knt. 1603; d. 1642/3; m. (1) Jane da. of Sir Wm. Gascoigne, she d. s.p. 1624; m. (2) Dorothy da. of Sir Ralph Delaval, issue John.

Conv. 1615, 1616; lands first seized 1618, rent £66 13s. 4d., discharged 1620.

Tenants . . . of WILLIAM HODGSON gentleman (36) owe £8 17s. 9⅓d. p.a. . . . of a messuage and 60 acres of land in Gateside a.v. £13 6s. 8d. . . . same day. . . .

And £84 8s. 10⅔d. . . . Total £93 6s. 8d.

36. 3rd s. of Robt. Hodgson of N. Hebburn & Anne da. of Rich. Langley of Grimsthorpe, co. York (he was executed for harbouring priests in 1586); aged 11 years in 1609; h. to his bro. Sir Robt. Hodgson, in Hebburn & Winlaton; sometime of Elswick & Lintsgreen; bur. at Ryton 14 Jan. 1661/2; m. Margaret da. of Sir Tho. Haggerston, issue, (Sir) Francis, Alice w. of Sir Tho. Tempest, Troth, Mary w. of Robt. Brandling.

Conv. 1624, 1625. Compounded 27 Sept. 1637 to pay 100s. p.a. plus 8½ years' arrearages; refused Protestation 1642 (*SS* 135, 24); under sequestration 1645-51 (*SS* 111, pp. 57, 73).

Tenants . . . of ELIZABETH HEDLEY of Lintsgreene widow (37) owe £17 15s. 6⅔d. p.a. . . . of two messuages and 300 acres of land, meadow and pasture in Lints, Lintsgreene, Overlints and Netherlints for the term of her life, a.v. £26 13s. 4d. . . . same day. . . .

And £168 17s. 9⅓d. . . . Total £186 13s. 4d.

But they ought not . . . mem. 1654 Hil. term. . . . Quit.

Tenants . . . of the aforesaid Elizabeth Hedley owe 28s. 10⅔d. p.a. . . . of a close called Birdside in Gateshead divided into three several closes a.v. 16s. 8d. . . . of 7 Burgages in Gateside a.v. 26s. 8d. . . . same day. . . .

And £13 14s. 5⅓d. . . . Total £15 3s. 4d.

"But they ought not to be sumoned for the same debt Nor ought the same farm to be hereafter charged By consideration of the Barons annoted as above among the comon businesses of Hillary term 1654. So they are Quitt."[1]

37. Da. of Rich. Hodgson (Mayor of Newcastle 1549, 1555, 1580) & Isabel da. of Jas. Lawson of Nesham; aunt of Wm. Hodgson above; m. Nicholas Hedley of Newcastle & Lints; in prison for recusancy 1582; convicted 12 times 1583-1628; widow 1604, land and goods seized 1605; lands leased to Geo. Bartram 1610, at £20 9s. 3½d. p.a., payments traced to 1616; in 1629 comp. to pay £20 p.a., payments traced to 1632.

Tenants . . . of JOHN HODGSON of Bywell Andrew in the county of Northumberland, gentleman (38) owe 66s. 8d. p.a. . . . of a messuage called Fenhall in Lanchester a.v. 100s. . . . same day. . . .

And £31 13s. 4d. . . . Total £35.

38. Eld. s. of Lancelot Hodgson of Lanchester & Jesmond, & Mary da. of Wm. Lee of Brandon & Esh, steward to the Earl of Westmorland; hostman of Newcastle 1656; mortgaged property in Jesmond 1642, & with Anne his wife & Lancelot his son alienated the surface lands there in 1659. The Bywell estate (a messuage & 56 acres) was seized 1626, & in 1632 he compounded, with Mary his mother, to pay £13 6s. 8d. p.a. *plus* 3 years' arrearages, and £26 13s. 4d. more p.a. after the death of Chas. Hedworth (his mother's step-father). In 1638 bond was taken for payment of £60.

Conv. of Brancepeth, 1630; in 1655 (of Jesmond) refused the Oath of Abjuration.

Tenants . . . of PETER FORCER (39) owe £10 p.a. . . . of a messuage & 60 acres in Kelloe a.v. £15 . . . same day. . . .

And £95. . . . Total £105.

But they ought not . . . insufficiency of the inquisition . . . mem. 13 Car. Mich. term in a process touching John Forcer. . . . Quit.

39. 4th s. & eventual h. of Tho. Forcer (no. 4) & Margaret Trollopp; nuncupative will 24 May 1626; inq. p.m. 1 Aug. 1626; m. Katherine

[1] The Rolls for the Commonwealth years are written in English, as also additions made during those years.

da. of Robt. Hodgson of Hebburn & Anne Langley, issue, John, Francis, Thomas, Peter, Robert, Mary w. of Wm. Eure, Anne.

Conv. with Katherine his wife, 1624, 1626.

Tenants . . . of HUGH SMITH of Trimdon (40) owe 16d. p.a. . . . of a messuage in Trimdon a.v. 2s. . . . same day. . . .

And 12s. 8d. . . . Total 14s.

40. Conv. 1624 (labourer), 1625, 1626.

Tenants . . . of ISABELLA HARDINGE (41) of Hollingside owe £26 13s. 4d. p.a. . . . of an annuity of £40 out of lands and tenements in Hollingside for the term of her life . . . same day. . . .

And £253 6s. 8d. . . . Total £280.

Look in Roll 14 in *Ebor* regarding this rent and arrears.

41. Da. of Ralph Harding of Hollinside, par. Whickham, & Isabel Radcliffe of Stranton; living in 1631 aged 80.

Conv. 1605, 1606/7, 1615, 1624, of Hollinside, ind. of Tanfield, 1628.

Tenants . . . of CHARLES HALL of Greenecrofte (42) owe £6 13s. 4d. p.a. . . . of an annuity of £10 out of Greenecrofte . . . same day. . . .

And £63 6s. 8d. . . . Total £70.

42. See no. 23.

Tenants . . . of DOROTHY GARGRAVE (43) owe 13s. 4d. p.a. . . . of a messuage and 10 acres in Hetton-le-Hole a.v. 20s. . . . same day. . . .

And £6 6s. 8d. . . . Total £7.

But they ought not . . . because of the conformity of the same Dorothy . . . mem. 15 Car. Mich. term. . . . Quit.

43. See no. 26.

Tenants . . . of MARGARET BELLASIS (44) late wife of Brian Bellasis Esq. deceased and now wife of Thomas Swinburne knt. . . . owe £13 6s. 8d. p.a. . . . of 10 messuages, 10 cottages, 30 acres of land, 200 of meadow, 300 of pasture and 200 of moor in Redmarshall, a.v. £20, of which she is seized in freehold for the term of her life . . . same day. . . .

And £126 13s. 4d. . . . Total £140.

But they ought not . . . insufficiency of the inquisition and for that the said Margaret died about Easter 1637 . . . mem. . . . 14 Car. Mich. term. . . . Quit.

44. Da. of Wm. Lee of Brandon & Elizabeth da. of Tho. Lawson of Usworth; m. (1) Ralph Claxton, probably the Ralph Claxton eld. s. of Wm. Claxton of Wynyard, o.v.p. before 1597; she had the Redmarshall property in dower; m. (2) Brian Bellasis of Morton House (d. 1608), issue, (Sir) William (Sheriff of Durham), Richard, Mary w. of Gerard Salvin, Joan w. of John Vasey, Elizabeth, Margaret; m. (3) Sir Tho. Swinburne of Edlingham, North/d. Bur. St. Oswald's, Durh. 27 Feb. 1636/7.

Conv. as Margaret Bellasis, 1606/7 (New Elvet); lands seized 1609 & leased to John Richardson at £12 p.a. rent paid to May 1622.

Conv. as Margaret Swinburne 1615, 1624, 1625, 1626; registered her abode in Elvet 1616.

In 1634 her son, Sir Wm. Bellasis, as Sheriff, collected under a writ of *fieri facias* the third part of a sum (unspecified) owing for goods.

Tenants . . . of GEORGE SWALWELL (45) of Wolveston yeoman owe 40s. p.a. . . . of a messuage, 20 acres of land, 30 of meadow and 40 of pasture by lease from the Dean and Chapter of Durham for the term of the life of Anne his wife . . . same day. . . .

And £19. . . . Total £21.

45. See no. 8.

In 1634 he compounded to pay 53s. 4d. p.a.; in 1638 he owed £9 6s. 8d., and Sir Wm. Bellasis collected 70s.

Proceedings against him in the Court of High Commission "for a Popish seducer" 1634 (*SS* 34, pp. 77, 171).

A person of the same name was executed in 1594 for being reconciled to the Church of Rome.

Tenants . . . of ALICE GARRIE of Sadburie widow (46) owe 3s. 4d. p.a. . . . of the third part of a cottage and 3 acres in Sadburie a.v. 5s. for the term of her life, . . . same day. . . .

And 30s. 20d. . . . Total 35s.

46. See no. 10.

Tenants . . . of WILLIAM EWRIE knt. (47) owe £20 p.a. . . . of Bradley and 40 acres of land, 50 of meadow and 100 of pasture in Bradley, a.v. £30, in fee . . . same day. . . .

And £190. . . . Total £210.

But they ought not . . . mem. . . . 13 Car. Trin. term. . . . Quit.

47. See nos. 6, 12.

Tenants . . . of PETER WALBANCK of Pearcebrigg (48) owe 40s. p.a. . . . of a messuage and 20 acres of land, 30 of meadow and 40 of pasture, a.v. 60s. . . . in freehold for the term of 3 years still to come . . . same day. . . .

And £19. . . . Total £21.

48. See no. 14.

Tenants of ISABELLA KILLINGHALL (49) owe £13 6s. 8d. p.a. . . . of an annuity of £20 out of the lands and tenements of Henry Killinghall of Middleton George during the natural life of the aforesaid Isabella, to be paid at the feasts of the Purification of the blessed virgin Mary and St. Peter ad vincula.

And £126 13s. 4d. . . . Total £140.

But they ought not . . . insufficiency and incertitude of the inquisition and for that the said Isabella died about the month of February 1627 and for the cause noted in another part of the roll in the farm of the tenants of the lands of Dorothy Hodgson. And they are Quit.

49. A Killinghall of Middleton George, married to Christopher Ewbank (no. 62).

Conv. with her husband 1597, 1600, 1605, 1606/7; both imprisoned 1612.

Tenants . . . of WILLIAM PORRETT (50) owe 13s. 4d. p.a. . . . of a burgage in Hartlepool, a pasture for a beast and pasture for a horse appurtaining to the same burgage in Hartlepool, a.v. 20s. of which he is seized in fee.

And £6 6s. 8d. . . . Total £7.

But they ought not . . . conformity of the said William . . . mem. . . . 14 Car. Mich. term. . . . Quit.

50. Conv. with Margaret his wife 1624, 1625, 1626, ind. 1628.

Tenants . . . of GEORGE CONYERS knt. (51) late of Sockburn owe £4 p.a. . . . of the manor of Sockburn, an orchard, 30 acres of land, 100 of meadow and 300 of pasture in Sockburn . . . in fee . . . into the King's hands 9 *Aug.* 3 *Car.* by John Calverley . . . as is contained in Roll 3 in *Item Adhuc Item (4) Res Ebor.*

And £38. . . . Total £42.

But they ought not . . . insufficiency of the inquisition and for the reason noted in another farm of the same tenants. . . . Quit.

51. See no. 29.

Tenants . . . of NICHOLAS SALKEILD (52) owe 6s. 8d. p.a. . . . of a messuage and garden in Coniscliffe a.v. 10s. . . . in fee . . . same day. . . .

And 63s. 4d. . . . Total 70s.

52. 2nd s. of Lancelot Salkeld & Elizabeth da. of Nicholas Bardsey; with his bros. Lancelot & Francis in 1597 took a lease of property in Over Coniscliffe, & in 1606 with Wm. & Anthony Porter acquired land in Coniscliffe; bur. at Coniscliffe 20 Oct. 1638.

Conv. 1624, 1625; ind. with Margaret his wife 1628.

Tenants . . . of JAMES MEDCALFE (53) owe 26s. 8d. p.a. . . . of a messuage and 20 acres of land in Hamsterley a.v. 40s. . . . in fee . . . same day. . . .

And £12 13s. 4d. . . . Total £14.

[in margin: "et pro terr' in Rackwoodhill."]

53. Conv. with Barbara his wife 1624, 1625, 1626, ind. 1628. In 1632 comp. to pay 100s. p.a., payment for first year traced; 1634 lands seized at £22 13s. 4d. p.a., goods at £53 19s. 6d. Died *c.* 1637 (*SS* 111, 290).

Tenants . . . of FRANCIS LAWSON Esq. (54) owe £53 6s. 8d. p.a. . . . of the manor of Thorpebulmer a.v. £80 held in fee.

And £506 13s. 4d. . . . Total £560.

But they ought not . . . insufficiency and incertitude of the inquisition . . . mem. 13 Car. Hil. term in a process touching Isabella Wicliff. . . . Quit.

54. Eld. s. of Wm. Lawson of Newcastle & Thorpe Bulmer, & Katherine da. of Rowland Beadnall; found insane 1610; inq. p.m. 1621; m. Elizabeth . . . she remar. Lancelot Holtby (see no. 109).

(Isabel Wycliff was sister to Franc. Lawson & wife to Franc. Wycliffe of Preston-le-Skerne.)

Conv. with Elizabeth his wife 1606/7, 1609.

Tenants . . . of RALPH HALL of Greenecrofte in the par. of Lanchester (55) owe £6 13s. 4d. p.a. . . . of the manor of Greenecrofte with the appurtenances, and of 16 messuages, 4 cottages, 10 tofts, 10 gardens, 8 orchards, 100 acres of land, 200 of meadow, 30 of pasture, 100 of woodland, 100 of moor, 60 of bog, 100 of peat and 200 of broom and heath, with the appurtenances in Greenecrofte and Espes in the aforesaid par. of Lanchester, annual value in all, charges excluded, £10 . . . held in fee . . . into the King's hands

1 Sept. 2 Car. by John Calverley knt. . . . as is contained in Roll 2 in *Item Adhuc Item (2) Res Ebor.*

And £63 6s. 8d. . . . Total £70.

55. Eld. s. of Wm. Hall of Greencroft & Alice Tempest (cf. no. 23); m. Alice (probably da. of Sir Wm. Blakeston & Alice Claxton), issue, William, George.

Conv. with Alice his wife 1615, 1624, 1625, 1626, ind. 1628; 1617 lands seized, rent £4 4s. 8d., no payments traced. 1629 comp. to pay 40s. p.a.

Tenants . . . of WILLIAM CLOPTON gentleman recusant (56) owe £133 6s. 8d. p.a. . . . of the manor of Gatenby in the occupation of Marmaduke Langdale knt. a.v. £200 . . . into the King's hands *28 March 12 Car.* by the very Reverend in Christ Thomas Bishop of Durham and other commissioners. . . .

And £66 13s. 4d. from last year. Total £200.

But they ought not . . . Mem. 13 Car. Easter term.

And they are Quit.

56. See no. 27.

rot. *Item Adhuc Res Ebor.*

Tenants . . . of MARGARET BELLASIS (57) late wife of Brian Bellasis deceased and now wife of Thomas Swinburne knt. owe £13 6s. 8d. p.a. . . . of 10 messuages, 10 cottages, 30 acres of land, 200 of meadow, 300 of pasture and 200 of moor, with the appurtenances in Redmarshall a.v. £20 . . . in freehold for the term of her life. Into the King's hands *1 Sept. 2 Car.* by John Calverley . . . as is contained in Roll 4 in *Adhuc Item Ebor.*

And £106 13s. 4d. . . . Total £120.

But they ought not . . . insufficiency of the inquisition and for that the said Margaret died about the feast of Easter 1637 . . . mem. 14 Car. Mich term. . . . Quit.

57. See no. 44.

Tenants . . . of ROBERT PORRETT (58) owe IIIs. 1⅓d. p.a. . . . of a messuage called le friers in Hartlepool and 2 acres of land appurtaining a.v. 66s. 8d. . . . in fee. And of the tithes of grain of the villages of Hart and Throston of which he is possessed by lease from Richard Lumley knt. for the term of 14 years yet to come a.v. 100s. seized the same day and year. As is contained in Roll 3 in *Item Adhuc Item (2) Res Ebor.*

And £13 17s. 9⅓d. . . . And for the past 8 years £44 8s. 11⅓d. Total £63 17s. 10d.

But they ought not . . . mem. 1656 Mich. . . . Quit.

[in margin: "C. sed non pro x s.]

58. One of the family who, after 1605, acquired "the Friars".

Conv. with Isabella his wife 1624, 1625, 1626; ind. 1628 (no wife); conv. with Rich. & Tho. Porrett 1630. For Wm. Porrett his son, see no. 50.

Present seizure of 1626 also included £122 for goods. In 1630 he compounded to pay £6 13s. 4d. p.a.; owed for ½ year in 1636. Sheriff's charges for the same year included £300 arrears.

Proceedings against him in the Court of High Commission in 1635 for "scandalous words" (*SS* 34, p. 146).

Tenants . . . of REBECCA SALVIN (59) owe £20 p.a. . . . of an annuity of £30 out of the manor of Heworth of which she is seized in her own right in freehold for the term of her life.

And £50 . . . and £160 for the last 8 years. Total £230.

But they ought not . . . mem. 1656 Trin. term in a process touching Robert Collingwood and Gilbert Crouch. . . . Quit.

[in margin: "sed non pro hoc anno."]

59. See no. 3.

Tenants . . . of DOROTHY HODGSON (60) owe 17s. 9⅓d p.a. . . . of an annual rent of 26s. 8d. out of lands at Readhall in the par. of Middleton George . . . for the term of her life.

Into the King's hands *9 Aug. 3 Car.* by John Calverley knt. . . . as is contained in Roll 3 in *Item Adhuc Item (4) Res Ebor.*

And 26s. 8d. And £7 2s. 2⅔d. for the past 8 years. Total £9 6s. 8d.

But they ought not . . . insufficiency of the inquisition and for that the said Dorothy in fact was never seized of the aforesaid annuity . . . mem. 14 Car. Trin. term in a process touching William Killinghall. . . . Quit.

60. See no. 11.

Tenants . . . of JANE HOPPER (61) owe 40s. p.a. . . . of the half of an annuity renewed yearly from corn tithes in the village of Shincliffe by lease from the Dean and Chapter of Durham . . . same day . . . as is contained in Roll 3 in *Item Adhuc Item (3) Res Ebor.*

And 60s. And £16. . . . Total £21.

61. Probably the widow of Hugh Hopper of Durham, draper (d. 1605). Conv. (wife of Hugh Hopper) 1605; as widow conv. 1615, registered her abode 1616, conv. 1624, 1626, ind. 1628. In 1629 compounded for goods seized at £17 10s. to pay 50s p.a.; payments traced to 1632.

The property described above "late belonging to Mrs. Jane Hopper and Thos Hopper her son" was under sequestration in 1645 (*SS* 111, 247). "Thos. son to Hughe Hopper" bapt. St. Oswald's 1 Aug. 1602.

Alexander Stratton knt. lord Lawrenston owes £4 8s. 11d. p.a. for the two parts of an annuity of £20 out of the lands of Henry Killinghall parcel of the property of CHRISTOPHER EWBANCK (62) recusant, to be held from 9 Apr. 9 Jac. for the term of 41 years to pay one third of the two third parts above mentioned, viz £4 8s. 11d. as is contained in Roll 9 Jac. in *Adhuc Item Ebor.*

And £73 7s. 1d. . . . And £35 11s. 4d. . . . Total £113 7s. 4d.

But he ought not . . . insufficiency and incertitude of the inquisition and for that the said Christopher Ewbanck was seized of the annuity only for the lifetime of Isabella his wife who died about the month of February 1627 . . . mem. . . . for the reason noted above in the farm of the lands of Dorothy Hodgson.

And he is Quit.

62. Conv. 1597, 1600; goods seized at £20 6s. 8d., *fieri facias* ordered, discharged by order of the Court 1600; conv. 1604, 1605, 1606/7. See no. 49.

The same Alexander owes 44s. 5½d. p.a. . . . of a tenement in Shipley a.v. 36s. 8d. . . . of a tenement with appurtenances in Haughton in the par. of Denton in the tenancy of Lancelot Shalter a.v. 36s. 8d. And of a tenement in Denton with appurtenances in the tenancy of John Garth a.v. 9s. and of a close with appurtenances in Denton in the tenancy of the said John a.v. 40s. And of a close called Carlebury close in Denton aforesaid in the tenancy of Simon Dent a.v. 36s. 8d. Parcels of the lands of ANNE MARSHALL (63) widow there.

And £35 11s. 4d. . . . And £17 15s. 8d. . . . Total £55 11s. 5½d.

But he ought not . . . the incertitude of the inquisition and because the said Anne was seized only for the term of her life and died about the Annunciation 10 Jac. . . . mem. 14 Car. Hil. term. . . . Quit.

63. Da. of George Tonge of West Thickley & Helen da. of John Lambton; m. Richard eld. s. of Gilbert Marshall of Newcastle & Denton, & Agnes da. of Cuthb. Brakenbury of Selaby; issue Cuthbert, Henry. Rich. Marshall was bur. at Denton 7 Oct. 1608.

Conv. with her husb. 1606/7, as widow 1609; property leased to Alex. Stratton 9 April 1611.

Tenants . . . of JOHN CLAXTON Esq. (64) owe 66s. 8d. p.a. . . . of a messuage, 30 acres of land 30 of meadow and 40 of pasture with appurtenances in Plawsworth a.v. 100s. Into the King's hands *1 Sept. 2 Car.* by John Calverley knt. . . . as is contained in Roll 3 in *Item Adhuc Item(2) Res Ebor.*

And £8 6s. 8d. . . . And £26 13s. 4d. . . . Total £38 6s. 8d. But they ought not . . . Mem. 14 Car. Mich. term. . . . Quit.

64. S. & h. of Sir John Claxton of Nettlesworth (d. Jan. 1637/8) & Mary da. of Anthony Wrenn of Binchester; above 9 years old in 1609; living in Gilesgate in Durham city 1649; m. Jane da. of Francis Tunstall of Scargill, co. York.

Conv. 1616; with Jane his wife 1624, 1625, 1626; in 1629 with his father comp. to pay £50 p.a. on Westmorton, Knitsley, Nettlesworth & a fourth of Ricknall Grange, £75 owing in 1636. *Quietus* granted by reason of his conformity, Mich. 1638.

Tenants . . . of DOROTHY CONSTABLE of North Biddick widow (65) owe £25 6s. 8d. p.a. . . . of one third of a messuage, 100 acres of land, 100 of meadow and 100 of pasture in Gt. Kelloe a.v. £10, and of divers messuages in West Auckland . . . same day. . . .

Owing for 1 year ending at the feast of the Annunciation b.m.v. 2 Car.

But they ought not . . . by reason of an order . . . 13 Car. Mich. . . . for that the said Dorothy Constable died about 11 July 1627. . . . Quit.

The heirs and administrators of the aforesaid Dorothy Constable owe £25 6s. 8d. charged upon them by order of the Court, Mich. 13 Car. on behalf of the Remembrancer of the Treasurer for a farm of £25 6s. 8d. owed for the year ending at the Annunciation b.m.v. 2 Car. As is contained immediately above.

But they ought not to be summoned for the same, by reason of an order or decree of the Exchequer of Michaelmas term 13 Car. on the part of the Remembrancer of the Treasurer, remaining in the book of orders or decrees, where it is ordered by the Barons that the heirs, executors and administrators of the aforesaid Dorothy are not to be summoned with regard to the £25 6s. 8d. on the behalf of the said lord King. . . . Quit.

65. See no. 16.

Tenants . . . of RICHARD HIXON of Preston-le-Skerne gentleman (66) recusant owe £160 p.a. . . . of a capital messuage in Morton and 200 acres of land, meadow and pasture adjoining the said messuage, a.v. £100 of which he is seized in his own right in fee; and . . . of a capital messuage and 22 oxgangs of land meadow and pasture in Preston-le-Skerne in the par. of Aykliff in the said county then and late in the tenancy or occupation of John Witham of Cliffe Esq. or his assigns, a.v. £140, of which he is seized in his own right in fee . . . into the King's hands *28 March 12 Car.* by the very Reverend Thomas Bishop of Durham and other Commissioners. . . .

And £80 for the past half year. Total £240.

But they ought not . . . by reason of the conformity of the said Richard . . . Mem. 13 Car. Easter term. . . . Quit.

66. S. & h. of Edward Hixon of Preston-le-Skerne (d. 1612/13) & Anne Read (no. 5); bur. at Aycliffe "the recusant delinquent" 16 Dec. 1640; m. Isabel . . . issue Margery, Joan, Anne, wife of Geo. Porter.

Conv. with Isabel his wife 1624, 1625 (Chester), 1626 (Tribley). In Sept. 1637 comp. to pay £6 13s. 4d. p.a. for the recusancy of Isabel his wife.

The same Richard Hixon owes £32 for the worth of goods and chattels, viz. 5 horses, found the same day and year and a return made, by reason of the recusancy of the aforesaid Richard Hixon. He is Quit.

Tenants . . . of THOMAS TOWERS (67) late of Preston-le-Skerne deceased recusant owe £26 13s. 4d. p.a. . . . of a messuage in Preston and 10 oxgangs of land in the tenancy of Francis Wicliffe gentleman, a.v. £40 . . . same day. . . .

And £13 6s. 8d. Total £40.

But they ought not . . . for that the said Thomas Towers at the time of his conviction was not seized of the premises in his own right in fee as was supposed at the inquisition but he sold the premises before his conviction and the taking of the said inquisition . . . mem. 13 Car. Trin. term in a process touching William Wicliffe. . . . Quit.

67. A member of an old-established family in Preston-le-Skerne, probably s. of Tho. Towers & Elizabeth Claxton, mar. at Aycliffe 28 July 1584; termed "the younger" in 1625; m. Anne. . . .

Conv. with Anne his wife 1615 (Preston), 1624, 1625, 1626 (Darlington).

Tenants . . . of ROBERT BUTLER of Sockeburne (68) owe £17 15s. 6⅔d. p.a. . . . of the manor of Girsbie in the county of York a.v. £26 13s. 4d. . . . same day. . . .

And £8 17s. 9⅓d. Total £26 13s. 4d.

But they ought not . . . because of the insufficiency and incertitude of the inquisition . . . mem. 13 Car. Mich. term in a process touching William Conyers. . . . Quit.

68. Conv. 1624 of Sockburn gent., 1625 yeoman.

Tenants . . . of RALPH ROOKESBIE of Harverton in the par. of Chester (69) owe £46 13s. 4d. p.a. . . . of a capital messuage called Saltwesside now in the tenancy of Alexander Hall or his assigns a.v. £70 . . . in fee.

And £23 6s. 8d. Total £70.

But they ought not . . . Mem. 13 Car. Mich. term in a process touching Alexander Hall holder of the premises. . . . Quit.

69. S. of Ralph Rookesbie; m. Mary da. of Ralph Hedworth of Harraton & Jane da. of Nich. Rutland.

Conv. of Gateshead gent. with Ralph Rooksby Esq. & his wife, & Robert Rooksby gent., 1624; conv. of Harraton 1630, of Elvet with . . . his wife 1632. In 1632 he comp. to pay 40s. p.a. on his personal estate *plus* 3½ years arrearages; in 1655/6, then of Callaly, North/d. he refused the Oath of Abjuration.

Cf. *SS* 111, p. 324.

Tenants . . . of JOHN CLAXTON Esq. (70) of Nettlesworth in the par. of Chester owe £93 6s. 8d. p.a. . . . of a capital messuage in Preston and divers cottages and tenements and 20 oxgangs of land in the tenure of John Conyers bart. or his assigns of which he is seized in his own right in fee.

And £46 13s. 4d. Total £140.

But they ought not . . . Mem. 13 Car. Hil. term in a process touching John Conyers Francis Wicliffe and James Clement. . . . Quit.

70. See no. 64.

Tenants . . . of the aforesaid John Claxton recusant owe £10 p.a. . . . of a tenement in Preston and 5 oxgangs of land meadow and pasture now in the tenure of John Clement gentleman a.v. £15 . . . in fee.

And 100s. Total £15.

But they ought not . . . for the cause noted immediately above in another farm of the same tenants. . . . Quit.

Tenants . . . of John Claxton Esq. owe £9 11s. 1⅓d. p.a. . . . of a parcel of land in Preston called Carrlaine now in the tenure of Francis Wicliffe gentleman a.v. £14 6s. 8d. . . . in fee.

And £4 15s. 6⅔d. Total £14 6s. 8d.

But they ought not . . . for the cause noted above in another farm of the same tenants. . . . Quit.

ANTHONY GARGRAVE (71) of St. Ellen Auckland in the aforesaid county [*blank*][1] £10 for the price or value of 4 steers, 30 sheep, a mare and foal, seized into the King's hands and there returned the same day and year.

71. Conv. 1630; refused Protestation 1642 (*SS* 135, pp. 65, 68).

Tenants . . . of MABELLA GIBBIN and ANNE GIBBIN (72) of St. Ellen Auckland recusants owe 40s. p.a. . . . of certain lands, namely a messuage and 16 acres of meadow adjoining the said messuage a.v. 60s. in Morly.

And 20s. Total 60s.

72. Conv. 1624 with Tho. & Jane Gibbon, 1630 with Jane & Christopher Gibbon (no. 229); ind. with Janet their mother, of Morlie 1628.

In 1638 the above rent had mounted to £6, & the Sheriff collected 20s. In 1642 Anne Gibbon was returned as a recusant of Auckland St. Helen.

Tenants . . . of ELIZABETH ESHE (73) of Wakerfield in the said county owe 66s. 8d. p.a. . . . of a cottage in Wakerfield and 15 acres of land meadow and pasture in the par. of Standropp a.v. 100s.

And 33s. 4d. Total 100s.

Look in Roll 14 in *Res Ebor.* regarding this farm and arrears.

73. Conv. with Henry Eshe of Wakerfield, par. Staindrop, gent. 1632.

[1] The word "deb' (owes)" is added only when the account has been discharged.

The same Elizabeth Eshe owes 100s. for the price of 11 cows there returned.

Look in Roll 14 in *Res Ebor. etc.*

KATHERINE GREAME (74) of Aycliffe widow ( ) £10 the value of money counted there.

74. Conv. 1624, 1626, ind. 1628, conv. 1632.

Tenants . . . of JOHN SALVIN gentleman (75) of the city of Durham owe £58 p.a. . . . of a capital messuage in Heworth and 20 acres of land meadow and pasture adjoining a.v. above charges £87 . . . in fee . . . same day. . . .

And £29. . . . Total £87.

But they ought not . . . by reason of the conformity of the said John . . . mem. 14 Car. Hil. term. . . . Quit.

75. See no. 28.

THOMAS HALL (76) of Chilton in the par. of Merrington owes £78 10s. for the price of goods, viz. 4 steers, 18 sheep, a horse and 5 cows found at the same time, and also for certain grain and other goods there.

But he ought not . . . by reason of the conformity of the said Thomas . . . mem. 14 Car. Mich. term. . . . Quit.

76. 4th s. of Francis Hall of Newsham & Margaret da. of John Tunstall of Long Newton; m. Elizabeth da. of Tho. Wilbore of Knottingley, co. York and had issue; living, of Hornby Hall, 1640.

Conv. of par. Eaglescliffe (Newsham) 1624.

JOHN HALL (77) ( ) £20 for the like, viz. a horse, 3 cows and other goods returned at the same time.

77. Bro. of Tho. Hall above; bapt. 26 Mar. 1598; sometime servant to the Countess of Arundel; will 17 Mar. 1639/40, then of Walworth, pr. 1640.

Conv. of Gt. Chilton, 1630.

Tenants . . . of JOHN SWINBURNE of Capheaton in Northumberland Esq. (78) owe £66 13s. 4d. p.a. . . . of a capital messuage called Halliwell in the par. of Branspith in county Durham a.v. £100 . . . in fee . . . into the hands of the King *28 Mar. 12 Car.* . . .

And £33 6s. 8d. Total £100.

But they ought not . . . insufficiency and incertitude of the inquisition and because the aforesaid John Swinburne was never seized of the said premises . . . mem. 14 Car. Mich. term in a process touching Henry Widdrington and William Swinburne holders of the premises. . . . Quit.

78. Eld. s. of Wm. Swinburne of Capheaton & Margaret da. of John Swinburne of Edlingham; o.v.p. murdered by Capt. John Salkeld, Feb. 1642/3 (NCH II, p. 131 f.n.); m. (1) Dorothy da. of Cuthb. Heron of Chipchace; (2) Isabel da. of Sir Tho. Tempest of Stella, issue, Isabel w. of Geo. Forcer, Troth w. of Hen. Grey of Bitchfield.

Conv. at Morpeth, 13 Jan. 1629/30 with his father & step-mother (Janet Bee), of Symondburne; was included under his father's composition, 16 Oct. 1629, to pay £70 p.a.

Tenants . . . of THOMAS CLAXTON (79) of Waterhouse owe £12 p.a. . . . of a lease in Waterhouse worth £18 p.a. . . . into the King's hands as above.

And £6. . . . Total £18.

But they ought not . . . insufficiency etc. . . . mem. 14 Car. Trin. term in a process touching Thomas Claxton holder of the premises. . . . Quit.

79. S. & h. of Wm. Claxton of Waterhouse & Grace da. of John Trollopp of Thornley (she was sentenced to death in 1594 for harbouring the seminary priest John Boast, but afterwards reprieved); aged 30 in 1615; sometime of Upper Bitchburn; m. Mary da. of Oswald Metcalfe of Hornby, co. York, issue Barbara w. of Wm. Witham of Fawside.

Conv. of Waterhouse, with his wife, 1615, of Witton-le-Wear with his wife, 1624, 1625, 1626, ind. 1628; land in Bitchburn seized 1626; comp. 1632 to pay 40s. p.a. on a moiety of Upper Bitchburn; refused Protestation 1642.

Not the same person as Thomas Claxton, no. 80.

Tenants . . . of Thomas Eury of Bradley (   ) £10 13s. 4d. p.a. being two parts of an annuity of £16 for the term of life of THOMAS CLAXTON of Willington (80) recusant, payable by Thomas Eury to the aforesaid Thomas Claxton.

And 106s. 8d. . . . Total £16.

Look in Roll 14 in *Res Ebor.* regarding this rent and arrears.

80. Ind. 1628, conv. with Jane his wife 1630; refused Protestation 1642. Thomas Eure, eld. s. of Sir Wm. Eure (no. 6) was also ind. 1628.

The same Thomas Claxton ( ) 70s. for the price of goods and chattels returned at the same time.

Tenants . . . of ROBERT THAYLOR (81) of Waterhouse owe 53s. 4d. p.a. . . . of a tenement in Waterhouse a.v. £4.
And 26s. 8d. . . . Total £4.

81. Conv. with Elizabeth his wife 1625, 1626; owed 30s. for goods 1627; refused Protestation 1642.

The same Robert Thaylor ( ) £10 for the price of goods returned at the same time.

Tenants . . . of WILLIAM THAILOR (82) of Waterhouse owe £10 13s. 4d. p.a. . . . of a tenement in Waterhouse a.v. £16. . . .
And 106s. 8d. . . . Total £16.

82. Conv. 1624, 1625, 1626, ind. 1628; (. . .) his wife 1624, 1625, 1628; goods owned in common with Sampson Trollopp and Christopher Rowell (no. 85) seized at £26 13s. 4d. in 1626; owed 66s. 8d. for goods 1627.
The above £16 was included among the Sheriff's charges in 1638: he distrained upon goods and chattels, and collected 15s.

Tenants . . . of JOHN SMITH of Durham gentleman (83) owe £19 6s. 8d. p.a. . . . of a tenement in Waterhouse a.v. £29. . . .
And £9 13s. 4d. . . . Total £29.
But they ought not . . . insufficiency etc. . . . and for the reason noted above in a process touching Thomas Claxton and the aforesaid John Smith. . . . Quit.

83. 2nd s. of George Smythe of Esh & Margaret da. of Sir Edw. Gage of Framfield, Sussex; of Embleton (Elmeden); d. in Paris, 1649. M. Margaret da. of Sir Bertram Bulmer of Tursdale, issue, George, William, John (d. 1651), Edward, Thomas; Margaret & Alexia, Benedictine nuns.
Was included under his father's composition of 6 Nov. 1630 to pay £130 p.a.; in 1632 comp. for himself and wife for Barmton at £10 p.a.

Tenants . . . of NICHOLAS HOPPER (84) of Eastbrandon owe £6 p.a. . . . of a tenement a.v. £9.
And 60s. . . . Total £9.

84. Conv. of Brancepeth with Margaret his wife, 1625; ind. of Hillhouse (no wife) 1628.

The same Nicholas Hopper ( ) £20 for the price of goods. . .

CHRISTOPHER ROWELL (85) of Waterhouse (   ) £10 for the like.

85. Conv. 1624, 1625, 1626 (Brandon), ind. 1628 (Waterhouse), conv. 1630; goods seized 1626 (cf. no. 82); owed 20s. in 1627.

Tenants . . . of JOHN HODGSON of Eastbrandon (86) owe £33 6s. 8d. p.a. . . . of the half of a capital messuage in Eastbrandon a.v. £50 of which he is seized for the term of 9 years.

And £16 13s. 4d. . . . Total £50.

Look in Roll 14 in *Ebor.* regarding this rent and arrears.

86. See no. 38.

The same John Hodgson of Eastbrandon (   ) £100 for the price of goods. . . .

[in margin: *C scri*]

C scri Tenants . . . of THOMAS PINCKNEY of Brandon (87) owe £4 p.a. . . . of a tenement a.v. £6.

And 40s. . . . Total £6.

87. 2nd s. of Martin Pinkney of East Brandon (d. 1623) & Anne da. of Tho. Batmanson of Broomhall; bapt. 23 May 1602 (Brancepeth); bur. 3 Feb. 1676/7 (Esh); m. Isabel sister of Tho. Pickering of Brancepeth, issue, Thomas, Miles, Anne.

Conv. 1624, 1625, 1626; owed for goods 1626, 1627; conv. with his wife 1630; with Anne Pinckney his mother comp. 30 Sept. 1637 to pay 40s. p.a. *plus* 8½ years' arrearages; refused Protestation 1642; estate under sequestration 1645/51, petitioned for relief 1650 (*SS* 111, p. 54). Tho. Pinkney and his wife recusants of Esh, 1665; conv. of Ushaw (Tho. Pinkney sen.) 1674.

C scri The same Thomas Pinckney (   ) £30 . . . goods.

C scri Tenants . . . of ANNE PINCKNEY of Brandon (88) owe 40s. p.a. for two parts of an annuity of 60s. for the term of her life. . . .

And 20s. . . . Total 60s.

88. Da. of Tho. Batmanson of Broomhall, Durham (d. 1615) by his wife Anne; m. at Ryton 4 May 1590 Martin Pinkney of East Brandon; issue, Miles (seminary priest), Thomas (no. 87), Katherine, Helen.

Conv. of Brandon 1624, 1625, 1626; owed for goods 1626, 1627; ind. 1628. Comp. with her son, as above, 1637.

Tenants . . . of ANNE TREWITT of Tuddoe (89) owe 66s. 8d. p.a. . . . an annuity of 100s. . . . for the term of her life. . . .

And 33s. 4d. . . . Total 100s.

89. Anne wife of Henry Trewhitt conv. 1624, ind. 1628; Anne Trewitt widow conv. 1632. 100s. collected under a *fieri facias* 1638.

The same Anne Trewitt ( ) £6 . . . goods. . . .

Tenants . . . of BARBARA COLEMAN (90) of Tuddoe owe 20s. p.a. . . of a tenement in Tuddoe a.v. 30s.

And 10s. . . . Total 30s.

90. Barbara wife of Tho. Coleman conv. 1615, 1624, ind. 1628; widow, conv. 1632.

The same Barbara Coleman ( ) 40s. . . . goods. . . .

JOHN POTTER sen of Tuddoe and JOHN POTTER jun. of the same (91) ( ) 40s. . . . goods. . . .

91. John Potter tailor & Margaret his wife conv. 1624, ind. 1628. John Potter & Anne his wife conv. 1625.

JOHN SIDGESWICKE (92) of the same ( ) 20s. for the like. . . .

92. Conv. with Mary his wife 1632; refused Protestation 1642.

Tenants . . . of ISABELLA JACKSON of Tuddoe (93) owe 53s. 4d. p.a. . . . of a cottage in Tuddoe and 4 acres a.v. £4 . . . in fee.

And 26s. 8d. . . Total £4

93. Conv. wife of Wm. Jackson of Tuddoe 1606/7; widow 1624, ind. 1628, conv. 1632; owed £4 on goods 1635.

40s. of the above £4 was collected by the Sheriff, 1638.

The same Isabella Jackson ( ) 100s. . . . goods. . . .

Tenants . . . of JOHN HEDWORTH (94) of Chester-in-le-Streete owe £10 8s. 10⅔d. p.a. . . . of one acre of meadow a.v. 13s. 4d. . . . of 3 oxgangs of land, meadow & pasture in Witham a.v. £15 . . . in fee.

And 104s. 5⅓d. . . . Total £15 13s. 4d.

94. Conv. with Anne his wife 1624, 1625, 1626; proceedings against him in the Court of High Commission for contempt 1636 (*SS* 34, p. 169); owed £25 on above rent 1639, £8 distrained; refused Protestation 1642.

The same John Hedworth ( ) £4 . . . goods. . . .

WILLIAM JACKSON (95) of Chester ( ) £10 . . . goods. . . .

95. Possibly a son of Tho. Jackson of Harraton & Mary da. of John Watson; no record of conviction unless he was the Wm. Jackson of Hedleyhope conv. 1626, & of Greencroft ind. 1628.

Tenants . . . of ELIZABETH LAWES of Chester widow (96) owe 13s. 4d. p.a. . . . of a tenement in Chester a.v. 20s. . . . in fee. . . .
And 6s. 8d. . . . Total 20s.

96. Conv. wife of James Lawes of Chester 1630, widow 1632.

The same Elizabeth Lawes ( ) 66s. 8d. . . . goods. . . .

ANNE COMYN (97) of Chester ( ) £6 13s. 4d. for the like.

97. No other reference, unless she is the Anne (Agnes) Comyn spr. of St. Giles, Durham, conv. 1625, 1626, 1632.

JANE CUTHBERT (98) of Orpeth in the par. of Chester owes £10 for the like viz. 2 oxen & 2 cows.
But she ought not . . . because of the conformity of the said Jane . . . mem. 14 Car. Mich. term. . . . Quit.

98. Thomas Cuthbert of Urpeth and Jane his wife conv. 1632.

Tenants . . . of ROBERT CONYERS of Harverton in the par. of Chester (99) owe £26 13s. 4d. p..a . . . of coal mines in Harverton a.v. £40 . . . in fee. . . .
And £13 6s. 8d. . . . Total £40.
Look in Roll 1649 in *Ebor.* regarding this rent and arrears.

99. Probably the Robert Conyers of Elvet conv. with his wife 1632.

Tenants . . . of ELIZABETH DIXON widow (100) of Magna Lumley owe 22s. 2⅔d. p.a. . . . of a third part of a farm in Lumley a.v. 33s. 4d.
And 11s. 1⅓d. . . . Total 33s. 4d.

100. Elizabeth wife of Edward Dixon of Lumley labourer conv. 1624, 1625, 1626.

C scri ROBERT ATKINSON (101) of Parva Lumley ( ) £8 . . . goods. . . .

101. Conv. 1624, 1626, ind. 1628, with Margery his wife, of Lumley castle; comp. 14 Aug. 1637 to pay for his personal estate 40s. p.a. Refused Protestation 1642.

JOHN LIDDELL of Lambton (102) (   ) 66s. 8d. for the value of a horse.

[Margin: *Jo de Chester est idem gen' ut J. J. dicit.*]

C scri

102. Compounded "recusant convicted" 26 July 1637 to pay for his personal estate etc. 40s. p.a., no arrearages. Refused Protestation (of Plawsworth), 1642.

Tenants . . . of GEORGE WRAY (103) of Ambell in the county of Northumberland gentleman owe £13 6s. 8d. p.a. . . . of an annuity of £20 out of certain lands in Plawsworth in the county of Durham now in the possession or occupation of Jane Hutchinson widow and Anne Hutchinson, a.v. £20, from which he is possessed of the said annuity for the term of his life.

And £6 13s. 4d. . . . Total £20.

But they ought not . . . insufficiency of the inquisition . . . mem. 14 Car. Hil. term. . . . Quit.

103. 4th s. of Sir Wm. Wray of Beamish (d. 1629) & Jane da. of Wm. Selby of Whitehouse; of Lemington, North/d. (*SS* 111, pp. 385 et seq.); bur. 26 July 1670; m. Elizabeth da. of Robert Brandling of Felling, issue, Thomas.

RALPH HARBERT (104) of Holemyers in the par. of Chester (   ) 66s. 8d. for the value of a horse and a cow.

104. S. of Ralph Harbert (d. 1634); under age 1608.

Conv. of Harraton (Ralph Harbottle) 1630; of Elvet 1632; refused Protestation 1642.

30s. of the above 66s. 8d. was collected by the Sheriff under distraint, in 1638.

C. scri ANNE GARNETT (105) of Blaikewell in the par. of Darlington owes 13s. 4d. p.a. rent for two parts of half a tenement in Blaikewell for the term of her life a.v. 20s.

And 6s. 8d. . . . Total 20s.

105. Possibly widow of the Robert Garnett who owned property in Blackwell in 1620 (Surtees, *Durham* III, 369).

Conv. (widow) with George Garnett 1624; with her children George and Anne ind. 1628, conv. 1632; owed £6 for goods 1635, then of Coniscliffe; comp. 27 July 1637 for property described above and for one third of tithes of Marton & Dishford, co. York, & for her personal estate, to pay 40s. p.a. *plus* 8½ years' arrearages.

C pro bon' infrascript' tenen' per Cop' Cur' manerii de Lanchester ut per dict' Cop' ostens' patet

Tenants . . . of GEORGE GARNETT (106) of the same owe £26 13s. 4d. p.a. . . . of a tenement and 6 oxgangs of land, arable meadow and pasture, now in the tenure or occupation of Christofer Bierlye gentleman a.v. £40.

And £13 6s. 8d. . . . Total £40.

106. S. of Anne Garnett above; conv. as above. Compounded 27 Sept. 1637 for his personal estate to pay 40s. p.a. *plus* 5½ years' arrearages; had paid £8 by Pentecost 1639. Refused Protestation 1642; under sequestration as Papist 1645-55 (*SS* 111, p. 73).

Copyhold lands were not to be seized for recusancy (Judges Rulings) See Temple Newsham MSS. quoted by Dom Hugh Bowler in *Recusant History*, vol. IV, no. 5, April 1958, p. 194: c. 1628-33.

The same George Garnett ( ) £4 . . . goods, viz. 2 cows.

C scri Tenants . . . of ANNE HUTTON widow (107) of Cockerton owe £4 8s. 10⅔d. p.a. . . . of a messuage in Cockerton for the term of her life and 26 acres of land meadow and pasture a.v. £6 13s. 4d.

And 44s. 5⅓d. . . . Total £6 13s. 4d.

107. Da. of Francis Parkinson of Whessoe; m. at Witton Gilbert 16 Oct. 1597, Robert Hutton of Cockerton & Woodham (d. 1633); issue, Thomas (no. 163), William, Thomazine.

Conv. (wife of Robt. Hutton) 1624, 1625, ind. 1628; compounded 20 Mar. 1637/8 to pay 66s. 8d. p.a. & increments after deaths of Thomazine Hutton & Margaret w. of Cuthb. Foster of Byland.

C scri The same Anne Hutton ( ) £6 for the value of 3 cows.

C scri Tenants . . . of THOMAS HARRISON (108) of Sadbury in the par. of Long Newton owe £8 17s. 9⅓d. p.a. . . . of a messuage and 4 oxgangs of land . . . in fee a.v. £13 6s. 8d.

And £4 8s. 10⅔d. . . . Total £13 6s. 8d.

108. Conv. of Long Newton yeoman, 1625, 1630; comp. 28 July 1637 to pay £4 10s. p.a. *plus* 2½ years' arrearages.

Tenants . . . of ELIZABETH LAWSON (109) now wife of Lancelot Holtby of Helmedon gentleman owe £57 15s. 6⅔d. p.a. . . . of a third of the manor of Thorpe Bulmer by way of jointure a.v. £86 13s. 4d.

And £28 17s. 9⅓d. . . . Total £86 13s. 4d.

But they ought not . . . because of the insufficiency . . . and for the reason noted in *Adhuc Res Ebor.* in the farm of Francis Lawson. . . . Quit.

109. Widow of Francis Lawson (no. 54); remar. Lancelot s. of George Holtby of Scackleton, co. York.

Conv. with Franc. Lawson 1606/7, 1609; wife of Franc. Lawson, 1615; wife of Lanc. Holtby ind. 1628.

C scri Tenants . . . of ROBERT CUTHBERT (110) of Lamesley owe £18 4s. 5⅓d. p.a. . . . of 5 acres of land in Lamesley a.v. 66s. 8d. . . . in fee; and of a tenement there with appurtenances a.v. £24.

And £9 2s. 2⅔d. . . . Total £27 6s. 8d.

110. 1st conviction not traced. Compounded 14 Aug. 1637, on a cottage & 5 acres called Kibblesworth, a tenement called Ridinge & 100 acres held at the will of Ralph Lambton, & for his personal estate, to pay 66s. 8d. p.a. *plus* 2½ years' arrearages. With Margaret his wife, conv. 1674 (Nether Eighton).

C scri The same Robert Cuthbert (   ) £41 . . . goods, viz. 4 oxen, 4 cows, 8 horses . . . seized as above. . . .

Tenants . . . of ROBERT MARLYE (111) of Kibblesworth owe 17s. 9⅓d. p.a. . . . of a cottage and 2 acres of land now in the possession of Anthony Marlye or his assigns a.v. 26s. 8d.

And 8s. 10⅔d. . . . Total 26s. 8d.

111. Conv. 1632; refused Protestation 1642.

Tenants . . . of THOMAS SMIRK (112) of the chap. of St. Margaret's in Durham owe 5s. 4d. p.a. . . . of a cottage for the term of 34 years or thereabouts a.v. 8s.

And 2s. 8d. . . . Total 8s.

112. Probably s. of the Thomas Smirk & Alison Spark, mar. 9 June 1594, at St. Margaret's, Durham.

Convicted, with (. .) his wife and Alice, wife of Tho. Smirke, 1626; proceedings against him in the Court of High Commission for clandestine marriage & private baptisms, 1637-8 (*SS* 34, pp. 172, 186); possibly the Tho. Smirke mar. to An Sympson at St. Margaret's, 22 Aug. 1630. Refused Protestation 1642.

The same Thomas Smirk (   ) 60s. . . . 18 sheep. . . .

Tenants . . . of JOHN TEASDELL of the same (113) owe 13s. 4d. p.a. . . . of a cottage in Durham for the term of 30 years held of the Dean and Chapter of Durham a.v. 20s.

And 6s. 8d. . . . Total 20s.

113. Refused Protestation 1642.
Jane wife of John Teasdale of Crossgate conv. 1626, ind. 1628.

Tenants . . . of JOHN ADAMSON (114) of the same owe 6s. 8d. p.a. . . . of a cottage held of the Dean and Chapter a.v. 10s.

And 3s. 4d. . . . Total 10s.

But they ought not . . . insufficiency of the inquisition . . . mem. 14 Car. Hil. term . . . Quit.

114. Conv. 1626, ind. 1628, conv. 1632 (slater); owed 40s. for goods, charged to sheriff 1636. Refused Protestation 1642.

rot. *Item Adhuc Item Res Ebor.*

Tenants . . . of ROBERT BURNE (115) of Durham owe 6s. 8d. p.a. . . . of a tenement there a.v. above all charges 10s. . . . in fee. . . . Into the King's hands *28 March 12 Car.* . . .

And 3s. 4d. . . . Total 10s.

115. Conv. with (. .) his wife, of Farnton Hall, Bishop Wearmouth, 1625; ind. with Jane his wife, of Washington, 1628; refused Protestation 1642.

Tenants . . . of WILLIAM JOHNSON (116) of the same, weaver, owe 13s. 4d. p.a. . . . of a tenement in Durham a.v. 20s.

And 6s. 8d. . . . Total 20s.

116. Conv. with John and Robert Johnson, of St. Oswald's, Durham, 1624.

The same William Johnson (   ) 60s. . . . goods. . . .

Tenants . . . of JOHN JOHNSON (117) of Fieldhouse in the chap. of St. Margaret's in Durham owe 4s. 5⅓d. p.a. . . . of a tenement a.v. 6s. 8d.

And 2s. 2⅔d. . . . Total 6s. 8d.

117. See entry above; possibly the John Johnson weaver mar. to Margaret . . . 28 June 1607 (St. Nicholas, Durham).
John Johnson of Elvet, weaver, conv. 1615; refused Protestation 1642.

Tenants . . . of JOHN FORCER (118) of Harberhouse owe £20 p.a.

. . . of a capital messuage and 200 acres of land . . . in fee, a.v. £30.

And £10. . . . Total £30.

118. Eld. s. of Peter Forcer (no. 39); under age 1626, wardship granted to Sir Tho. Riddell of Gateshead; Colonel in Royalist forces; bur. 31 Aug. 1665 (par. reg. St. Margaret's, Durh.); m. Jane da. of Sir Tho. Riddell; issue, George (heir), Peter, Jane w. of Philip Hodgson of Tone. Estate sequestered for recusancy and delinquency 1644, included in 2nd Act for Sale (*SS* 111, p. 209).

MARGARET GARFOOTE (119) of Durham (   ) 40s. for goods. . . .

119. Wife of Michael Garfoote, wheelwright, of Harber House. Conv. 1606/7, 1615, 1624.

C scri RICHARD JACKSON (120) of Bladon, par. of Ryton, (   ) £20 for goods viz. 6 cows and 2 horses.

120. Anne wife of Richard Jackson conv. 1626, 1630. Proceedings against him in the Court of High Commission for clandestine marriage & private baptisms, 1635 (*SS* 34, 114); convicted for the first time April 1636 & compounded the same month for messuage and goods, to pay 50s. p.a.

C scri MARMADUKE JACKSON (121) of the same (   ) £20 for goods, viz. 10 horses and 4 cows.

121. Comp. 11 April 1636 "convicted recusant" to pay 40s. p.a. for personal estate. Refused Protestation 1642.

JOHN WALKER (122) of the same owes £28 . . . 4 oxen 2 horses 2 cows.

But he ought not to be summoned for the same . . . because of his conformity . . . mem. 14 Car. Mich. term. . . Quit.

122. Conv. 1630, with (. .) his wife.

JOHN GARRY (123) of the same (   ) £10 . . . goods.

123. Conv. of St. Giles, Durham, 1624, 1625; of Bladon comp. 12 Aug. 1637 to pay 40s. p.a. for personal estate *plus* 2½ years' arrearages.

Tenants . . . of JOHN RUDDERFORTH (124) of Blackhall owe £8 17s. 9⅓d. p.a. . . . of a messuage and 40 acres of land meadow and pasture . . . a water mill . . . a fuller's mill a.v. £13 6s. 8d. . . . in fee.

And £4 8s. 10⅔d. . . . Total £13 6s. 8d.

124. See note on Charles Rudderford (no. 20). Refused Protestation 1642.

C scri JOHN ODDYE (125) of Stella ( ) £12 . . . 2 cows 2 horses 2 oxen. . . .

125. (or Addy); comp. 12 April 1636 to pay 40s. p.a. for goods; arrearages from Martinmas 1633 "because not convicted before then." Refused Protestation 1642 (John Addy jun.)

C scri Tenants . . . of JOHN LIDDELL (126) of the same owe 66s. 8d. p.a. . . . of a tenement there a.v. 100s.

And 33s. 4d. . . . Total 100s.

126. Conv. 1626, 1630; with (. .) his wife 1632; comp. 12 Apr. 1636 to pay 60s. p.a.

C scri Tenants . . . of JANE WRAY (127) widow of Beamish owe £66 13s. 4d. p.a. . . . of 300 acres of land meadow and pasture for the term of her life a.v. £100

And £33 6s. 8d. . . . Total £100.

Look in Roll 22 of this King in *Ebor.* regarding this rent and arrears.

127. Da. of Wm. Selby of Newcastle & Elizabeth da. of Gerard Fenwick of Newcastle; m. Sir Wm. Wray of Beamish (d. 1629); issue, Thomas, William, Henry, George (no. 103), Dorothy w. of Robt. Millott (no. 17). Conv. 1624, 1625, 1626.

With her son Thomas, comp. Nov. 1630 to pay £70 p.a. £770 paid and composition discharged 1645/6, Jane Wray having died Aug. 1640.

C scri The same Lady Jane Wray ( ) £50 . . . 6 oxen 4 horses 6 cows and other goods. . . .

THOMAS PEARSON (128) of Stanlye ( ) 40s. . . . goods.

128. Conv. with Ursula his wife 1632; refused Protestation 1642.

CHRISTOPHER BARNES (129) of the same ( ) £4 . . . goods.

129. Conv. of St. Oswald's, Durham, 1624; refused Protestation 1642, then of Tanfield.

THOMAS SELBYE (130) of Tanfeild ( ) 30s. . . . goods.

130. Not identified with certainty; (possibly the 4th s. of Sir Wm. Selby of Winlaton and Shortflatt, and Elizabeth da. of Wm. Widdrington; m. Dorothy da. of John Swinburne of Blackheddon; refused Protestation 1642; conv. with Dorothy his wife 1674, 1680).

ROBERT CARRE jun. (131) of the same ( ) 40s. . . . goods.

131. Possibly a s. of Robert Carr of Tanfield whose wife Jane was conv. 1615, 1624, 1626, ind. 1628.

ANTHONY STEPHENSON (132) of the same ( ) 40s. . . . goods.

132. Conv. of Harraton, with Jane his wife, 1632.

MARY JOPLYN (133) of the same ( ) 40s. . . . goods.

133. Conv. 1632. £6 for goods charged to sheriff 1636. 16s. out of 40s., the value of a cow, was collected by the sheriff in 1638.

GEORGE JOPLYN (134) of the same ( ) 40s. . . . goods. . . .

134. Conv. 1624, 1626; ind. with (. .) his wife 1628.

WILLIAM RAWE (135) of the same ( ) £12 . . . goods. . . .

135. Probably s. of Wm. Rawe (no. 146).
Wm. Rawe jun. of Lunshouse and Isabella his wife conv. 1626. A Wm. Rawe refused Protestation 1642 (Lanchester).

WILLIAM DUNNE (136) of the same ( ) 40s. . . . a horse. . . .

136. Wm. Dunn sen. conv. with (. .) his wife 1626, ind. with Magdalen his wife 1628.

NICHOLAS GALLYE jun. (137) of the same ( ) £6 13s. 4d. . . . 2 oxen, a horse. . . .

137. Conv. 1632; refused Protestation 1642.

WILLIAM ROBSON (138) of Barmeston par. of Washington ( ) 40s. . . . a cow. . . .

138. Conv. 1624; with Mary his wife conv. 1626, ind. 1628; refused Protestation 1642.

Tenants . . . of ROBERT MANNERS (139) of Hebborne owe 53s. 4d. p.a. . . . of a tenement annual value £4.
And 26s. 8d. . . . Total £4.

139. Servant to Ald. Richard Hodgson; administration of the goods of Robt. Manners granted to Anne his wife, 19 Jan. 1638/9.
Anne (Agnes) his wife conv. 1606/7, presented by churchwardens of Jarrow 1609, conv. 1615, 1616.
Robert Manners and Anne his wife conv. 1624, 1625, 1630.
Arrears of above rent amounting to £6 13s. 4d. appear among monies charged to sheriff, 1638; 60s. recovered.

The same Robert Manners ( ) £8 . . . 4 cows. . . .

C scri Tenants . . . of RALPH HALL (140) of Greencroft par. of Lanchester Esq. owe £40 p.a. . . . of a capital messuage and 200 acres of land meadow and pasture . . . in fee, a.v. £60.
And £20. . . . Total £60.

140. See no. 55. Comp. 31 Jan. 1636/7 to pay £13 6s. 8d. p.a. *plus* 7½ years' arrearages to be paid by 15 instalments.
Cf. *SS* 111, p. 229.

C scri The same Ralph Hall ( ) £8 10s. . . . 3 cows and a horse.

Tenants . . . of DOROTHY GARGRAVE (141) of Hetton in le Hole par. of Houghton in le Spring widow owe 66s. 8d. p.a. . . . of a close in Hetton for the term of her life by way of jointure a.v. 100s.
And 33s. 4d. . . . Total 100s.
but they ought not . . . because of her conformity . . . mem. 15 Car. Mich. term. . . . Quit.
141. See nos. 26, 43.
Tenants of the lands and tenements of Robert Porrett father of William Porrett of Trimdon owe £20 p.a. being two parts of an annuity of £30 for the term of life of the aforesaid WILLIAM PORRETT (142) recusant out of the lands of the aforesaid Robert Porrett.
And £10. . . . Total £30.
But they ought not . . . by reason of the conformity of William Porrett . . . mem. 14 Car. Mich, term. . . . Quit.

142. See no. 50.

C scri Tenants . . . of WILLIAM THOMPSON (143) of Trimdon owe £66 13s. 4d. p.a. . . . of a lease for the term of 1000 years of a messuage and 30 acres a.v. £100.
And £33 6s. 8d. . . . Total £100.

143. Conv. 1615, 1624, 1625, 1626; ind. 1628, conv. 1632; and cf. *SS* 111, p. 359.
Comp. 27 July 1637 to pay 50s. p.a. plus 6½ years' arrearages.

C scri The same William Thompson ( ) £10 . . . 4 cows 3 steers and a horse. . . .

NICHOLAS PORTER (144) of Greencroft ( ) 106s. 8d. . . . 2 cows 10 sheep. . . .

144. Possibly s. of Nich. Porter of Shieldraw (d. 1642); termed *jun.* in 1628, when prosecuted in the Court of High Commission for a clandestine marriage with Anne Bierley (*SS* 34, p. 14).

Conv. with (. .) his wife 1626, then of Lintsgreen.

ELLINOR FORCER (145) of the same (   ) £13 . . . 2 oxen a horse, 3 cows. . . .

145. Da. of Thomas Forcer (no. 4). Ind. of Greencroft 1628, conv. of Harber House 1630.

C. pro bon' Tenants . . . of WILLIAM RAWE (146) of the same owe 53s. 4d. p.a. . . . of the moiety of a tenement called Lumshouse a.v. £4.

And 26s. 4d. . . . Total £4.

146. Probably s. of Wm. Rawe of St. Margaret's, Durham (will 1587, *SS* 112, p. 124); m. at Lanchester 6 Dec. 1590, Elinor (Emmot) Elmett; issue, William, bapt. 1596 (see no. 135).

Conv. with Elinor his wife 1606/7; fined £40 in Court of High Commission for contempt in non-appearance, 1607; both presented by churchwardens of Lanchester, 1609; conv. with his wife, 1615, 1624, 1625, 1626, 1630. Comp. in 1629 to pay 40s. p.a.; payments traced to 1632.

"William son of William Rawe of St. Margarets, Durham, absent in France without licence with the privity of his father", 1581 (S.P. Dom. Eliz. 150/95).

C scri The same William Rawe (   ) £8 . . . 2 cows 20 sheep. . . .

JOHN WILSON of Mounckwarmough (147) (   ) £4 . . . 2 cows. . . .

147. Conv. of Whickham, labourer, 1624, 1625; listed as having removed 1626; comp. in 1638 to pay 53s. 4d. p.a.

C scri Tenants . . . of JOHN HUTCHINSON (148) of Burnhouse in the said par. of Lanchester owe £8 p.a. . . . of a tenement of which he is possessed for the term of 8 years . . . of another tenement in Billingside and 16 acres of land. . . .

And £4. . . . Total £12.

148. See no. 24; his previous composition (1635) was for goods only.

C scri The same John Hutchinson (   ) £40 . . . 4 oxen 2 horses 3 cows 4 steers 40 sheep. . . .

C pro bon' terr' infrascript' ten' per Cop' Cur' de Episcopo Dunelmen' ut de manerio de Lanchester prout per dict' Cop' ostens' patet Tenants . . . of WILLIAM LAWS (149) of Kiopeth owe £6 13s. 4d. p.a. . . . of a messuage and 60 acres a.v. £10.

And 66s. 8d. . . . Total £10.

149. Possibly the William Lawes of Bursblades conv. in 1626 with Anne his wife. Mar. before 1637 Katherine da. of Anthony Meaburn of Pontop and Katherine Emerson (*SS* 34, p. 119); comp. 1629 to pay 40s. p.a., payments traced to 1632. Conv. at the Old Bailey 1632/3; under sequestration 1645-55 (*SS* 111, p. 73).

C scri EDWARD JOPLIN (150) of the par. of Lanchester (   ) £8 10s. . . . 2 cows 2 steers. . . .

150. Proceedings for clandestine marriage 1635 (*SS* 34, p. 140); "fled" in 1637; never compounded.

C scri Tenants . . . of PETER WYTHAM (151) of Fawside gentleman owe £4 8s. 10⅔d. p.a. . . . of a messuage and 30 acres a.v. £6 13s. 4d.

And £2 4s. 5⅓d. . . . Total £6 13s. 4d.

151. 3rd s. of Anthony Wytham of Cliffe, co. York, & Anne da. of John Middleton of Stokeld. M. Jane . . . , issue John.

Conv. of Twisell 1615; of par. Chester with Jane his wife, 1625, 1626 (Tribley); comp. 8 Sept. 1637 to pay 60s. p.a. *plus* 8 years' arrearages; refused Protestation 1642; under sequestration 1651 (*SS* 111, p. 58).

C scri The same Peter Wytham (   ) £21 10s. . . . 4 cows 1 horse 40 sheep. . . .

C scri Tenants . . . of GEORGE TAYLOR (152) owe 44s. 5⅓d. p.a. . . . of a tenement and 12 acres a.v. 66s. 8d.

And 22s. 2⅔d. . . . Total 66s. 8d.

But they ought not . . . mem. Mich. term 1656 in a process touching Thomas Taylor. . . . Quit.

152. Conv. 1630; comp. 17 March 1637/8 to pay 46s. 8d. p.a., no arrearages. Proceedings for conveying popish priests, and for clandestine marriage, 1635 (*SS* 34, p. 141).

C scri Tenants . . . of JOHN HODGSON (153) of Mannor-house owe £30 p.a. . . . of a messuage and 15 acres . . . and of all the small tithes belonging to the prebend of Lanchester

And £15. . . . Total £45.

153. See no. 15.

C. pro bon' terr' tent' per Cop' Cur' manerii de Buttsfeild prout per Cop' ostens' patet Tenants . . . of JOHN WINTER (154) of Eastbuttsfeilde owe £4 13s. 4d. p.a. of a tenement and 20 acres. . . .
And £2 6s. 8d. . . . Total £7.

154. Conv. 1624, 1625, 1626 (Copighill); ind. with Anne his wife 1628. Comp. for goods worth £10 10s. to pay 30s. p.a. 1629; payments traced to 1632. Refused Protestation 1642. Under sequestration 1645-51.

JOHN ILEY of Hamstells (155) ( ) £15 . . . 3 cows 2 steers 20 sheep. . . .

155. Conv. 1624; with Elizabeth his wife 1625, 1626, ind. 1628.

C scri WILLIAM ILEY (156) of the same ( ) £10 . . . 2 cows 2 steers 20 sheep. . . .

156. Conv. with Anne his wife 1624, 1625, ind. 1628, conv. (Esh) 1630. Comp. as of Ford, 17 March 1637/8 to pay 46s. 8d. p.a., no arrearages. Refused Protestation 1642.

C pro bon' terr' tent' per Cop' Cur' Decan' de Lanchester prout patet per Cop' Tenants . . . of LANCELOT TAILOR (157) of Westrawe owe 33s. 4d. p.a. . . . of a tenement and 8 acres. . . .
And 16s. 8d. . . . Total 50s.

157. "Lanclott Tayler and Elisabeth Mayr" mar. at Lanchester, 15 May 1582.
Conv. with Elizabeth his wife 1624, 1625 (Newbiggin), ind. 1628. Comp. for goods (Lanc. Taylor sen.) of West Rawe in 1629 to pay 40s. p.a., payments traced to 1632.
The present Lancelot Taylor was possibly a son of the above; a Lancelot Taylor was prosecuted in the Court of High Commission for private baptisms in 1635.

C scri Tenants . . . of MARY BLAKESTON (158) of Seaton widow owe £11 6s. 8d. p.a. . . . of the third part of a messuage and 60 acres. . . .
And £5 13s. 4d. . . . Total £17.
Look in 21 Car. in *Ebor.* regarding this rent and arrears.

158. Da. of Martin Hallyman of Lumley & wife of Ralph Blakeston (d. 1635).
Ralph Blakeston & Mary his wife conv. 1612, 1618, 1624, 1625, 1626; ind. 1628, conv. 1630. Ralph Blakeston compounded 18 Dec. 1629 to

pay £14 p.a. £21 was owing at his death, discharged 14 Car. Mary Blakeston is here charged with rent for her widow's portion; but she had already (11 Feb. 1635/6) comp. to pay £4 13s. 4d. p.a., 1st payment due at Martinmas 1635, no arrearages previous to this.

C scri The same Mary Blakeston (   ) £37 . . . 6 cows 8 steers and heifers 3 calves 19 sheep a horse and other goods. . . .

C scri Tenants . . . of JOHN ERRINGTON (159) of Yarum in the co. of York Esq. owe £44 8s. 10⅔d. p.a. . . . of a capital messuage in Elton in the co. of Durham and 20 oxgangs of land . . . in fee, a.v. £66 13s. 4d.

And £22 4s. 5⅓d. . . . Total £66 13s. 4d.

"But they ought not to bee therefore sum̃oned. Neither ought ye sd. yearely Rent to be hereafter charged By consideration of ye Barons Annoted on ye Trears. Remembrance. Viz. amongst ye Com̃on businesse of Hillary terme in ye yeare 1654 Roll. And they are Quitt."

159. S. of Tho. Errington of Yarm and Elton (d. 1595) & Jane da. of Robt. Clavering of Callaly, North/d; Colonel in the service of Charles I; d. 1666, "Mr. John Errington, maximus natu, Papist, bur. 31 Dec. 1666, Elton" (Mickleton MSS., quoted by Surtees, *Durham* III, 209). M. Mary . . . , issue John.

No previous record found among Durham entries.

See note on no. 37.

Tenants . . . of KATHERINE LADY CONYERS (160) widow of Sockburne recusant owe £44 8s. 10⅔d. p.a. . . . of a third of the manor of Sockburne for the term of her life a.v. £66 13s. 4d.

And £22 4s. 5⅓d. . . . Total £66 13s. 4d.

But they ought not . . . insufficiency of the inquisition . . . mem. 14 Car. Mich. term. . . . Quit.

160. Da. of Anthony Bulmer of Tursdale & Diana da. of Franc. Metham of Wigginthorpe, co. York; m. Sir Geo. Conyers (no. 29).

Conv. (wife of Geo. Conyers) 1605, 1606/7, 1615; with Geo. Conyers, 1624, 1625; as widow comp. in 1632 to pay 60s. p.a. *plus* 3 years' arrearages. 30s. & 30s. arrearages paid in 1632.

ROBERT ELSTOB (161) of Stillington (   ) £4 . . . a cow a horse.

161. A Robert Elstob of par. Sedgefield was convicted with (   ) his wife, 1624, 1625. Proceedings against him for clandestine marriage 1633 (*SS* 34, p. 74).

C scri MARGARET HALL (162) of Newsome in the par. of Egglescliffe (   ) £30 . . . 10 cows 40 sheep. . . .

162. Da. of John Tunstall of Scargill & Long Newton, & Josiana da. of Ralph Rokeby of Marske; d. 1643; m.i. Eaglescliffe; mar. Francis s. of Chr. Hall of Newsham (d. 1611), issue, Christopher, Francis, John (no. 77), Thomas (no. 76), William, Anthony, Helen w. of Chr. Gaynes (serving on present jury), Jane w. of John Jenison, Dorothy w. of Tho. Hutton, Katherine w. of Tho. Lascelles.

Conv. (w. of Franc. Hall) 1605, 1606/7; (widow) conv. 1615, ind. 1628, conv. (of Long Newton) 1633. Comp. 27 Oct. 1636 to pay 40s. p.a. *plus* 7 years arrearages.

C ux' eius scri Tenants . . . of THOMAS HUTTON gentleman (163) late of Newsham deceased owe £6 13s. 4d. p.a. . . . of a tenement in Woodham and 30 acres of land, a.v. £10.

And 66s. 8d. . . . Total £10.

163. Eld. s. of Robt. Hutton of Cockerton & Woodham, & Anne Parkinson (no. 107); d. 1630. M. Dorothy da. of Margaret Hall above; issue, Francis, Thomas, Dorothy w. of Tho. Crosier.

Conv. 1624; with his wife conv. 1625, ind. 1628, conv. 1630.

C scri Tenants . . . of DOROTHY HUTTON widow (164) late wife of the aforesaid Thomas Hutton deceased owe 44s. 5⅓d. p.a. . . . of a third part of the tenement by way of jointure now in the occupation of Walter Forest. . . .

And 22s. 2⅔d. . . . Total 66s. 8d.

164. Widow of Tho. Hutton above.

With her husband, ind. 1628, conv. 1630. Comp. 27 Oct. 1636 to pay 60s. p.a. *plus* 7 years' arrearages (her late husband not having compounded); under sequestration 1642-55 (*SS* 111, p. 73).

Tenants . . . of JOHN ERRINGTON (165) of Yarum in the co. of York Esq. owe £10 13s. 4d. p.a. . . . 2 oxgangs of land in the par. of Eaglescliffe . . . in fee, a.v. £16. . . .

And £5 6s. 8d. . . . Total £16.

But they ought not . . . Hil. term 1656. . . . Quit.

165. See no. 159.

C scri Tenants . . . of JOHN SWINBURNE of Hamsterley Esq. (166) owe £66 13s. 4d. p.a. . . . of a capital messuage and 250 acres now in the occupation of John Hunter sen. and John Hunter jun. and others.

And £33 6s. 8d. . . . Total £100.

166. The same person as no. 78; inherited Hamsterley from his maternal grandfather John Swinburne of Edlingham (d. 1625); it was not included in his father's composition of 1629.

C scri The same John Swinburne (   ) £25 . . . 5 horses. . . .

JOHN DANBYE (167) of Meddomsley in the said county (   ) £14 . . . 2 horses. . . .

167. No record of conviction found. Refused Protestation 1642.

C pro bon' scri Tenants . . . of WILLIAM STEVENSON (168) of Knitslye owe £8 p.a. . . . of a lease in Knitslye of which he is possessed for the term of 9 years taken of George Baker or John Claxton Esq.
Total £12.

168. Conv. with Frances his wife 1624, 1625, 1626, ind. 1628; comp. in 1632 to pay 40s. p.a. *plus* 3 years' arrearages; paid 20s. rent and £3 arrearages in 1632.

Tenants . . . of WILLIAM NEWTON (169) of Bradley owe £6 13s. 4d. p.a. . . . of a messuage and 50 acres. . . .
Total £10.

169. See no. 22.

The same William Newton (   ) £19 11s. 8d. . . . 2 oxen 2 steers 2 horses 6 cows 5 sheep 3 calves. . . .

C scri Tenants . . . of WILLIAM BURNOPP (170) of Houns owe £10 13s. 4d. p.a. . . . of a messuage and 60 acres . . . in fee. . . .
Total £16.
But they ought not . . . 1656 Mich. term. . . . Quit.

170. Son of Martin Burnup, under age at his father's death in 1596: heir to his bro. Richard 1618; married . . . (Jane Burnop, widow, was seized of a moiety of the Howmes in 1675). Cf. *SS* 111, p. 138. Conv. with (. .) his wife 1630; comp. 25 Sept. 1637, to pay £6 p.a. *plus* 2 years' arrearages.

C scri The same William Burnopp (   ) £52 8s. . . . a horse and foal 80 sheep 4 calves 6 oxen 6 cows. . . .

C scri FRANCIS HODGSON (171) of Hamsterley (   ) £26 . . . 4 oxen 4 cows 2 steers 4 horses 19 sheep. . . .

171. Probably the same person as the Francis Hodgson of Collierley who compounded for himself and Dorothy Hodgson his mother (no. 11), 25 Sept. 1637 to pay 53s. 4d. p.a. Refused Protestation 1642.

C scri Tenants . . . of RALPH CATHERICK (172) of Fishburn in the par. of Sedgefield owe £10 13s. 4d. p.a. . . . of a messuage and 60 acres now in the tenure of the aforesaid Ralph and George Atkinson . . . in fee. . . .

Total £16.

Look in the Great Roll for 1654 regarding this rent and arrears.

172. See no. 9. Comp. with Ralph his son 1 March 1637/8 to pay 106s. 8d. p.a., all arrearages included.

Tenants . . . of WILLIAM STODDERT (173) of the same owe 10s. 8d. p.a. . . . of a tenement in Fishburn and a croft. . . .

Total 16s.

173. Conv. 1624; with Anne his wife 1632; refused Protestation 1642; Certificate of Composition 1644 (*SS* 111, p. 13).

The same William Stoddert (   ) 30s. . . . a cow. . . .

ROGER RICHARDSON (174) of Butterwick (   ) 30s. for the like. . .

174. Conv. with Alice his wife 1624, 1625, 1626, ind. 1628; owed 40s. for the value of 2 cows 1626; 40s. included in sheriff's charges 1636.

"Roger Richardson, servant to Mr. John Conyers," bur. 1 April 1661 (St. Oswald's, Durham).

Tenants . . . JOHN SMITH (175) of Durham gentleman owe £33 6s. 8d. p.a. . . . of the manor of Elmeden with appurtenances in the tenure or occupation of the said John a.v. £50 . . . in fee. . . .

Total £50.

Look in the Great Roll for 1649 in *Ebor.* regarding this rent and arrearages.

175. See no. 83.

Tenants . . . of URSULA MASON (176) of Barnard Castle widow owe £10 p.a. . . . of a tenement and 30 acres . . . for the duration of the life of Talbott Bowes knt. and Thomas Bowes gentleman.

176. Ursula wife of John Mason of Hungerknowle, conv. 1632. "Ursaley Mason" bur. 10 Oct. 1649 (par. reg. Barnard Castle).

C scri Rob. de Bradley pro bon' Trollop[1] Tenants . . . of ROBERT MERRIMAN (177) of Fetherstonhalgh in the co. of Northumberland gentleman owe £6 13s. 4d. p.a. . . . of a messuage called Eastyate and 500 acres for the term of 16 years. . . .

177. Mar. Merial da. of Gerard Salvin of Croxdale & Anne Blakeston; issue Merial and probably others; bur. St. Oswald's, 13 Aug. 1661, "Mr. Robert Meryman of Croxdale". "Mrs. Murill Merreman widow", bur. St. Oswald's, 19 Jan. 1675/6.

Conv. of Cleadon 1606, of Trimdon with Merial his wife 1615, of Witton-le-Wear (Wadley) 1624, 1625, 1626; comp. 1629 for goods, to pay £6 13s. 4d. p.a. Payments traced to 1632. Lands at Eastgate seized 1635. Proceedings against him "for a popish seducer" in the Court of High Commission, 1635 (*SS* 34, p. 100).

Tenants . . . of MARGERY STUBBS of Roochalside in the par. of Stanhope widow (178) owe £12 p.a. . . . of a tenement and 30 acres in the occupation of Christopher Harrison a.v. £18. . . .

Total £18.

But they ought not . . . by reason of her conformity . . . mem. 4 Car. Mich. term. . . . Quit.

178. Conv. 1632. A Margery Stubbs of Framwelgate ind. 1628, of Staindrop conv. 1630.

Tenants . . . of RALPH STUBBS (179) of Brandon Walls owe £8 13s. 4d. p.a. . . . of a tenement in Roochallside and 30 acres in the occupation of Isabel Johnson widow. . . .

Total £13.

179. Conv. 1619.

Tenants . . . of ROBERT EMMERSON in the par. of Stanhope (180) owe £20 p.a. . . . of a messuage and 100 acres in the occupation of Christopher Emmerson and George Bainbridge.

Total £30.

Look in Roll 14 Car. in *Ebor.* regarding this rent and arrears.

180. S. of Richard Emmerson and Elizabeth his wife; married, with 7 children, in 1652 (*SS* 111, p. 186). Estate sequestered and in 3rd Act for Sale; bought by Gilbert Crouch.

"Robert Emerson of Ludwell was drowned but not buried here because he dyed excommunicate", 19 Apr. 1667 (Stanhope par. reg.).

[1] Marginal note, unpunctuated. I can find no connection between Merriman and Trollop, or Trollop and Bradley.

Comp. 19 Aug. 1635 (of Sparkaley) for his personal estate, to pay 50s. p.a. *plus* arrearages from Martinmas 1635 only, "because not convicted before that".

C scri Tenants . . . of ELIZABETH EMMERSON of Pontasse in the aforesaid county widow (181) owes £8 13s. 4d. p.a. . . . of a tenement in Ludwell and 40 acres in the tenure of the aforesaid Elizabeth.
Total £13.

181. Widow of Richard Emmerson & mother of Robert above. Estate sequestered for recusancy 1644 (*SS* 111, p. 73).

C scri The same Elizabeth Emmerson ( ) £10 . . . goods. . . .

Tenants . . . of JOHN WRIGHT of Bradewood (182) owe £40 p.a. . . . of a farm of 40 acres of land meadow and pasture for the term of 7 years a.v. £60.
Total £60.
But they ought not . . . by reason of the conformity of the said John and for the cause noted immediately below.
The same John Wright owes £40 . . . 10 cows a horse 20 sheep.
But he ought not . . . mem. 14 Car. Mich. term. . . Quit.

182. A John Wright of *Winston* and Anne his wife were conv. 1626, ind. 1628.

WILLIAM RIDDELL knt. (183) of Gateside ( ) £20 . . . 2 horses.

183. S. & h. of Sir Tho. Riddell & Elizabeth da. of Sir John Conyers of Sockburn; matriculated at Univ. Coll. Oxf. 2 Dec. 1614; of Lincolns Inn 1623; knighted 17 July 1633; took part in the defence of Tynemouth castle & was committed to the Tower of London, 1644; in 1653 begged benefit of the Act of Pardon (*SS* 111, p. 321). M. Katherine da. of Sir Henry Widdrington; issue, George, William, Thomas, (probably) Peter S.J., Robert secular priest, Henry, Katherine, Jane, Margaret.
Conv. with Katherine his wife 1624, 1625, 1626, ind. 1628; refused Protestation 1642.

C scri Tenants . . . of WILLIAM CLAPTON (185) of Sledwisley gentleman owe £20 p.a. . . . of a water mill in Barnard Castle now in the occupation of Matthew Stoddert or his assigns. . . .
Total £30.
But they ought not . . . by consideration of the Barons . . .

mem. 1650 Hil. term in a process touching Matthew Stoddert. . . . Quit.

185. See nos. 27, 56. 20s. of the above £30 was collected by the sheriff, 1638.

Tenants . . . of ELLENOR CARLETON (186) of Wolsingham in the said county widow owe £26 13s. 4d. p.a. . . . of an annuity of £40 for the term of her life by way of jointure. . . .
Total £40.

186. Conv. 1630.

Tenants . . . of JOHN TROLLOP sen. of Thorneley (187) in the par. of Kelloe owe £133 6s. 8d. p.a. . . . of the manor of Little Eden in the par. of Easington in the tenure of Nicholas Heath gentleman or his assigns. And of divers other lands in Morden in the par. of Sedgefield now in the tenure of George Martin and John Calverlye gentlemen, of Durham, and others a.v. £200.
Total £200.
Look in the following Roll in *Res Ebor.* regarding this rent and arrears.

187. S. of Francis Trollop of Eden (d. 1595) & Margaret da. of Francis Tunstall of Scargill; h. to his gr.father John Trollop; recovered, under the entail, estates forfeited by the attainder of the latter in 1570; joined the Royal standard 1641; under sequestration 1645, estate included in 3rd Act for Sale 1652; d. 1668. M. (1) Elizabeth da. of Sir Wm. Blakeston of Blakeston; issue, John, outlawed for manslaughter 1637; m. (2) Isabel da. of George Holtby of Scackleton, co. York: issue, Michael & William, both killed in the royal service.
Conv. with Elizabeth his wife 1604, 1606/7; with Isabel his wife 1624, 1625, 1626, ind. 1628; Little Eden seized in 1626 & leased to Wm. Carr of Cocken at £15 p.a.; payments traced to 1627.
Comp. 12 Oct. 1629 for himself and John his son to pay £15 p.a. *plus* 2 years' arrears; payments traced to 1633; comp. again, 29 Sept. 1637 to pay £133 6s. 8d. p.a. Quittance granted 14 Car. Easter term, when £333 6s. 8d. remained to be paid.

HENRY SMITH (188) of Thorneley ( ) £10 . . . 2 cows and divers other goods. . . .

188. Conv. with Mary his wife 1630. Proceedings in Court of High Commission for contempt in not repairing to the parish church, 1630 (*SS* 34, p. 21); refused Protestation 1642. Inventory of household goods sequestered, 1644 (*SS* 111, p. 27).

A Henry Smith of Thornley and (. .) his wife conv. 1676; (no wife) 1680.

JOHN TROLLOPP of Thornley aforesaid yeoman (189) ( ) £11 . . 3 cows. . . .

189. A dependent at Thornley, possibly "little" John Trollopp (cf. *SS* 111, p. 27).
Conv. 1615.

GRACE WILSON (190) of the same widow ( ) 40s. . . . goods. . . .

190. Most probably Grace da. of "old" John Trollopp of Thornley, serving-man, & Grace his wife; as Grace Trollopp convicted with them 1596, 1599, 1600; as Grace wife of Robert Wilson conv. (with the above) 1606/7, 1615; with Robert Wilson, conv. 1624, 1625, 1626, 1632.

KATHERINE ANDREWE (191) of the same widow ( ) 40s. . . . goods. . . .

191. William Andrewe and Katherine his wife conv. 1624, 1625, 1626; Katherine ind. (alone) 1628; as widow conv. 1632.

MICHAEL JOPLYN (192) of Windgate in the par. of Kelloe ( ) £6 . . . goods. . . .

192. Conv. 1624, 1626, ind. 1628 (labourer, Wheatliehill), conv. 1632. Goods seized at £4, 1627. Refused Protestation 1642. A Michael Joplyn of Coxhoe conv. 1674, 1680.

Tenants . . . of RICHARD BOOTH (193) late of the aforesaid parish owe £40 p.a. . . . of a capital messuage called Whitehurworth and 120 acres of land, arable meadow and pasture, a.v. £60 . . . in fee. . . .
Total £60.
But they ought not . . . because of an order or decree of the Exchequer . . . by reason of the conformity of Ralph son and heir of the aforesaid Richard . . . mem. 14 Car. Hil. term. . . . Quit.

193. S. & eventual h. of Robt. Booth of Old Durham & Katherine da. of Wm. Layton of Sproxton, co. York; she remar. Chas. Radcliffe. M. Barbara da. of Humphrey Blakeston of Fulthorpe; issue, Ralph, Robert, George, Dorothy, Mary.
Conv. with his wife 1615, 1624, 1625, 1626; lands seized 1608, and valued at 100s. p.a., two parts leased to Robt. Walker and Rich. Brasse at 22s. 3d. p.a. Goods seized at 40s. at the same time and redeemed by R. W. & R. B. for 13s. 4d. Rent payments traced to 1620. Land & goods seized again 1626, 1627.

Tenants . . . of BARBARA BOOTH (194) widow of the same late wife of Richard Booth owe £13 6s. 8d. p.a. . . . of a third part of the aforesaid messuage for the term of her life.
Total £20.
Look in Roll 14 in *Res Ebor.* regarding this rent and arrears.

194. See Richard Booth above. £10 of the above £20 collected by distraint, 1638. Listed as Papist of Croxdale 1665.

FRANCES TROLLOPP (195) of Kelloe ( ) £12 . . . goods. . . .

195. Conv. 1632 with Michael, Dorothy & Wm. Trollopp.

C scri Tenants . . . of ROBERT HARRINGTON (196) of the same, gentleman, owe 40s. p a. . . . of a cottage and 6 acres during the life of one Elizabeth Woodmasse a.v. 60s.
Total 60s.

196. Mar. at Witton-le-Wear, 9 Feb. 1612/13, Mary da. of Sir John Conyers of Sockburn & Agnes Bowes of Streatlam.
With Mary his wife, conv. 1615, of North Hebburn; 1624, 1625, 1626, ind. 1628, of Kelloe; comp. 27 July 1637 to pay 50s. p.a. *plus* 8 years' arrearages. Refused Protestation 1642.

C. scri The same Robert Harrington ( ) £12 . . . goods. . . .

JOHN TROLLOPP (197) of Kello labourer ( ) 60s. . . . goods. . . .

197. One of the many John Trollopps dependent upon the main family. Refused Protestation 1642.

Tenants . . . of RALPH LITTLEFAIRE (198) of the same owe 40s. p.a. . . . of a cottage and 6 acres for the term of his life.
Total 60s.

198. Servant to Tho. Forcer (no. 4) who bequeathed him the cottage (*SS* 142, p. 151).
Conv. 1626 (labourer); with Anne his wife 1632. Goods seized at £4, 1626. Refused Protestation 1642.

The same Ralph ( ) £12 . . . goods. . . .

JOHN WINTER (199) ( ) £7 10s. . . . goods. . . .

199. Conv. 1606/7, 1616; (tailor, with Margaret his wife) conv. 1624, 1626, ind. 1628; conv. (alone) 1632. Refused Protestation 1642.

GEORGE WINTER (200) ( ) £7 . . . goods. . . .

200. Conv. 1624; with (. .) his wife 1625, (tailor) with Katherine his wife 1626; ind. (alone) 1628. Goods seized at 60s. 1627.

GEORGE TIPLADY (201) ( ) £11 . . . goods. . . .

201. Conv. 1624 (carpenter); with Elizabeth his wife 1632. Refused Protestation 1642.

FRANCIS HODGSON (202) ( ) £6 . . . goods. . . .

202. Not identified.

C pro bon' scri Tenants . . . of GEORGE COMYN (203) of the par. of St. Nicholas in Durham weaver owe 26s. 8d. p.a. . . . of a cottage a.v. 40s.

Total 40s.

203. Conv. (par. of St. Nich.) with Elizabeth Comyn widow, 1626. Comp. for himself and Elizabeth his mother to pay £2 p.a. 1630. Goods seized at £215, including £200 for "mercery wares" 1635.

[Another George Comyn of Durham was named in the latter list of seizures.]

C scri The same George Comyn ( ) £6 . . . goods. . . .

Tenants . . . ALICE BUCKLYE (204) of the same spinster owe 40s. p.a. . . . of a cottage and a croft . . in fee. . . .

Total 60s.

204. Conv. 1624, 1626.

JANE MARSHALL (205) widow of the same ( ) 40s. . . . goods. . . .

205. Jane wife of William Marshall of Elvet conv. 1606/7; widow 1626.

CHARLES HALL (206) of the same ( ) 66s. 8d. . . . goods. . . .

206. Possibly the same person as no. 42; implements seized at 40s. 1635; refused Protestation 1642.

MARGARET BROWNE (207) of the same ( ) 40s. . . . goods. . . .

207. See nos. 25, 32.

EDWARD BROWNE (208) of the same ( ) £10 . . . goods. . . .

208. Ind. (glazier) 1628; conv. with Margery his wife 1632. Comp. 1634 to pay 40s. p.a. *plus* 5½ years' arrearages. Owed 1 year's rent & 2½ years' arrearages in 1636. Refused Protestation 1642.

CUTHBERT TAYLOR (209) of the same ( ) 40s. . . . goods. . . .

209. Conv. (tailor) 1626, with (. .) his wife 1632. Refused Protestation 1642.

JOHN SERVANT (210) of the same ( ) £6 13s. 4d. . . . goods. . . .

210. Conv. with Frances his wife, 1624, 1626; ind. with Jane his wife 1628, conv. 1632. Proceedings against him in the Court of High Commission 1633, for clandestine marriage with Jane Pinkney, performed by Mr Foord a popish priest (either Rev. Francis Ford, secular priest, or Dom John Placid Hartburn *alias* Foorde, O.S.B.) (*SS* 34, p. 74).

"John Servant, draper-tailor" bur. 13 Aug. 1656, St. Oswald's, Durham.

20s. of the above £6 13s. 4d. was collected by the sheriff, 1638.

JOHANNA BOANE (211) of Billingham ( ) £33 13s. 4d. . . . for the like in money counted there.

211. Da. of John Bone of Billingham & Margaret da. of Simon Welbery of Castle Eden.

Conv. 1615, 1624, 1625, ind. 1628, conv. 1632.

Tenants . . . of GEORGE SWALLWELL (212) of Woolveston owe £4 p.a. . . . of the moiety of a farm there for the term of two years. Total £6.

212. See nos. 8, 45.

Tenants . . . of RICHARD HUNTLEY (213) of Townburdon in the aforesaid county owe £6 13s. 4d. p.a. . . . of a tenement in Burdon and 60 acres of land meadow and pasture.

Total £10.

But they ought not . . . insufficiency of the inquisition . . . mem. 14 Car. Hil. term. . . . Quit.

213. Conv. 1624, 1626, 1632; refused Protestation 1642.

"*ex*[r]." GEORGE SIMSON (214) of Sunderland ( ) £13 . . . for the like. . . .

214. No record of conviction found; possibly the reason for the note "exoneratur". Refused Protestation 1642.

rot. *Item Adhuc Item Item Res Ebor.*

C scri Tenants . . . of RALPH HUNTLYE (215) of Shadford in the par. of Pittington and ELIZABETH HUNTLYE his mother owe £6 13s. 4d. p.a. . . . of a tenement and 60 acres. . . .

Total £10.

215. Conv. (jun.) 1624, 1625, 1626; proceedings in the Court of High Commission for clandestine marriage & private baptisms 1635 (*SS* 34, p. 114 & Surtees, *Durham* I, p. 118).

Comp. for himself & Elizabeth his mother, 27 July 1637, to pay 73s. 4d. p.a. *plus* 8 years' arrearages. Refused Protestation 1642. Under sequestration as papist, 1651 (*SS* 111, p. 57).

C scri The same Ralph Huntlye ( ) £6 for the price of 3 cows and a steer.

C scri Tenants . . . of JANE YONGE (216) of Edderacres in the par. of Esington owe £4 p.a. . . . of an annuity of £6 for the term of her life.

Total £6.

216. Widow of Christopher Young of Ederacres (d. 1623); probably the "Jennet Young of Ederakers" bur. 16 June 1645 (Easington par. reg.). Had issue (*Arch. Ael.* (4) I, 149).

Conv. 1626, ind. 1628, conv. 1630, 1632. Comp. 27 July 1637, to pay 40s. p.a. *plus* 8 years' arrearages. At Martinmas 1638 owed a total of £18.

C scri The same Jane owes 100s. . . . 2 cows.

Look regarding the rent and arrears and the debt in Roll 1653 in *Dunelm.*

C scri Tenants . . . of KATHERINE BYERS (217) of Shotton owe 53s. 4d. p.a. . . . of the fourth part of a farm there a.v. 40s., and a farm in Stranton a.v. 40s.

Total £4.

217. Katherine wife of James Byers of Easington conv. 1630.

The same Katherine Byers ( ) £20 . . . goods. . . .

C scri THOMAS DAWSON of Middleton George (218) owes £50 . . . 6 oxen 3 cows 60 sheep a horse 2 foals.

218. Thomas Dawson of Sadberge conv. 2 Oct. 1633; comp. 28 July 1637 to pay 50s. p.a. *plus* 3½ years' arrearages. Refused Protestation 1642.

Tenants . . . of WILLIAM PRESTON SAYER (*sic*) gentleman (219) of

Preston owe 100s. p.a. . . . of a messuage and 5 oxgangs of land meadow and pasture a.v. £7 10s.

Total £7 10s.

219. 3rd s. of John Sayer of Worsall & Dorothy Bulmer; probably dead before 1644 (*SS* 111, p. 19); m. Gertrude . . . issue Dorothy w. of John Errington.

Conv. with Gertrude his wife 1624, 1626, ind. 1628, conv. 1630.

The same William Sayer (   ) £30 . . . goods. . . .

FRANCIS SCURRY (220) of Preston on Tease (   ) 100s. . . . goods. . . .

220. Conv. with Margaret his wife 1630, 1633; refused Protestation 1642; under sequestration 1644 (*SS* 111, p. 19).

Tenants . . . of MARGARET SCURRY (221) of the same widow owe 26s. 8d. p.a. . . . of a tenement and one oxgang.

221. Margaret wife of John Scurry conv. 1616, 1626, 1633.

The same Margaret (   ) £8 . . . goods. . . .

Tenants . . . of James Lawson deceased late of Neesome Esq. owe £13 6s. 8d. p.a. . . . of an annuity of £20 issuing out of the aforesaid lands payable to MARY LAWSON (222) of Hurworth widow Recusant, for the term of her life. . . .

Total £20.

222. The widow of James Lawson (d. 1628) was *Frances*, da. of Walter Vavasour of Hazelwood, co. York. Mary Lawson is possibly his aunt, described here as widow in error for spinster.

Mary Lawson spinster conv. 1624, 1626, 1632, 1633.

WILLIAM JOHNSON (223) of the same (   ) £4 . . . goods. . . .

223. Conv. with (. .) his wife 1633; refused Protestation 1642. "Marian Johnson, widow, of Hurworth" listed as Papist 1665.

JOHN WAYTIN sen. (224) of the same (   ) £6 13s. 4d. . . . a horse and a mare.

224. Probably bro. of William Waytin of Nesham, whose son was John Waytin jun.

Conv. 1606/7 with Elizabeth his wife, & William Waytin & Jane his wife; conv. 1633 with (. .) his wife, William and Jane, & John jun. & his wife.

FRANCIS EMMERSON (225) of Whitton in the par. of Grindon ( ) £16 . . . 5 cows 30 sheep 1 horse. . . .

225. Of the family of William Emmerson below.
Refused Protestation 1642.

C scri Tenants . . . of WILLIAM EMERSON of Barmton (226) in the par. of Haughton owe £26 13s. 4d. p.a. . . . of the third part of a messuage in Cornforth and 200 acres of arable pasture and meadow in right of Anne his wife, now in the occupation of Robert Widhouse a.v. £20 . . . and of another messuage in Thorpethewles and 200 acres in the tenure or occupation of Alexander Davison of Newcastle gentleman or his assigns a.v. £20.
And £13 6s. 8d. . . . Total £40.

226. S. of George Emmerson of Barmton & Margaret his wife; m. Anne . . . ; she was probably one of the 3 heiresses of John Shaw of Cornforth, possibly the one whose third had passed (before 1644) to Matthew Smyth of Barmton (cf. Surtees, *Durham* III, p. 15, & *SS* 111, p. 8).
Comp. 1632 for a moiety of Barmton, to pay 40s. p.a. *plus* 3 years' arrearages; rent & 1st instalment of arrearages paid 1632.

C scri Tenants . . . of RICHARD FOSTER (227) of Rotforth in the par. of Hamsterley owe £33 6s. 8d. p.a. . . . of 4 messuages and 100 acres of arable meadow and pasture . . . in fee a.v. £50 in the occupation of William Maddison Tunstall Toes and others.
Total £50.

227. See no. 1.

C scri TUNSTALL TOES (228) of the same ( ) £16 . . . 4 oxen 4 cows 20 sheep 2 horses. . . .

228. Conv. with Jane his wife 1624, 1625, 1626, ind. 1628. Comp. 1632 to pay £3 p.a.; no record of payment. 1634, goods seized at £10 6s. 8d. and land at £20 4s. 10d. p.a. Comp. 1 March 1637/8 to pay £4 p.a., arrearages included.

Tenants . . . of CHRISTOPHER GIBBIN (229) of Hamsterley owe 17s. 9⅓d. p.a. . . . of a cottage and 3 acres in the occupation of John Farr. . . .
Total 26s. 8d.

229. Ind. of Morley, Auckland St. Helen, with Mabel & Anne Gibbon (no. 72) 1628; conv. 1632.

C scri WILLIAM ACCROID (230) of Witton gentleman ( ) £40 . . . a cow a horse and other goods. . . .

230. Conv. 1632. In 1634 goods were seized at £92 3s. 4d., including £80 for "malt stock". Comp. 1 March 1637/8 to pay £5 p.a., arrearages included.

Tenants . . . of ROBERT MERRIMAN (231) of Fetherstonhaugh in the co. of Northumberland owe £19 6s. 8d. p.a. . . . of the third part of a capital messuage in Wadley in co. Durham and 50 acres of land meadow and pasture of which he is seized for the term of 9 years a.v. 60s. and of a farm in Macuele (or Matuele) and 40 acres a.v. £26.

Total £29.

231. See no. 177.

C scri Tenants . . . of BARTHOLOMEW MALAND (232) of Whitworth in the co. of Durham owe £10 p.a. . . . of a tenement and 40 acres adjoining with appurtenances a.v. £15.

Total £15.

232. Conv. 1632. Comp. 17 Aug. 1637 to pay 40s. p.a. *plus* 1½ years' arrearages. Refused Protestation 1642.

C scri The same Bartholomew Maland ( ) £6 . . goods. . . .

C scri LAWRENCE COPELAND (233) of Over Coniscliffe ( ) £14 . . . 4 cows 2 horses. . . .

233. Conv. 1624, 1625, 1626. Goods seized at £15, 1627, owed £18 in 1635. Comp. 21 Apr. 1636 to pay 66s. 8d. p.a. Payment for 1st half-year traced. Refused Protestation 1642.

C scri JOHN CONN (234) of the same ( ) £16 . . . 4 oxen 2 horses 2 cows. . . .

234. S. of John Conn (d. 1611) & Isabella Blakelock; bapt. 25 Sept. 1599 (Coniscliffe reg.); m. . . . ; issue, Isabel, Thomas, Christopher, Elizabeth. Bur. 26 Jan. 1689 (Coniscliffe).

Conv. 1624, ind. 1628; owed £16 for goods 1635. Comp. 12 Aug. 1637 to pay 45s. p.a., arrearages included.

FRANCIS THIRKELT (235) of the same ( ) 17s. 4d. . . . 1 cow 1 horse. . . .

235. With Anne his wife conv. 1624, 1625, 1626, ind. 1628 (labourer); owed 100s. for goods 1635; refused Protestation 1642.

C scri Tenants . . . of JOHN HILDRETH (236) of Pearsbridge owe £4 p.a. . . . of a tenement and 60 acres of arable meadow and pasture . . . for the term of 3 lives. . . .

Total £6.

236. Conv. with Faith his wife 1626; ind. 1628, conv. 1633. Had compounded 23 March 1635/6 to pay 50s. p.a.

Refused Protestation 1642.

C scri The same John Hildreth (   ) £13 13s. 4d. . . . 2 oxen 4 cows 4 steers 20 sheep a mare & a foal. . . .

Tenants . . . of PETER WABANCKE (237) of the same owe £4 p.a. . . . of a tenement and 60 acres. . . .

Total £6.

237. See nos. 14, 48.

Tenants . . . of Henry Birkebecke gentleman owe 66s. 8d. p.a. . . . of an annuity of 100s. payable to MARGARET LANCASTER (238) of Pearsbridge by the aforesaid Henry Birkebecke, he being possessed of the same. . . .

Total 100s.

238. Margaret wife of Ambrose Lancaster conv. 1615; wid. 1625, 1626. Fine between Henry Birkbeck, & Ambrose Lancaster & Margaret his wife, 15 July 9 Jac. (Surtees, *Durham* IV, p. 30).

Tenants . . . of THOMAS PATTISON (239) of the par. of St. Giles in Durham owe 12s. p.a. . . . of a cottage and garden. . . .

Total 18s.

239. See nos. 18, 31.

The same Thomas Pattison (   ) 40s. . . . goods. . . .

Tenants . . . of MARGARET CHILTON (240) of the same owe 12s. p.a. . . . of a tenement and garden a.v. 18s. . . . in fee. . . .

Total 18s.

240. Conv. 1624, widow. Said to have conformed, 1626.

The same Margaret (   ) 40s. . . . goods. . . .

Tenants . . . of ANNE FRISELL (241) of the same owe 4s. 5⅓d. p.a. . . . of a cottage and garden a.v. 6s. 8d. . . . in fee. . . .

Total 6s. 8d.

241. As wife of John Frisell (no. 33) conv. 1624, 1625, 1626, ind. 1628, conv. 1630; widow, conv. 1632.

The same Anne (   ) 20s. . . . goods. . . .

C pro modo inde Tenants . . . of ANTHONY METCALFE (242) of Elvitt in Durham owe £66 13s. 4d. p.a. . . . "maner' de Corbon [*an error for* miner' de carbon'] ibidem infra capellariam sancte Margarete" a.v. £100.
Total £100.

242. With Mary his wife conv. 1625, 1626 (Whickham), ind. 1628 (St. Oswald's). Comp. 19 Aug. 1637 to pay 60s. p.a.

C scri The same Anthony Metcalfe (   ) £14 . . . a horse 2 cows and other goods. . . .

Tenants . . . of GEORGE HUNTER (243) of the same owe 26s. 8d. p.a. . . . of a tenement . . . in fee. . . .
Total 40s.

243. Conv. 1632, tailor. Signed Protestation 1642.

The same George Hunter (   ) 53s. 4d. . . . a horse. . . .

Tenants of RALPH DENHAM (244) of Houghton in le side owe 13s. 4d. p.a. . . . of a cottage and croft a.v. 20s.
Total 20s.

244. Ralph Denham and Margaret his wife conv. 1624, 1626; said to have conformed 1626. Owed £40 for goods 1635.

The same Ralph Denham (   ) £30 . . . 9 cows 30 sheep a mare and a foal. . . .

C scri MARTIN BATMANSON (245) of Eshe (   ) £6 13s. 4d. . . . 2 cows 2 calves 2 oxen. . . .

245. 2nd s. of William Batmanson of Ushaw (d. 1605) & Margaret Taylor; bapt. 7 Apr. 1595 (Esh); m. Anne . . . , issue, Margaret (bapt. 1634), Mary, Anne, Elizabeth.
Conv. 1624, 1625, 1626, ind. 1628, conv. 1630. Comp. 17 March 1637/8 to pay 46s. 8d. p.a. arrearages included. Refused Protestation 1642.

ROBERT JOPLYN (246) of the same (   ) 40s. . . . a cow. . . .

246. Conv. 1624 (tailor, Esh), 1625, 1626 (tailor, Rowley); ind. 1628 (Ushaw).

C scri LANCELOT TAYLOR (247) of the same (   ) 100s. . . . a cow a mare 10 sheep. . . .

247. With Mary his wife conv. 1624, 1625, ind. 1628; goods seized at £4 12s. 8d., 1626 (Haghouse). Comp. (Lanc. Taylor jun. Esh) in 1632 to pay 40s. p.a.

C scri Tenants . . . of AGNES DUCKETT (248) of Burdon par. of Houghton widow owe 66s. 8d. p.a. . . . of a lease in Great Burdon held of the Dean and Chapter of Durham of which she is seized for the term of 4 years a.v. 100s.

Total 100s.

248. Conv. 1626, ind. 1628; owed £15 for goods, 1635. Comp. 27 Oct. 1636 to pay 40s. p.a. *plus* 7 years' arrearages.

C scri The same Agnes Duckett (   ) £22 . . . 8 cows 40 sheep a mare 2 foals 2 steers 3 calves. . . .

Gabriel Redman owes 26s. 8d. p.a. . . . of the half of a capital messuage called Heyworth in the par. of Ackley, and of divers other messuages lands and tenements parcel of the lands of REBECCA SALVIN (249) widow as is contained in Roll 9 Car. in *Item Ebor*. and in the Exannual Roll.

And £21 6s. 8d. for the 16 years last past. Total £22 13s. 4d.

249. See no. 3.

Tenants . . . of REBECCA SALVIN of Elvett widow owe £21 6s. 8d. p.a. . . . of certain goods and chattels of the annual value of £30 and of a messuage with appurtenances in Elvett a.v. 40s. remaining in the Kings hands as is contained in the preceding Roll in *Adhuc Ebor*. and in the Exannual Roll

And £64 for 3 years including this year. Total £86 13s. 4d.

But they ought not . . . mem. 1656 Trin. term in a process touching Robert Collingwood & Gilbert Crouch.

And they are Quit.

C scri Tenants . . . of CUTHBERT BROWNE (184) of Gateside owe 13s. 4d. p.a. . . . a cottage.

Total 20s.

184. Conv. 1632; comp. 26 Sept. 1637 to pay £46s. 8d. p.a. including arrears. Refused Protestation 1642.

APPENDIX A

Compositions made with the Lord Wentworth between Martinmas 1636 and Martinmas 1637, extracted from the *Comp.* rotulets of Recusant Roll 12 Car. (E.377/44).

D. RADO HALL de Greencrofte gen' pro redd' duarum partium manerii de Greencrofte in paroch' de Lanchester et terr' tent' et heredit' eidem spectan' et pro personal' stat' in bonis Prius composuit ad solvend' vi li. xiii s. iiii d. et modo ad solvend' ad fest' Pentecostis et sci Martini equaliter per annum xiii li. vi s. viii d.

Hic in onere pro viii annis et dimid' anni finit' ad fest' sci Martini hoc anno Cxiii li. vi s. viii d.

RALPH HALL of Greencrofte gentleman in debt for the rent of two parts of the manor of Greencrofte in the parish of Lanchester and of the lands tenements and hereditaments thereto belonging and for his personal estate in goods Formerly he compounded[1] to pay £6 13s. 4d. a year and now to pay £13 6s. 8d. a year at the feasts of Pentecost and Martinmas in equal parts.

He is charged for the 8½ years ending at Martinmas this year. £113 6s. 8d.

D. Johne Pulford de Windsore in com' Berk' Ar' pro redd' Recusancie ISABELL BELLASIS uxor' Jacobi Bellasis de Owlton in Episcopat' Dunelm' Ar' illa exist' recusan' convict' solvend' singulis annis durante eorum junct' vita et eius recusancia per annum vi li. xiii s. iiii d.

Pro redd' omn' bonor' et catall' et pro personal' stat' BARTHI ADDYE de Swallwell solvend' durante vita et eius recus' per annum lx s.

Necnon pro redd' omn' bonor' et catall' et pro personal' stat' JOHNIS LIDDELL de Ryton solvend' durante vita et eius recus' per annum lx s.

In toto solvend' ad fest' sci Martini et Pentecostis per annum xii li. xiii s. iiii d.

[1] With Sir John Savile.

Hic in onere pro uno anno et dimid' anni finit' ad Pent' hoc anno 1637 atting' ad xix li. Un' mediet' solvend' super confirmacionem compositionis cum commissariis in partibus boreal' que fuit secundo die Octobris 1637 et alter' mediet' solvend' est ad vel ante finition' termini sci Martini tunc proxime sequent'

Necnon pro redd' premiss' pro dimidio unius anni finit' ad fest' sci Martini hoc anno vi li. vi s. viii d.

In toto xxv li. vi s. viii d.

John Pulford of Windsore in the county of Berkshire Esq. in debt for the rent of the Recusancy of ISABELLA BELLASIS wife of James Bellasis of Owlton in the Bishopric of Durham Esq. she being a Recusant convict to pay for each year during their joint life and her recusancy £6 13s. 4d. yearly.

And for rent for the goods and chattels and for the personal estate of BARTHOLOMEW ADDYE of Swallwell to pay during his life and recusancy 60s. yearly.

Also for rent for all the goods and chattels and for the personal estate of JOHN LIDDELL of Ryton to pay during his life and recusancy 60s. yearly.

In all, to pay at the feasts of Martinmas and Pentecost, £12 13s. 4d. yearly.

He is charged for a year and a half ending at Pentecost this year 1637, amounting to £19; he is to pay one half upon the confirmation of this composition with the Commissioners in the Northern parts, which was on the 2nd October 1637, and the other half at or before the end of the Martinmas term immediately following.

Also for rent of the premises for the half year ending at Martinmas this year £6 6s. 8d.

In all £25 6s. 8d.

JOHN LIDDELL of Chester in debt . . . 40s. p.a. . . . charged for ½ year		20s.	
ROBERT HARRINGTON of Kelloe . . . 50s. p.a. . . . 8½ years	£21	5s.	
RALPH HUNTLEY of Shawdforth and ELIZABETH his mother . . . by composition 27 July 1637 . . . 73s. 4d. p.a. . . . 8½ years	£31	3s.	4d.
JANE YOUNGE of the par. of Esington . . . 40s. p.a. . . . 8 years	£16	0	0

WILLIAM THOMPSON of Trimdon . . . 50s. p.a. . . . 6½ years	£16 5s. 0
ANNE GARNETT of Blackwell . . . 40s. p.a. . . . 8½ years	£17 0 0
THOMAS HARRISON of Sadbury . . . £4 10s. p.a. . . . 2½ years	£11 5s. 0
THOMAS DAWSON of Middleton George . . . 50s. p.a. . . . 3½ years	£8 15s. 0
JOHN CONN of Nether Coniscliffe . . . 45s. p.a. . . . ½ year	22s. 6d.
JOHN GARRY of Winlayton . . . 40s. p.a. . . . 2½ years	100s.
ROBERT ATKINSON of Lumley . . . 40s. p.a. . . . 1½ years	60s.
ROBERT CUTHBERT of Rideinge . . . 66s. 8d. p.a. . . . 2½ years	£8 6s. 8d.
BARTHOLOMEW MALHAM of Whitworth . . . 40s. p.a. . . . 1½ years	60s.
ANTHONY METCALFE of the City of Durham . . . 60s. p.a. . . . 1½ years	£4 10s. 0
Richard Hickson of Preston on Skerne . . . being conformable for the recusancy of ISABELLA his wife . . . £6 13s. 4d. p.a. . . . ½ year	66s. 8d.
PETER WITHAM of Fawside . . . 60s. p.a. . . . 8½ years	£25 10s. 0
WILLIAM BURNOPP of le Howmes . . £6 p.a. . . . 2½ years	£15 0 0
FRANCIS HODGSON of Collierley & DOROTHY HODGSON his mother . . . 53s. 4d. p.a. . . . ½ year	26s. 8d.
GEORGE FAIREHAIRE of the City of Durham in lieu of all arrears of rent above mentioned to be paid at Martinmas this year £4. Also rent for a burgage called Elvett to pay 13s. 4d. p.a. in addition to the former composition made with Lord Wentworth . . . ½ year	£4 6s. 8d.
CUTHBERT BROWNE of Gateside . . . 46s. 8d. p.a. . . . ½ year	23s. 4d.
WILLIAM HODGSON of Lintsgreen . . . 100s. p.a. . . . 8½ years	£42 10s. 0

GEORGE GARNETT of Blackwell . . . 40s. p.a. . . . 6 years £12 0 0

THOMAS PINKNEY of East Brandon & ANNE PINKNEY his mother . . . previously compounded to pay 13s. 4d. p.a.[1] and now to pay 40s. p.a. . . . 8½ years £17 0 0

APPENDIX B

Compositions made with Lord Wentworth between Martinmas 1637 and Martinmas 1638, extracted from the following Roll, 13 Car. (E.377/45).

JOHN HODGSON of le Mannorhouse & JANE HODGSON his mother . . . £10 p.a. . . . 8½ years ending Martinmas 1637

RALPH CATTERICK of Fishburn & RALPH CATTERICK his son . . . 106s. 8d. p.a. . . . quit of all arrears

WILLIAM AIKCROYD of St. Ellen Auckland . . . 100s. p.a. . . . quit of all arrears

TUNSTALL TOES of Hamsterley . . . £4 p.a. . . . quit of all arrears

GEORGE TAILOR of Lanchester . . . 46s. 8d. p.a. . . . quit . . .

MARTIN BATMANSON of Eshe . . . 46s. 8d. p.a. . . . quit . . .

WILLIAM ILEY of Ford . . . 46s. 8d. p.a. . . . quit. . . .

ANNE HUTTON of Cockerton . . . 66s. 8d. p.a. . . . 1½ years ending Martinmas 1637

[1] With Sir John Savile.

INDEX I (Recusants' Estates 1717-1778)

References in th.s index are to pages

PART I

PERSONS

INDEX I

Part II

PLACES

INDEX II (Recusants' Roll 1636-7)

References in this index are to the numbered items

Part 1

PERSONS

INDEX II

Part II

PLACES